A
PRACTICAL GUIDE
TO
LEGAL WRITING
AND
LEGAL METHOD

A PRACTICAL GUIDE TO LEGAL WRITING AND LEGAL METHOD

JOHN C. DERNBACH
RICHARD V. SINGLETON II

FRED B. ROTHMAN & CO.
Littleton, Colorado 80127
1981

Library of Congress Cataloging in Publication Data

DERNBACH, JOHN C.
    A practical guide to legal writing and legal
method.

    Bibliography: p.
    1. Legal composition.   2. Law—United States—
Language.   3. Law—United States—Methodology.
I. Singleton, Richard V.   II. Title.
KF250.D47   808'.00634   81-771
ISBN 0-8377-0513-4   AACR2

©1981 by John C. Dernbach and
Richard V. Singleton II

Printed in the United States of America

Summary of Contents

PART D: THE BRIEF

APPENDIXES

Table of Contents

Foreword

LAWYERS are articulate about nearly everything, it seems, except the craft of lawyering. Virtually all good lawyers can recognize and appreciate a first-rate brief or memorandum; few, if any, can describe intelligibly the process by which such documents are created. One learns the craft of lawyering by doing and observing, relying on one's own instinct, talent, and judgment, assisted by occasional criticism from peers, teachers and more experienced lawyers. Unfortunately, senior lawyers and law teachers have lacked time and incentive to organize their basic shared insights into a convenient form that allows them to be communicated economically to younger lawyers.

This book is a long step in the right direction. It is an insightful, systematic articulation of what goes into good legal analysis and writing. It de-mystifies the process of thinking and writing clearly. This is a simple book; it is written more for the average than the exceptional law student and lawyer. Those who pride themselves on their sophistication, however, may find that a clear articulation of basics provides a secure foundation for more complicated intellectual maneuvers.

Dernbach and Singleton have made available a full course of instruction with exercises for those who might wish to adopt their method of teaching legal writing. The text stands alone, however, and can be used in a wide range of course formats. Virtually anyone who must teach lawyering skills will find something in this book that will help young lawyers to master the fundamentals of legal writing.

SALLYANNE PAYTON
Associate Professor of Law
University of Michigan

Acknowledgments

THE original work for this book was funded by an educational development grant from Wayne State University.

Many friends and colleagues provided support and constructive criticism. Special thanks, however, go to Cheryl Scott, Sally Payton, Laura J. Hess, Kathy Yorkievitz, and the 1980-81 legal writing staff at Wayne State University Law School.

We are also grateful to Emblem T. Collins, who patiently typed and retyped this manuscript.

Our greatest debt is to our legal writing students at Wayne State University Law School, to whom we dedicate this book. We hope they learned as much from us as we learned from them.

Introduction

A GOOD lawyer is much more than a professional. A good lawyer is a craftsman, applying his or her talents with imagination, diligence, and skill. Although the practice of law requires a combination of negotiating, counseling, research, and advocacy skills, there is one skill upon which all others depend. The good lawyer, the craftsman, must be able to write effectively.

Effective legal writing combines two elements—legal method and writing. Legal method is a process of applying legal rules to specific factual situations and drawing justifiable and well-organized conclusions. Law school, it is often said, is designed to teach you to "think like a lawyer." The myriad of legal rules presented in torts, civil procedure, property, and other courses are important, but law school courses should also instill the logic or method of law. A good lawyer knows how to resolve a particular problem, even though he or she may not yet know the relevant legal rules.

A thorough understanding of the legal problem-solving process is of little value, however, unless the analysis can be communicated on paper. Good legal writing is essentially the same as good writing in general. Legal writing is clear, precise, and complete, yet fully understandable to a lay person. Although it may seem surprising, good legal writing is not a legalistic style of Latin phrases and archaic words.

Effective legal writing is hard work. Nothing is included without good reason, and nothing of significance is omitted. Each word, each sentence, is chosen or structured with care. If the document reads smoothly and intelligently, it is not usually because it was easy to write. The reverse is more often true; the document that was easy to write is often muddled. The beauty of good craftsmanship is that the final product masks the painstaking and difficult process by which it was created. The good writer—the craftsman—makes it *look* easy.

This book is designed as a legal writing text, primarily for first year law students. Its value as a learning tool is based on two premises. First, the fundamental principles of legal writing and legal method can be reduced to a series of fairly simple rules or guidelines. Second, these rules can best be learned by practice, particularly by working through highly focused exercises. Although there is widespread agreement on the importance of practice, there is less certainty about the content of the lessons preceding the practice. Too often students are taught general concepts and highly technical details while the basic rules of legal analysis and legal writing are ignored or overlooked.

This book tries to fill that gap by providing practical guidance in the basic skills of legal writing and legal method.* Each chapter covers a specific topic such as organization, precedent, or advocacy. Most chapters set out a short series of rules. These rules are explained, justified, and then illustrated with hypothetical legal problems. The book shows good and bad ways of applying these rules to the problems and explains why one way is better than the other. Exercises of varying complexity, which afford an opportunity to learn and apply the rules, are provided at the end of each chapter (except Chapters 7 and 12). The illustrations and the exercises are based on altered or abridged versions of real cases and statutes. (Citations are set out in the Bibliography.)

The materials in this book are intended to be straightforward, manageable, and easy to understand. After the rules are understood in this context, they can be applied to legal writing assignments and to more complex situations. With time and practice, the finer points of legal writing and legal method can be mastered. This book cannot make you a legal craftsman; it is intended only to provide a solid foundation for the further development of your skills.

J.C.D.
R.V.S.

Detroit, Michigan
November 15, 1980

---

*Grammar, legal research, and citation form are not discussed. These subjects are covered in detail elsewhere, and there is little value in summarizing them here.

PART A

INTRODUCTION TO LAW

1

Rules and Policies

DEFINING law is a difficult philosophical problem, but law can initially be understood as a series of rules and policies for regulating behavior in society, the creation or application of which requires the participation of the government. Rules describe what behavior is impermissible, what procedures are to be followed to accomplish certain ends, and what happens to those who do not follow them. Legal rules come about when the legislature enacts a statute, when the governor or president signs an executive order, when a court resolves a dispute, when Congress ratifies a treaty with another nation, or when a government agency promulgates administrative rules.

Policies are the underlying values or purposes for rules, and they vary greatly in scope and abstractness. A building code provision requiring a certain kind of insulation for apartment buildings will probably be premised on technical judgments concerning the safety or efficiency of certain materials. Affirmative action programs in education or employment, by contrast, are rooted in far more abstract (but no less important) views about equality. Sometimes these policies are articulated clearly, but frequently they are stated unclearly or simply not stated at all. Often, a single rule is buttressed by several policy considerations.

Rules and policies are important in many ways. They provide a means of resolving or avoiding disputes peaceably, predictably, and more or less efficiently. They attempt to promote socially desirable goals. They define relationships among individuals and groups and help people arrange their business or conduct with greater security. Rules are thus a source of social norms, requiring certain behavior in particular situations, and a source of expectations, permitting people to plan their actions.

Rules and policies do not exist in a vacuum. Legal rules are not etched in stone for eternity, nor do they necessarily reflect the "natural" order of things. Legal rules are supported by certain values or beliefs about the way people should conduct their affairs. When the values or beliefs change, legal change will often follow.

The evolution of the law regarding gender-based discrimination is illustrative. In 1872, the Supreme Court of the United States decided that the federal Constitution did not prevent Illinois from refusing to license an otherwise qualified woman to practice law in that state. The legislature had said, in effect, that only men could be lawyers. Justice Bradley, writing for himself and two other justices, commented:

> The paramount destiny and mission of woman are to fulfil the noble and benign offices of wife and mother. This is the law of the Creator. And the rules of civil society must be adapted to the general constitution of things, and cannot be based upon exceptional cases . . . . I am not prepared to say that it is one of her fundamental rights and privileges to be admitted into every office and position, including those which require highly special qualifications and demanding special responsibilities.*

Although the Court's recent sex discrimination decisions leave some doubt about how equal it believes women really are, there can be little question that its outlook has undergone a marked change in the past century. It is difficult to imagine the Court drawing the same conclusion today as it did in 1872, particularly with the increasing number of women enrolled in law schools, practicing law, and judging cases. As Justice Brennan, referring to the *Bradwell* case, wrote in a 1974 opinion:

> There can be no doubt that our Nation has had a long and unfortunate history of sex discrimination. Traditionally, such discrimination was rationalized by an attitude of "romantic paternalism" which, in practical effect, put women, not on a pedestal, but in a cage.†

This change in the Court's attitude, and ultimately in the law, came as a direct result of changing public views about the role of women. This is not to suggest that judicial (or even legislative) decisions are made only after a poll is taken; the point is rather that public attitudes and values define the environment in which these decisions are made. All such decisions, in addition, involve choices among competing values. Judges and legislators

---

*Bradwell v. Illinois, 83 U.S. (16 Wall.) 130, 141-42 (1872).
†Frontiero v. Richardson, 411 U.S. 677, 684 (1974) (footnote omitted).

4 INTRODUCTION TO LAW   PART A

must constantly reconcile competing policy considerations. At what point, for example, does a criminal defendant's right to a fair trial limit the public's right to full media reporting of that trial? When can a person's right to run her business as she sees fit be limited by society for the protection of her employees? You will be constantly probing the cases you read for the justness of their rules and policies.

The importance of recognizing that value choices support legal rules cannot be overstated. You will need to explain and weigh competing policies in your office memos. As an advocate, moreover, you will be writing briefs to explain why certain policies outweigh others, and you will have to appeal to the values of your audience to do so.

Value choices are also important for their social implications. Your clients will have an obvious interest in your work as a lawyer, but your work will also be affecting the way society operates. Lawyers have obligations to their clients, but they also have obligations to society, and that tension is not always easy to resolve. If you successfully help a company develop a shopping mall just outside a city, for instance, you will have a significant effect on local land use, transportation, and housing patterns. If you successfully represent a landowner's group seeking to block that development, you will prevent those effects but cause others. Whichever side you represent, you will be arguing for the social good your clients ostensibly seek. "Justice" and "the social good" have many meanings, and you will develop and refine your own understanding of these concepts as you study law.

The following exercises are intended to show you some of the difficult problems judges and legislators face. As you answer the questions posed in the exercises, ask yourself where your policy or value judgments come from, whether other judgments might be more appropriate, and what consequences your judgments would have. In addition, keep in mind these three criteria for good legal rules:

1. Rules should be created and applied to accomplish articulated goals. Rules impose burdens on people, and they can be justified only in terms of more important social purposes.

2. Rules should state simply and precisely what actions are forbidden, required, or accepted. The more ambiguous the rules, the more they confuse people, and the less likely they are to accomplish their purposes.

3. Rules must be capable of achieving the desired outcome without creating other significant and undesirable side effects. Ineffective or counterproductive rules help no one.

Exercise 1-A

1. Assume you are a state legislator voting on the following bills. State whether you would vote for or against these bills and explain your decisions.

(a) A bill requiring persons who ride motorcycles to wear protective helmets.

(b) A bill requiring companies that produce food or beverages for public consumption to place warning labels on products known to contain cancer-causing agents.

(c) A bill requiring couples applying for a marriage license to undergo twelve hours of psychological counseling and testing before the license is granted so they can better determine whether marriage is appropriate for them.

(d) A bill prohibiting any person from smoking tobacco.

2. Are your decisions consistent with one another? Explain.

3. Do you think it is important that your decisions be consistent? Is it more important that judicial decisions be consistent? Explain.

Exercise 1-B

1. Assume you are a trial judge. Decide each of the following cases according to your idea of a just result, and explain the reasons for your decision. Do not refer to any of the other cases in making your decision, and do not invent additional facts.

(a) Sally Hyde was arrested and charged with possession of marijuana at the annual "Hash Bash," an unofficial celebration of spring that drew 2,000 people. She objected to her prosecution because most of the other people there also possessed marijuana. There were no other arrests for drug possession, and the police said she was arrested at random "as an example to others." Does Hyde have a valid defense? Explain.

(b) Hiram Price was arrested and charged with armed robbery shortly after three men stole $20,000 from the Crabtree National Bank. Two of the men escaped without a trace. Price objected to his prosecution on the ground that he should not be tried unless the other two were tried with him. Does Price have a valid defense? Explain.

(c) Jennifer Flick was arrested for driving sixty-four miles per hour in a fifty-five mile per hour zone. She objected to her prosecution because she had just been passed by two trucks and a car, all traveling five to ten miles per hour faster than she. Most of the other vehicles were traveling at the speed limit. Does Flick have a valid defense? Explain.

(d) Denise Gilman was arrested for cohabitation with a male friend. She was an outspoken and militant advocate for better housing, integrated schools, and improved social services in Motor City. The cohabitation law had not been enforced for years. She objected to her arrest on the ground that she was being unfairly singled out. Does Gilman have a valid defense? Explain.

2. Using your decisions in these four cases and the reasons you gave, frame a rule that will reconcile your conclusions. Remember that your statement of the rule should be clear and precise. Justify your rule.

2

Case Analysis

COURTS in our society decide what the law means and how it should be applied to specific situations. Sometimes courts interpret rules that are codified in statutes, regulations, or constitutions. At other times they make their own rules as they decide cases, forming a body of judge-made law known as common law.

Judicial decisions are the result of a great deal of time and hard work on the part of lawyers, judges, and all other participants in the litigation process. Disputes are first heard in trial courts. Whether one party is suing another for breach of contract, or whether the state is prosecuting someone for manslaughter, the case is heard in a trial court. The trial court has two responsibilities. First, it decides what actually occurred in the case. For example, where was the defendant on the night of June 25? Sometimes the parties agree on the facts, but often they do not. Different witnesses may have different stories. The court will hear the testimony of these witnesses, and will examine other evidence to determine which version of the facts is correct. Sometimes a jury determines the facts; sometimes the job belongs to the judge. Second, the trial court is required to determine what legal rules should be used to decide a particular case. Counsel for the opposing parties will make arguments, but the judge makes the final decision. In light of both the law and the facts, the court then decides which party prevails.

The losing party may challenge the decision in a higher or appellate court if that party believes the trial judge made a mistake that affected the outcome in stating or applying the relevant legal rules. Appellate courts must accept the factual record from the trial court; the only remaining issues are legal ones. The appellate court will examine the legal rule or rules at issue, sometimes upholding the trial court decision, and sometimes reversing it. Unlike trial courts, whose responsibilities are limited largely to ascertaining what actually happened and doing justice in individual cases, appellate courts must think about a range of situations far beyond the facts of the case and the broader policy implications of what the trial court has done. Since appellate courts review decisions by many trial courts under them, they also help insure that the rules are understood and applied uniformly.

Courts record their decisions in opinions, which describe what the dispute was about and why the court decided it in the way it did. These opinions deserve a great deal of careful study. Since courts rely on earlier cases in resolving disputes (see Chapter 3), cases have enormous value in predicting what a court might do in a specific situation and in persuading a court to reach a particular conclusion. Your ability to understand what these cases mean is thus a necessary skill in analyzing or writing about any legal problem.*

Although judicial opinions can contain many things, five components are of great importance. These are a description of the facts, a statement of the legal issues presented for decision, the relevant rules of law, the holding (the rule of law applied to the particular facts of the case), and the policies and reasons that support the holding.

Consider, for example, the following judicial opinion:

State v. Jones (1971)

(1) Jones appeals from his conviction for possession of marijuana. (2) When the police stopped and searched Jones's van, they found an ounce of marijuana in a backpack in the far rear of the vehicle. (3) Although Jones admitted he knew the marijuana was there, he defended against the charge by claiming that the backpack and drugs belonged to a hitchhiker who had been riding with him and who had accidentally left them in the van. (4) In this state, it is presumed that drugs are in the possession of the person who controls them. (5) The issue in this case is whether the marijuana was within Jones's control even though it was in a backpack in the rear of his van. (6) The fact that the backpack and drugs may have been owned by someone else is irrelevant. (7) Public policy dictates that possession should not be synonymous with ownership because the difficulty of proving

---

*As a law student, you will analyze cases on a daily basis, and you may write case briefs for class. Most of the cases you will read will be appellate court opinions. A case brief, not to be confused with the brief described in Part D of this book, is a written summary of the basic components of a case. Writing case briefs will aid your understanding of cases as you study them and help you recall the details of cases during classroom discussion. Although this chapter is not designed to teach the mechanics of case briefing, a good case brief will contain the elements described here.

ownership would permit too many drug offenders to evade prosecution. (8) It is sensible to assume that anything inside a vehicle is within the control of the driver. (9) We hold that Jones possessed marijuana because the backpack was within Jones's van and thus under his control. Affirmed.

All of the essential elements of a case are in the above example. Sentences 1, 2, and 3 tell you the facts of the case. Sentence 1 sets out the procedural facts; sentences 2 and 3 give the legally relevant facts. Sentence 5 is the issue presented for decision by the appellate court. Sentence 4 gives the rule of law applicable to this factual situation. Sentence 9 is the court's holding. Sentences 6, 7, and 8 are reasons and policies that support the holding. Although few cases lend themselves to such ready analysis, the skill of case analysis is still not hard to master.

You should, however, be aware of three major difficulties. The first is learning how to think in reverse. The opinion is the end product of a lawsuit. You have to start with this end product and work backwards to unravel what the dispute was about, what happened in the trial court, and what happened on appeal. This process is akin to discovering the secret of a competitor's product through reverse engineering. The second problem is understanding the interplay between the basic components of a judicial opinion. All the components of a case—facts, issues, rules, holdings, reasons, and policies—are related. One element cannot be understood without understanding the others. Case analysis is thus largely a circuitous process. You will constantly revise your understanding of the elements as you begin to fit them together. The third problem is that not all of the elements may be expressed. Since all five elements should be present in any opinion, when you do not see one of the elements identified, you must read between the lines to pinpoint that element as precisely as you can.

The remainder of this chapter is designed to give you a method for analyzing cases. Each component of a case will be discussed separately with an emphasis on identifying and understanding that component. Because of the web-like nature of a judicial opinion, no method will result in instant identification or understanding of the components. As you polish your skills, you will develop a style that suits your particular abilities and needs. You should also understand that the components can be identified in a variety of orders, and that different judicial opinions lend themselves to different identification schemes. The following method should prove helpful as a starting point and framework for your analysis.

1. Carefully Read the Opinion

The first step in case analysis is to read the case carefully. Although several readings are usually required before you can completely understand a case, during your initial reading you simply want to gain a general understanding of who the parties were, how the dispute originated, and what effect the court's decision had on the parties. You will also form tentative theories concerning the basic components of the opinion, which you will test and clarify during later readings. After you have acquired a basic understanding of the facts of the case and the "real world" implications of the court's decision, a possible next step is to figure out what the court decided.

2. *Identify the Holding*

The holding is the actual decision in the case. It is the answer to the legal question presented to the court. Identifying the holding requires you to study the opinion and determine what the court *actually decided* in the case. Holdings can be either express or implied. Express holdings are easy to identify because they are announced as such. In an express holding, for example, a court might state:

> We hold that driving a car at eighty miles per hour is *prima facie* reckless driving.

Although identifying express holdings appears easy from this example, there is a hidden danger. Courts sometimes inadvertently state they are ruling one way when, in fact, they are deciding the case a different way. To avoid being misled, concentrate on what the court actually did in the case, rather than on what it said.

Implied holdings are usually harder to identify than express holdings because you can rely only on the court's actions. The court gives its ultimate decision and the reasons supporting it, but does not tell you what rule it has formulated or followed. In an implied holding, for example, a court might state:

> The trial court found defendant guilty of reckless driving without any testimony that defendant was, in fact, operating his car in a reckless manner. Anyone who drives at eighty miles per hour is forced to dodge and weave through traffic at a high rate of speed. This conduct is inherently reckless and endangers the well-being of others. Affirmed.

The court's holding is the same as in the first example, but here the judge did not expressly state it. Both holdings, however, are equally important.

Do not confuse implied holdings with the reasons for the decision. Sometimes these two elements are hard to distinguish. Remember that the holding is the actual decision, and that the reasons or policies are the justifications given for that decision. The two concepts can be distinguished by a simple but useful idea: each issue usually has only one holding, but each holding may be supported by several reasons.

*   *   *   *   *

Study the following judicial opinion and the three proposed holdings for the case:

State v. Klein (1969)

Casey Klein appeals from his conviction for burglary. Klein was apprehended reaching into a house with a ten-foot-long tree snips he had modified into a long pair of tweezers. He admitted to the police that he intended to steal a mink coat lying on a chair near an open window.

Appellant Klein denies that he could properly have been convicted of burglary. The maximum offense, he argues, is attempted larceny, since that crime requires only an attempt to steal the property of another. The prosecutor, however, correctly sought and won a conviction for burglary.

Generally, burglary occurs only if the defendant is physically present in the house; he must actually penetrate the enclosure of the dwelling. Although the defendant in this case never entered the house, he did extend his tree snips through the window. There is no meaningful difference between the snips and his arm since the penetration by the snips was merely an extension of Klein's person. Crime has run rampant in recent decades and this type of activity must be discouraged. Burglary carries a greater penalty than attempted larceny and this penalty will more effectively deter such crimes. We therefore hold that the need to deter such activities renders defendant's actions burglary.

ANSWER A: A defendant may properly be convicted of burglary during a high crime period where his conviction will deter similar actions, even if he was not physically present in the building.

ANSWER B: For the purposes of burglary, a tree snips is the same as a human arm.

ANSWER C: The protrusion of a tree snips held by defendant into a dwelling satisfies the penetration element of burglary even if the defendant's body does not enter the dwelling.

The actual holding of the case is contained in Answer C. It shows how the relevant legal rule was found applicable to the facts of this case. Answer C does not justify the holding; it is simply a statement of what the court decided. This is the rule that subsequent courts will apply or distinguish.

Answer A is what the court said it was holding, but not what it actually held. Deterring crime is a reason the court gave for deciding the case the way it did, but reasons and holdings are different things. The holding, again, is what the court actually decided in the case. Answer A reflects the court's confusing way of stating a policy justification for the decision, but it is not the court's holding.

Answer B sounds more like a holding and less like a reason than Answer A. It does not, however, offer a very useful holding. A tree snips may be the same as a human arm, but that statement fails to explain what legal rule is involved. In addition, the court *reasoned* that there was no meaningful difference between a tree snips and a human arm for purposes of satisfying the penetration requirement. Thus, Answer B also turns out to be a reason.

3. Identify the Issue

Cases usually develop because the parties disagree over the application of one or more rules of law to a particular fact situation. The issue is the legal question that must be resolved before a case can be decided. Notice the interplay between holdings and issues; holdings are the legal answers to the issues.

The issue in a case, like the holding, can be express or implied. Many times the court will tell you the issue. For example: "The question presented in this case is whether a snowmobile is a motor vehicle within the meaning of the Michigan Motor Vehicle Code." This is an express issue. Sometimes a court will tell you the issue is one thing when a close reading of the case will demonstrate that it is something else. Sometimes the court will not tell you the issue. When this happens, you must read the case carefully and identify the issue from the holding and the reasons that support the holding. The holding helps identify the issue because the holding is usually a positive statement of the issue. Once you have identified the holding in a case, you should have little trouble spotting the issue.

* * * * *

Study the following opinion and three suggested issues:

Johnson v. Silk (1969)

Alice Silk and Fran Johnson, university students who had recently met, decided to use Silk's small sports car to drive to their home town for the weekend. Silk told Johnson she would pay all their traveling expenses to repay Johnson for tutoring Silk before the midterm examination in Silk's Chinese philosophy class. Shortly after they started out, Silk lost control of her car and it struck a construction barrel on the side of the road. Johnson suffered severe injuries and brought suit against Silk to recover damages. The trial court granted Silk's motion to dismiss, and Johnson appealed.

The state Automobile Guest Statute bars guest passengers from suing drivers for injuries they sustain in automobile accidents. The statute applies only if the passenger did not confer a substantial benefit on the driver that motivated the driver to provide the ride.

The trial court found that Johnson was barred from recovery because she "paid nothing for the ride." The issue in this case is whether Johnson assumed the risk of her own injury by riding on a busy highway in a small sports car. Johnson tutored Silk, and she did so before the ride with every expectation of repayment. It is not necessary that the substantial benefit motivating the ride be cash. Silk owed a favor to Johnson that she felt obligated to repay, and under general principles of fairness actually was bound to repay. The Guest Statute therefore is inapplicable. Reversed.

ANSWER A: Whether a passenger injured in an accident while riding in a small sports car on a busy highway is barred by assumption of risk from suing the driver of that car for damages.

ANSWER B: Whether a court can disregard the Automobile Guest Statute to reach a just and fair result.

ANSWER C: Whether a passenger's tutoring of a driver before a midterm examination constitutes a substantial benefit to bar application of the Automobile Guest Statute.

The correct statement of the issue is Answer C. The court had to decide whether the Automobile Guest Statute applied to this situation. Application of the statute turned on whether the passenger conferred a substantial benefit on the driver. This is the real issue. The court determined that Johnson's tutoring of Silk constituted a substantial benefit because Silk felt obligated to repay Johnson by providing the ride. The court, therefore, held the statute inapplicable, and this holding provides further evidence of the issue.

Answer A is what the court said the issue was, but it is not what the court decided. Since the issue and the holding are so closely related, you must look elsewhere for the issue. Assumption of risk, as you may know, is a defense to negligence. Most of this opinion, however, deals with the Automobile Guest Statute, and this is a good clue that the issue concerns the statute and not assumption of risk. Although few courts will err as obviously as this one did, you should remember that word and deed are not necessarily the same thing in judicial opinion writing.

Answer B may be your first reaction to what happened in this case, but issues must be defined in a legal context, not a political one. It is true that the court mentioned fairness in the opinion, but this was a reason for the ultimate decision even though the court mistakenly said it was the holding. This mistake points to an important lesson. Although holdings and issues are closely related, you must be very sure you have identified the correct holding before you use it to infer the issue in a case. Answer B does not define the legal issue.

4. Identify the Rule

Once you have determined the issue and holding, you should identify the rule. The rule is the general legal principle relevant to the particular factual situation presented. The rule is a synthesis of prior holdings in cases with similar facts. It can also be a statutory provision.

Identifying the rule involved in a particular case is relatively easy. The court will usually state what rule it is applying or why it is refusing to apply a certain rule. When the court does not state what rule applies, and you are unfamiliar with the area of law, you will have to infer the rule from the issues, holdings, and facts of the case.

Rules, issues, and holdings are closely related. The issue generally is whether the relevant rule will be applied to the case. The holding is the resolution of the issue—the determination whether the rule should be applied to the case. Stated another way, the holding is the rule modified by the facts of a particular case.

The following examples are illustrative:

Whitman v. Whitman (1971)

James Whitman's will left all of his property to his brother, George. James's wife challenged the validity of the will after James died, claiming that it did not express James's clear intent. She sought to present evidence, including her own testimony, that James actually wanted to give a substantial portion of his estate to her. The trial court excluded this evidence, and we affirm. The rule in this state is that an unambiguous will is conclusive as to the testator's intent unless it would contravene law or public policy. All other evidence must be excluded. Since James's wife sought to present precisely such evidence, and the will was not ambiguous, the trial court properly ruled the evidence inadmissible.

Identifying the rule in this case is simple because the court explained that "the rule in this state" is that an unambiguous will is conclusive as to the testator's intent. But consider this opinion:

Central Credit Co. v. Smith (1963)

Olan Company began to operate as a business before it was properly incorporated. Prior to proper incorporation, the company made sales and incurred debts. Olan's creditors are seeking to hold Smith and Jones, the incorporators and sole shareholders, personally liable for these debts. A corporation does not legally exist until it has been properly incorporated. Once properly incorporated, a creditor cannot proceed personally against the shareholders; the creditor must look to the corporate entity to satisfy its claim. The trial court properly found Smith and Jones personally liable for the debts. Affirmed.

Since the precise rule used by the court is not stated here, you must identify it by inference. The legal rules stated by the court and its holding in this case help the inquiry. A corporation's legal existence begins with proper incorporation, the court said. After that time, the corporation's shareholders are not personally liable for its debts. The court also held these shareholders personally liable for debts they incurred before incorporation. The court thus applied a corollary of the rules stated: a shareholder of a corporation can be held personally liable for debts incurred when the company is not properly incorporated.

5. Identify the Facts

After you understand the rule, holding, and issue, you will be able to identify the relevant facts of the case. During the initial reading of the case, you simply wanted a general knowledge of the facts. Now you are ready to reread them and determine which facts were important to the decision.

Judicial opinions usually contain a lengthy description of the facts because the court wants the reader to understand the situation completely. You should identify two kinds of facts—legally relevant facts and procedurally significant facts.

Legally relevant facts are those the court considered important in deciding the case. These facts are outcome-determinative; they affected the court's decision. Since facts are inextricably tied to legal issues and rules, it is impossible to know which facts are relevant without first knowing what the court decided. Sometimes a court will state precisely those facts it thought significant in deciding the case, and at other times you will have to guess those facts from the court's holding and reasons. There is no rule that indicates which facts are outcome-determinative, and no single fact is necessarily legally significant.

Procedurally significant facts describe at what stage in the case the trial judge erred by granting or denying a motion by one of the parties. These facts are routinely stated in appellate opinions. Procedural facts are important because the procedural posture of the case affects what legally relevant facts are available to the appellate court. When the parties agree on the facts, the trial court simply determines and applies the relevant law. If the parties disagree on the facts, a trial is held where they present witnesses and other evidence to support their story. Appellate courts are then confronted with more numerous and less consistent facts than if a case is resolved before trial. The procedural posture of the case also affects what the appellate court can do if it disagrees with the trial court. If the factual record is complete, the appellate court's decision should end the controversy; if the record is not complete, the appellate court will remand the case for more fact finding.

*   *   *   *   *

Consider the following opinion and factual statements:

Lost River Ditch Co. v. Brody (1923)

Defendant owns a small riparian tract on Apple Blossom Creek. In the fall of 1922 he began diverting 45,000 gallons of water a day from a pumphouse on that tract to a nonriparian parcel one-half mile from the stream. Defendant claimed he needed the water because he had just doubled the size of his herd. Plaintiff, who owned another riparian tract downstream on the creek, sued defendant for damages, claiming that any diversion of water from the watershed was impermissible. Although plaintiff was unable to prove any actual damages, the jury awarded him one dollar in nominal damages. We reverse. Diversion of water from the creek to a nonriparian tract without some evidence of damage does not provide a basis for recovery of nominal or any other damages.

ANSWER A: Defendant, who owned a small riparian tract on Apple Blossom Creek, diverted 45,000 gallons of water per day in the fall of 1922 to supply water for his recently doubled cattle herd. Plaintiff, a downstream riparian owner on the same creek, sued defendant for damages, claiming that any diversion of water from the riparian tract was prohibited. A jury awarded plaintiff one dollar in nominal damages even though he was unable to prove actual damages.

ANSWER B: Defendant, who owned a riparian tract on a creek, diverted water from the creek to a nonriparian tract. Plaintiff, a downstream riparian owner on the same creek, sued defendant for diverting the water. Plaintiff could not show actual damages, but a jury awarded him nominal damages.

Answer B is better because it contains only those facts the court used to decide the case and those facts needed to explain what happened in the trial court. Answer B contains nothing else; it is simple and succinct. Answer A is a slightly rewritten version of the facts stated in the case. It includes interesting details, but the name of the creek, the quantity of water diverted, the actual amount of the nominal damages, and other details have nothing to do with the legal rule or the procedurally significant facts of this case. Answer A also omits an important fact by ignoring the type of tract to which the water was diverted. Since the rule is applicable only to water diverted to a nonriparian tract, Answer A should have stated that the water was diverted from the creek to a nonriparian tract.

6. Identify the Policies and Reasons

Chapter 1 defines policies as the underlying purposes of legal rules. Policies also support the holding in a particular case. Whether a court is modifying the law in bold strokes to reach certain social goals or whether it is carefully limiting the scope of earlier decisions, it will usually advance some policy justification for its decision. Even when a court admits it reached a harsh or unfair result for the parties, it will still try to show how the effect of the decision is in the best interest of the public. In other cases, when the law dictates an outcome the court dislikes, the court may complain about the law and even suggest the desirability of legislative change, but it will still explain the policies underlying the law and the outcome. Policies are important because they define the future direction of the law.

The easiest way to identify policies is to first identify the holding. Once you have determined what the court decided, look for the social justifications for the court's decision. An illustration used earlier in this chapter involved a defendant who attempted to take a fur coat through a window using a tree snips. The court in that case held that use of the tree snips satisfied the penetration element of burglary even though no part of defendant's body entered the building. The court stated a broad policy in support of its conclusion by emphasizing the deterrent value of the more severe penalty for burglary and the high crime rate.

Some opinions contain no policy justification at all. In the water diversion illustration set out earlier in this chapter, for example, the court stated a rule and reversed the trial court without explaining the basis for the rule or its holding. A court is less likely to provide an explanation in cases such as this when the rule and its application are fairly well settled. Look to earlier decisions, if need be, to determine the policies underlying the rule.

Reasons are similar to, but narrower than, policies. Reasons are the steps in the logical process a court uses in arriving at its holding, or in justifying its adoption of a particular policy. Reasons can be simple explanations of how a legal rule or policy is applicable or inapplicable to the case, or more involved explanations of why the analysis from one area of the law is applicable to an entirely different area of the law. When studying cases, you should determine the exact reasoning process the court employed in reaching its holding on an issue. Only through understanding the reasons behind a court's decision can you understand what the decision actually means—or how broadly or narrowly the case might be interpreted.

In the burglary case, for example, the court stated that there was no meaningful difference between a human arm and the tree snips. This was a logical step the court took in arriving at its conclusion that there was a burglary. In addition, although the court did not say so, the penetration requirement would look ridiculous if it did not apply to a device that extended the reach of a burglar's arm to take items he might not otherwise be able to reach. While that was not an express reason articulated by the court, it must have been part of the court's reasoning process. The court's reasoning and conclusion were justified by the broad policy goal of deterring crime.

The close relationship between reasons and policies sometimes makes it difficult to distinguish between the two, but the following test is useful: reasons indicate how the court arrived at its holding; policies tell you why this holding is socially desirable. An opinion can make sense without any policy justifications, but it cannot make sense without reasons showing how the court arrived at its conclusions.

7. Check for Congruency

Once you have some idea of the important facts, the issue, the rule of law, the holding, and the reasons and policies, check these elements against one another to make sure they are congruent. There is an interplay between them that should be obvious by now. The court's holding will be a combination of the relevant rule of law and the significant facts. The issue is the holding stated in the form of a question: should this rule of law be applied to the particular facts of this case? The answer to the issue will be the holding. Policies and reasons form a basis for the holding. Such interaction makes the case an interlocking whole, and underscores why you cannot understand any one element without reference to the others. Always pause when you have gone this far to make sure the elements are in agreement.

8. In Multiple-Issue Cases, Analyze Each Issue
Separately

A case can contain more than one issue because there may have been several disagreements of law in the trial court that the appellate court was asked to resolve. Although an appellate court will frequently dispose of the entire case after resolving only one of these disagreements, many times the opinion will contain a discussion of several issues with a corresponding holding for each issue.

When a case contains several issues, analyze each issue separately. For each issue you must identify a rule, relevant facts, a holding, the precise issue, and the reasons and policies supporting the court's holding on that issue. Although the issues may be closely related, your analysis of each should be distinct. Once you have identified each issue presented in an opinion, follow the steps outlined in this chapter for dissecting them.

The following exercises are designed to introduce you to case analysis. Each opinion contains all of the components discussed in this chapter. Try to follow the format for case analysis given in this chapter for the first two exercises by simply listing the components in the order of identification. If you begin to develop your own style, try that style on the remaining exercise. Remember, the goal is to identify the various components as precisely as possible.

Exercise 2-A

Toad v. Userp (1972)

The appellee, Marvin Toad, operates a roadside stand where he sells hand-carved, three-legged wooden stools to tourists. Toad's business started slowly, but it has increased substantially in recent years. Toad now derives a modest income from his enterprise. From the start, he has advertised and referred to his stools as "Toad Stools." After Toad operated his stand for one year, the appellant, Boris Userp, began operating a similar stand and selling similar stools which Userp also called "Toad Stools." When Userp first opened his stand, Toad asked him not to use the name, "Toad Stools," but Userp did so for two years. Toad made no further effort to prevent the use of the name until he started this suit.

Toad filed suit alleging that the appellant had infringed on his trademark. Toad requested $500 in damages for lost sales and an injunction barring Userp from using the name, "Toad Stool." The trial court granted Toad's motion for summary judgment. Appellant Userp now contends that the trial court erred in finding a trademark infringement because Toad did not actively defend his use of the name.

Common law trademark principles can protect the name of a business or product, but that protection is not absolute. A person must actively defend that trademark against known infringements. If he or she does not actively defend the name, a competitor is free to use that name after two years. "Actively defend" means making diligent efforts, including lawsuits if necessary, and Toad has not made diligent efforts according to the traditional rule.

We must, however, distinguish between large businesses that have the capacity and the resources to litigate such claims, and small businesses that do not have these resources and should not be held to the same standards. The smaller the business, the easier it should be to satisfy the active defense requirement. When Toad approached Userp and asked him not to use the name, he satisfied that requirement. Therefore, Toad is entitled to common law trademark protection. Affirmed.

Exercise 2-B

Bronson v. Road Runner Shoe Co. (1976)

The appellee, Road Runner Shoe Co., is a Maryland Corporation that manufactures and sells running shoes. Twenty of the company's 100 employees work at its Maryland headquarters, while the remainder work at offices throughout the United States. The company, which sells to major retailers, has a fleet of trucks for delivering its shoes. The company employed George Granger as a general helper and driver for one of its delivery trucks.

Johnny Bronson filed suit against the company for injuries he sustained when one of the company's trucks, driven by Granger, jumped the median strip and struck him while he was jogging. It is undisputed that Bronson was using extreme care while jogging and was wearing a bright red jogging outfit. Bronson claimed he would never be able to jog again and that he has had emotional problems since the accident. Granger, who had not received permission to use the truck, was on his way to see his girlfriend during his lunch hour. The company gives Granger one hour to eat lunch, and he was speeding back to work when the incident occurred. Granger was nineteen years old at the time and a "hard worker who comes from a reputable family." Granger was earning money so he could go to college and major in business administration. Granger was arrested once when he was sixteen for drag racing on a public highway, but his case was dismissed. Granger had worked for the company two years when the incident occurred.

The trial court granted the company's motion for summary judgment. On appeal, Bronson argues that the company should be liable on the theory of *respondeat superior*. We agree.

The general rule is that an employer is liable for the acts of employees when they are acting within the scope of their authority. In this case, Granger did not have permission to use the truck during lunch and did not usually drive it then. However, Granger normally had exclusive possession of the keys during working hours, and the company had never objected to Granger's private use of the truck. Employers should be held liable for the torts of their employees. It is too easy for an employer to shrug off legal responsibility by saying the employee was not authorized to commit the act. Very few employers expressly authorize employees to commit tortious acts. Employers, by their position of authority, have control over employees. Employees who do not behave responsibly should be discharged. Reversed.

Exercise 2-C

State v. Phyron (1975)

Appellant set fire to an unoccupied building. The building had been deserted for many years and had been condemned as a "firetrap." The appellant poured several gallons of gasoline throughout the first floor of the building and then ignited it. The building burned to the ground in thirty minutes. The trial court found her guilty of arson, a felony in this state. The appellant does not contest that conviction here.

On the way to put out the fire, a fireman was killed when he fell off the back of the firetruck and was run over by a car which was both speeding and following the truck too closely. There was no way the driver of the car could have avoided the fireman. The driver of the car was charged and convicted of speeding and careless driving. Appellant was also found guilty of murder under the felony-murder rule. She appealed this conviction.

The felony-murder rule provides that if someone is killed during the commission of a felony, the defendant is guilty of murder of that person. The purpose of the rule is to deter people from committing felonies, particularly those which are inherently dangerous to human life. In this case, there is no doubt the fireman was killed during the commission of a felony.

Fires and arson are inherently dangerous to people in buildings, bystanders, the surrounding neighborhood, and the firemen summoned to combat the blaze. The appellant should have known that a firetruck would be summoned to put out the fire, but could not foresee someone would be following the truck too closely. Public policy dictates that there must be a limit to liability. The felony-murder rule borders on strict liability in criminal law. Any expansion should be carefully scrutinized. As with any principle of strict liability, there must be a causal connection. Reversed.

3

Precedent and
Stare Decisis

JUDGES have much freedom to modify legal rules and principles in accordance with social norms and their views of justice and common sense. The concepts of precedent and *stare decisis* serve as important checks on this judicial freedom and insure that the law develops in an orderly fashion.

One of the fundamental notions of our legal system is that courts should look to previous decisions on similar questions for guidance in deciding present cases. Previous decisions on similar questions are known as precedent, and their usefulness is premised on the idea that an issue, once properly decided, should not be decided again. Reliance on precedent helps insure that similar cases are decided according to the same basic principles and helps courts to process cases more efficiently. Durable rules also assist people in planning their activities, encourage confidence in the legal system, and reinforce the social norms they define.

The values that surround the notion of precedent are reinforced by the principle of *stare decisis*. Where precedent merely requires that courts look to previous decisions for guidance, *stare decisis* requies that a court follow its own decisions and the decisions of higher courts within the same jurisdiction. A state trial court, for example, must follow its own decisions and the decisions of appellate courts in that state; an intermediate appellate court must follow its own decisions and the decisions of the state's highest appellate court. Federal courts of appeal must generally follow their own prior decisions and those of the United States Supreme

21

Court, but they are not bound by decisions of federal district courts or other appellate courts.

Precedent, then, can be of two types—binding or persuasive. Where the doctrine of *stare decisis* applies, precedent is binding and a court's options are limited. A court must harmonize the result in the present case with past decisions. Only after explaining why previous cases are inapplicable may a court fashion new rules or modify existing ones; a court may never ignore or contradict binding precedent. Where the doctrine of *stare decisis* is not applicable, as with decisions from other jurisdictions or lower courts in the same jurisdiction, courts are free to follow previous decisions or ignore them. Although courts are not bound by such decisions, they remain persuasive because their reasoning can illuminate possible solutions to a problem.

In theory, the concept of binding precedent seems absolute. In practice, precedent and *stare decisis* are flexible rather than static concepts. The inherent ambiguities of judicial opinions and varying levels of interpretation allow judges significant latitude even when dealing with binding precedent. The interplay between the stated holding of a case, its underlying reasons, and its factual situation permits these differing interpretations. Viewed most narrowly, a case stands for a particular result on that set of facts. Such interpretations give the case little value, but courts often confine cases to narrow factual categories. Viewed more broadly, a case stands for the rule announced by the court—a straightforward interpretation that goes no further than the court's explicit statements about the scope of the case. Viewed most broadly, a case stands for its articulated policy or policies, and the reasons motivating the court's decision. Since the court was most concerned with the facts of the case before it, one travels on increasingly risky ground the further one ventures from those facts. The best guides in venturing from those facts are the articulated reasons and policies of the case.

Courts sometimes make broad statements about matters that have no bearing on the decision. Statements that are irrelevant to a court's decision are known as *dicta*. *Dicta* have little precedential value because they are not part of the reasoning process that led to the decision, and because courts are supposed to decide only the issues before them. While *dicta* have little precedential value, they are nonetheless important because courts sometimes rely on *dicta* as a basis for their decisions. *Dicta* are also valuable because they reflect what judges are thinking and indicate how the court is likely to rule if confronted with a similar situation in the future.

The various ways in which a case can be interpreted highlight the fundamental role that precedent and *stare decisis* play in the process of legal analysis. In his well-known book, *The Bramble Bush*, Professor Karl Llewellyn defines this range of interpretation in terms of "strict" and "loose" views of precedent. The "strict" view, applied to "unwelcome" precedent, limits the reach of prior cases to show that they are not applicable to the case at hand. It requires careful distinguishing of the facts and policies and reads such cases for their minimum value. The "loose" view, applied to "welcome" precedent, maximizes the reach of these cases to show how they are applicable. As Llewellyn points out, both approaches are "respectable, traditionally sound, [and] dogmatically correct."*

The varying levels of case interpretation permit flexibility within the confines of *stare decisis*. This flexibility is necessary to the legal system because it allows the law to adapt to evolving conditions and to accommodate new factual situations. Although there is much flexibility, the stabilizing effect of *stare decisis* should not be underestimated. When the rules are well defined and the factual situations are clearly similar or plainly different, *stare decisis* mechanically dictates the result. Even when the rule is ambiguous or the factual situation complex, *stare decisis* at least defines the starting point for analysis. This tension between restraint and freedom, between stability and change, is the essence of our legal system.

The following two cases illustrate these ideas. They concern the question of when a landlord should be held liable for negligently exposing his tenants to foreseeable criminal activities. After deciding the first case, *Brainerd v. Harvey,* in 1972, the same state appellate court was presented with an opportunity four years later, in *Douglas v. Archer Professional Building, Inc.,* to expand the scope of the rule to cover a different factual situation. The use of the first case in deciding the second illustrates the meaning and function of precedent and *stare decisis*.

Brainerd v. Harvey (1972)

> Plaintiff is an elderly man who lived in a small building in a high crime area. The building had poor lighting on its front porch and a continuously unlocked outer door. As plaintiff was about to enter the building one night, the outer door was jerked open by an unknown youth who had been hiding inside. The youth struck and robbed the plaintiff. Plaintiff brought suit against the landlord, but the trial judge granted defendant's motion for a directed verdict of no cause of action.
>
> We reverse. We have from time to time held that persons are liable for negligently exposing others to foreseeable criminal activities, and this is such a case. The inadequate lighting and locks were physical defects in a common area of the building under the landlord's control; this would be a far different case if the building had not contained such defects. The landlord's negligence in failing to repair them made it more likely than not that plaintiff would be victimized by a criminal attack.

*K. LLEWELLYN, THE BRAMBLE BUSH 66-69 (1930).

The trial court also erred in refusing to grant plaintiff a jury trial. Since plaintiff demanded a jury trial, he did not waive that right, even though he waited until the pretrial conference to make his demand. Remanded for a jury trial.

Douglas v. Archer Professional Building, Inc. (1976)

In 1968, a mental health clinic leased and began occupying an office on the fifth floor of the Archer Professional Building. About two years later, an outpatient at the center stabbed Carol Douglas, a physician with an office in the building, while both of them were riding in the building's elevator. Dr. Douglas brought suit against the owner of the building. At trial, the director of the clinic testified that the stabbing was the first such incident in his ten years of experience with such programs. There was also testimony that before the incident other tenants in the building had voiced concern over use of the elevators and stairwells by the clinic's patients. Dr. Douglas won a jury verdict for $115,000 in damages. We affirm.

We stated in *Brainerd v. Harvey* that landlords are liable for damages caused when they negligently expose others to foreseeable criminal attacks in common areas of buildings they lease. In both this case and *Brainerd* the attack occurred in an area of the building under the landlord's control and used by all tenants. Just as the landlord in *Brainerd* knew or should have known about the absence of adequate lighting and locks in the apartment building, the defendant here knew or should have known about the potentially dangerous condition in the professional building. Where the landlord is informed by his tenants that such a condition exists, he has a duty to investigate and take any possible preventive measures. The jury could properly find that the landlord's failure to do so was negligence.

Fisher, J., dissenting. The court here imposes unwarranted and unreasonable burdens on landlords by vastly extending their potential liability. In *Brainerd v. Harvey,* we expressly limited the landlord's liability to his failure to detect and repair dangerous physical conditions in common areas of leased buildings. Unlike *Brainerd,* where the apartment had poor lighting and an unlocked front door, this professional building had no physical defect that enabled the assault to occur. In *Brainerd,* we also limited liability to foreseeable criminal attacks, rather than those based merely on the subjective fears of some tenants in the building. The majority opinion suggests a medieval fear of persons who receive mental health care and will impede the state's goal of returning mental patients to the community.

Although the majority and dissenting opinions reach opposite conclusions in the *Douglas* case, they both rely on *Brainerd* for the basic principles of decision. Both opinions acknowledge that landlords should be liable when they negligently expose their tenants to foreseeable criminal attacks in common areas of buildings they lease. The principle of *stare decisis* requires the court to start from that position, rather than craft new and different rules or principles.

The division of the court in *Douglas* illustrates the flexibility of *stare decisis*. The majority interpreted *Brainerd* broadly as "welcome" precedent. Where the landlord is informed by his tenants of their subjective fears of a potentially dangerous condition in a common area of the building, the majority ruled, he has a duty to investigate the situation and take precautionary measures. The court departed from *Brainerd* by refusing to limit the landlord's liability to situations where there were physical defects in the building, or even to situations where there was tangible evidence suggesting the possibility of a criminal attack. The court responded to the different factual situation presented in *Douglas* by pushing the law in a different direction, even as it reasoned that it was merely following the *Brainerd* decision.

The dissenting opinion interpreted *Brainerd* more narrowly as "unwelcome" precedent. *Brainerd,* it concluded, conditions the landlord's liability on the presence of physical defects in the building and objective evidence suggesting the possibility of a criminal attack, neither of which were present in *Douglas.* The dissent also raised an objection about the effect of the court's decision on landlords in general and outpatient mental clinics in particular to support its narrow reading of *Brainerd.* The dissenting opinion is buttressed by *dicta* from *Brainerd* that states the case would be different if the building did not have physical defects. The statement is *dicta* because it was not necessary to the resolution of the *Brainerd* case, and was thus disregarded by the majority in *Douglas.*

These two cases illustrate the tension between change and stability that is central to the study and practice of law. Certain factors militate in favor of stability. The *Brainerd* decision altered business expectations and forced landlords to modify their practices to avoid liability. In addition, since the corporate owner was found liable in the second case, it paid damages pursuant to a rule that was not articulated until the owner was found to have breached it. After *Douglas,* landlords for other office buildings no doubt made significant changes in their leasing procedures and plans. Uncertainties would be magnified by any perception that the law in the area was subject to further modification.

Other arguments counseled for change. The injury to Carol Douglas underscored the majority's view that landlords should keep their common areas free of foreseeable criminal activity. Even if the risk seemed most apparent after the harm occurred, a court might reasonably conclude that a subjectively perceived risk of great bodily harm should be sufficient to warrant extra protective measures by the landlord. In addition, even though the defendant is liable under a new formulation of the rule, such liability is the only realistic incentive for encouraging a plaintiff to seek relief in court. *Douglas* was based on an evolving view of the landlord-tenant relationship. Although the arguments vary somewhat from case to case, the tension between change and stability remains.

Two additional considerations are necessary for a full understanding of the mechanics and policies of precedent and *stare decisis*. First, appellate courts are supposed to decide only as many issues as are necessary for the disposition of a case. As Chapter 2 points out, sometimes this requires courts to decide multiple issues. Each holding on an issue—regardless of the number of holdings—is precedent for later decisions. The court's holding in *Brainerd* concerning plaintiff's demand for a jury trial, as well as its holding on the negligence issue, are both precedent, and will have to be considered by future courts rendering decisions on the same issues.

Second, since appellate courts tend to make and apply law, while trial courts simply apply law, appellate courts have greater freedom in treating precedent than trial courts. Appellate courts sometimes find it impossible to use previous cases and still reconcile their decisions with their own values or social norms. When this happens, a court may simply overrule the previous cases and chart a new course rather than show how these cases may be distinguished. Courts usually justify overruling previous decisions by pointing to the outdated principles or poor reasoning that supported them. These decisions are often spectacular, as when the United States Supreme Court, in the 1954 case of *Brown v. Board of Education*,* held that a state could not constitutionally require racial segregation in public schools, overruling its 1896 *Plessy v. Ferguson*† decision permitting "separate but equal" accommodations. Cases may also be more subtly overruled; a series of decisions, for example, may chip away at the scope of an earlier rule or undercut its policy basis.

The exercises that follow are intended to show the limitations and flexibility inherent in the concepts of precedent and *stare decisis*.

Exercise 3-A

1. Assume you are a trial judge. In the case before you, Marie Elson, an elderly blind woman, defaulted on the land contract for her home. The real estate company wants to repossess the house and keep $15,000 in payments she has made thus far on the $21,000 contract. Elson does not contest her default, and she is willing to let the real estate company repossess the house. She does, however, insist on the return of the $15,000. The following case is the only relevant precedent:

   Aaron v. Erickson (1947)
   Appellant Aaron defaulted on a $30,000 land contract after making $12,000 in payments. The trial court denied Aaron's request for return of the $12,000. We affirm. There is a fundamental difference

---

*347 U.S. 483 (1954).
†163 U.S. 537 (1896).

in our law between land contracts and mortgages. A land contract is an installment plan under which the purchaser does not get title to the property until the last payment. Those who buy property on a mortgage have it financed through a third party and receive title immediately. It may be a hard result, but those who buy property on a land contract take the risk of losing everything for failure to make payments. If this were a mortgage, we would reach a different result.

(a) Decide whether Elson is entitled to have the money refunded, using the *Aaron* case as precedent. Justify your decision.

(b) Is your answer to question (a) consistent with your sense of a just result? Explain.

(c) Could you have used *Aaron* to support a decision contrary to the one you reached in question (a)? Explain.

2. Assume you are a trial judge in a civil action in which Fowler, the defendant, claims the court has no jurisdiction because service was obtained "by trickery and fraud." Fowler, a resident of another state, knew she was the possible subject of two civil actions in your state, one for a $5,000 damage deposit she had not returned to a merchant, and the other for a $200,000 insurance swindle. She wanted to resolve the first potential suit but not the second. To do this, she arranged a vacation in your state so she could pay off the merchant, who said he wanted "to avoid litigation over the deposit." She met the merchant at the airport and paid his deposit. The merchant, who also worked for the defrauded insurance company, then served papers on her for the insurance scheme. The following case is the only relevant precedent in your state:

Eckersly v. Ramon (1951)

Appellant Eckersly, a resident of this state, sought to bring an action against Ramon, a nonresident, for breach of contract. To secure service of process on Ramon, Eckersly requested several of Ramon's acquaintances to persuade Ramon that his mother, who also lives in this state, was terminally ill. Ramon agreed to come to this state to visit her. In reality, Ramon's mother was hiking in the Rocky Mountains. Ramon was met at the airport by Eckersly's agent, who served Ramon with papers in the contract action. The trial court rejected Ramon's claim that it lacked jurisdiction because service was fraudulently obtained. We disagree. Where plaintiffs resort to such shocking fraud to obtain service of process, the integrity of the entire judicial system is undermined. The trial court had no power to render judgment in this case. Reversed.

(a) Decide whether your court has jurisdiction, using the *Eckersly* case as precedent. Justify your decision.

(b) Is your answer to question (a) consistent with your sense of a just result? Explain.

(c) Could you have used *Eckersly* to support a decision contrary to the one you reached in question (a)? Explain.

3. Assume that you are a state appellate court judge. Elliot Buckler was charged

with reckless endangerment under the Motor Vehicle Code after the car he was driving left the road early one morning and struck a tree, killing a passenger. The trial judge instructed the jury that it could return a guilty verdict only if it was convinced beyond a reasonable doubt that the evidence showed Buckler had operated his motor vehicle in reckless disregard of the lives or safety of others. The judge then read a separate provision of the Motor Vehicle Code which prohibits driving while under the influence of alcohol. Although Buckler was not charged for violating this provision, there was evidence that he had been drinking heavily. The judge told the jury it could use Buckler's violation of this provision to determine his guilt for reckless endangerment. Buckler was convicted. On appeal, he seeks a new trial by challenging the trial judge's instructions that guilt for driving while under the influence of alcohol could be used to establish guilt for reckless endangerment.

There are two relevant cases in the state:

State v. Waterford (1909)

This action began on a criminal complaint charging defendant with reckless endangerment. The complaint charged that defendant recklessly ran his motor vehicle against the decedent and the horse that the decedent was riding, killing both. The defendant filed a demurrer, claiming that the complaint did not indicate the offense with sufficient clarity to notify the defendant specifically for what crime he was to be tried. The trial court overruled the demurrer, and the defendant was convicted. We affirm.

Operators of motor vehicles have a duty to obey the laws regarding the use of motor vehicles. Disregard of or inattention to this duty, as defined in any of the motor vehicle laws, constitutes recklessness. The complaint therefore properly used the words "reckless endangerment" to describe the manner in which the defendant acted, particularly considering his manifest drunkenness. This was not an innocent accident.

State v. Seperic (1958)

A criminal complaint charged the defendant with reckless endangerment in violation of the Motor Vehicle Code. He was convicted after a jury trial. The defendant argues on appeal that the statute violates the state constitution because it does not state with sufficient clarity what it prohibits. We disagree.

Motor vehicles play such an important role in our lives that reckless driving has come to have a commonly understood meaning—driving with wanton disregard for the lives or safety of other persons. The acts prohibited are sufficiently definite to persons of ordinary intelligence. The standard requires not only reckless operation but also operation that endangered the lives or safety of others. Nothing else is needed to establish reckless endangerment. Affirmed.

(a) The court in *Seperic* did not mention the *Waterford* decision. Does the holding in the later case nonetheless affect the validity of the earlier case? Why?

(b) How would you decide Buckler's case? Why? How would you use these cases to explain your decision?

(c) Could you use *Waterford* to support a decision contrary to the one you reached in question (b)? Could you use *Seperic* to support a decision contrary to the one you reached in question (b)? Explain.

Exercise 3-B

Assume you are a judge confronted with the following cases:

1. Ernie Tubbs and Ray Hoffman negotiated every word of the contract by which Tubbs sold his elaborate stereo system to Hoffman for $1,700. The contract provided that Tubbs would deliver the stereo to Hoffman's house, and that Hoffman would be obligated to accept the stereo and pay the full price even if it was damaged in transit. The stereo was damaged when Tubbs's truck was involved in an accident. Hoffman accepted the stereo, but he insisted on a deduction from the full price. Can Tubbs collect the $1,700 from Hoffman?

   Decide this case according to your idea of a just result, and state a rule that explains your decision.

2. Beth Goldberg insured her house on Louisiana's Gulf Coast for $50,000. The contract was identical in form to all other home insurance policies sold by the company. Goldberg's home was severely damaged by flooding from a hurricane, and she made a claim on her policy. The company denied the claim, stating that a line in the middle of the seven-page contract specifically excluded hurricane flooding from coverage. Beth had never read the contract. Can she recover for damage to her home?

   (a) Decide this case for Goldberg in a manner that is not inconsistent with your answer to question 1. State a rule that explains your decision in both cases, and describe the basis for your rule.

   (b) Decide this case for the insurance company in a manner that is not inconsistent with your answer to question 1. State a rule that explains your decision in both cases, and describe the basis for your rule.

   (c) Are you more comfortable deciding the case for Goldberg or the insurance company? Why?

3. Waldo Graff bought a refrigerator from his neighborhood appliance dealer for $400. Since he could not pay the full purchase price, he agreed in a contract to the dealer's financing scheme, which required a $30 payment each month for five years. Graff has a third grade education and is not good with figures, so he did not know (nor was he told) that the refrigerator would actually cost him $1,800. After he had paid the dealer $500, a friend explained the contract to him. He made no further payments. Can the dealer collect the remaining $1,300?

(a) Decide this case for the dealer in manner that is not inconsistent with your answer to question 2(a). State a rule that explains your decision and describe the basis for it.

(b) Decide this case for the dealer in a manner that is not inconsistent with your answer to question 2(b). State a rule that explains your decision and describe the basis for it.

(c) Decide this case for Graff in a manner that is not inconsistent with your answer to question 2(a). State a rule that explains your decision and describe the basis for it.

(d) Decide this case for Graff in a manner that is not inconsistent with your answer to question 2(b). State a rule that explains your decision and describe the basis for it.

(e) Which of the above decisions do you prefer? Why?

4. Look carefully at the rules you drafted in answer to questions 1, 2(c), and 3(e). Do they differ from one another? If so, how?

PART B

BASIC CONCEPTS OF LEGAL METHOD

4

Selecting Issues for Analysis

THE first step in solving a legal problem is to select the questions that merit analysis from the broad range of possible questions presented in the factual situation. Some of the questions presented by the fact situation might not require analysis because they are irrelevant to the inquiry; others might be excluded from detailed analysis because they have clear answers. Legal questions that merit analysis are known as issues, and they occur whenever there can be some reasonable disagreement whether a particular rule should be applied to a set of facts. Issues are the focal point of a legal controversy—the legal questions that must be resolved before a case can be decided.

Selecting issues for analysis is a tentative and ongoing process, requiring you to constantly change or sharpen the focus of your inquiry. The process involves four distinct steps. First, identify all legal questions relevant to your situation. Since the legal questions in a case are posed by the possible application of a rule to a set of facts, you must ascertain all rules that may affect the outcome of the case. Second, identify only those questions within the scope of the problem presented. This requires you to understand precisely what questions should be addressed. Third, determine the legal questions that merit discussion. Some questions have straightforward answers; some do not. The less one-sided a question is, the more it should be discussed. Fourth, categorize the legal questions as issues or sub-issues. This is important to insure proper organization when communicating your analysis. These steps need not be taken in any particular order. You might take some of the last steps first or combine others, depending on your knowledge of the relevant law and the nature of the problem. These rules for identifying issues that merit discussion in a legal document are best illustrated in the context of a specific problem.

*   *   *   *   *

Fred Brookson, a lifelong resident of Klamath Falls, Oregon, contacted your firm to see if he can file suit against Wendell Carter for injuries sustained as a result of an incident that occurred in southern Oregon. About three months ago, Brookson and his wife, Ellen, from whom he is now separated, participated in a political demonstration on a wharf extending into the Coos River. A group of people gathered around the demonstrators and began to heckle them. The two groups exchanged remarks and eventually the hecklers threw rocks and bottles at the demonstrators. A rock thrown by Carter, one of the hecklers, struck Ellen Brookson and injured her. Angered by his wife's injury, Fred Brookson approached Carter. Carter said he regretted injuring Ellen since he had been aiming at Fred. The two men then exchanged heated remarks. Without any provocation from Fred Brookson, Carter pulled out a knife, screamed "reactionary pig," and lunged at Brookson, intending to stab him. The knife struck the placard Brookson was holding. As Brookson jumped back to avoid being injured, he bumped into an unidentified demonstrator. The demonstrator, who apparently thought he was being attacked, struck Brookson several times and seriously injured him. Both Brooksons required hospital treatment after the incident. Fred Brookson's medical expenses came to about $15,000, while those of his estranged wife amounted to $2,000. In addition, both have lost weight, exhibit chronic anxiety, and have periods of insomnia.

Your senior attorney wants you to advise him of Fred Brookson's chances of successfully bringing an action against Carter for the injuries Carter inflicted on him. Carter grew up in California, but has spent the last three years living with his brother in Oregon. Carter's parents are citizens of Oregon. Your senior attorney believes it best to bring this action in federal district court due to the unpopular nature of the incident which gave rise to the injuries. What claims can Fred Brookson validly raise? Can a federal court exercise jurisdiction in this case?

Your preliminary research has turned up the following:

Buckeye Industries, Inc. v. Real Properties, Inc. (1972)

Appellee Real Properties, Inc. brought suit for damages to a warehouse it owned caused by the explosion of a boiler manufactured by appellant Buckeye Industries, Inc. Real Properties alleged damages of $85,000 in its complaint, and a jury awarded the company $70,000. Buckeye now complains that the federal district court lacked jurisdiction to hear the case. We disagree.

Section 1332(a)(1) of the federal Judicial Code vests federal district courts with jurisdiction to hear civil cases where the matter in controversy exceeds $10,000 and is between "citizens of different states." The only question is whether the parties meet the last requirement. Section 1332(c) of the federal Judicial Code states that, for purposes of diversity jurisdiction, a corporation is a citizen of the state of incorporation and of the state in which it has its principal place of business. Real Properties is a citizen of Texas because it is incorporated in Texas and does all of its business there. Buckeye is incorporated in Oklahoma and does all of its manufacturing there, but it has its executive offices in Texas. Nonetheless, we find Buckeye to be an Oklahoma citizen and therefore diversity jurisdiction is proper. Where a corporation is engaged in one business activity, substantially all of which occurs in one state, that state is the corporation's principal place of business even though the administrative decisions are made elsewhere. Affirmed.

Krebs v. Beechwood Aircraft Co. (1977)

Appellant Krebs filed suit in federal district court after the small plane in which he was flying crashed into the ocean off the New Jersey coast because of a defective engine mount. Krebs claimed admiralty jurisdiction under Section 1333 of the federal Judicial Code. The district court dismissed for want of jurisdiction and we affirm.

Federal courts are courts of limited jurisdiction. Absent an express grant of jurisdiction from Congress or the Constitution, the federal courts have no power to hear a case. Section 1333 of the Judicial Code vests the federal courts with jurisdiction over cases that are maritime in nature. Claims dealing with navigation, shipping, and commerce by sea are typically maritime in nature because they are inherently linked to the sea. Airplane crashes are not so linked. This chance relation with the sea does not render appellant's claim sufficiently maritime in nature to justify the exercise of federal admiralty jurisdiction.

Jansen v. McLeavy (1961)

Mabel Jansen brought suit against defendant for negligence and intentional infliction of emotional distress after defendant's car ran a stop sign and killed her young son. She witnessed the accident from her front yard. The jury awarded her $75,000 for the negligent death of her son and $50,000 for intentional infliction of emotional distress. Defendant appeals only the latter award, and we reverse.

The tort of intentional infliction of emotional distress requires some evidence that defendant intended to inflict the emotional distress on plaintiff. Although Jansen's mental distress was great, the driver did not intend to cause that distress. While some jurisdictions have allowed recovery in similar circumstances on a theory that defendant's conduct made it probable that mental suffering would result, we will continue to require intentional infliction in this state.

State Legal Encyclopedia

Battery § 2. Battery occurs whenever a person intends to cause harmful or offensive contact or touching to any person and by his actions causes harmful or offensive contact to such person which is not legally consented to or otherwise privileged. Since battery is intended to protect a person's body from intentional and unwanted contacts, its protection extends to anything so closely connected with the person's body as to be regarded as part of it. The wrongdoer is liable not only for physically injurious contacts but also for the mere unlawful touching of another. To recover more than nominal damages, though, the person touched must show actual harm.

The following rules should assist you in identifying issues that merit discussion in a legal document:

1. *Identify All Relevant Legal Questions*

The first step in identifying all the relevant questions is to identify all potentially applicable legal rules. These rules, in rough form, are the counterparts of the possible issues in a case. A legal question is posed by the possible application of a legal rule to a set of facts. To form the range of possible issues in a case, you have to ask whether these rules should be applied here or, if there is no question that they apply, what effect their application will have on the outcome.

Many legal rules are potentially applicable to any factual situation, but only a few will be useful in analyzing a particular problem. A rule is applicable to a factual situation when it so closely corresponds to the situation that it affects the rights and responsibilities of the persons involved. Some rules can be eliminated immediately as too far afield; others will clearly apply. The applicability of many rules, however, will be unclear. If there is any doubt whether the rule is relevant, identify it as potentially applicable. It is better to weed out a rule later as irrelevant than to discard a potentially applicable rule prematurely.

To identify potentially applicable rules, you must first decide what large body of law applies to your problem and do preliminary reading in that area. After you have identified a body of law, such as torts, determine what kind of tort or torts might have been committed and what defenses might be available. Reading background material such as treatises, legal encyclopedias, and annotations will focus your attention on the broad spectrum of rules encompassed by a particular body of law.

Once you have gained a general understanding of the large body of relevant law, you should tighten the focus of your inquiry by examining primary sources of rules, such as cases, statutes, constitutions, and administrative regulations. The entire process is one of comparison. You must examine all reasonable sources of legal rules and determine which of these rules, if any, match your factual situation closely enough to have a plausible effect on the outcome. At the simplest level, rules will be applied to the specific situations for which they were created. At a more abstract level, rules may be applied to different situations if is sensible to do so.

Relevant questions are of two kinds. The first involves legal rules that plainly affect the outcome because there can be little dispute that they are applicable. The second involves rules that may or may not affect the outcome. There is a certain threshold of plausibility concerning the possible application of these particular rules to the facts of your problem. Questions that do not reach this threshold are not relevant and should be discarded. The threshold is not always easy to determine, and there can be reasonable disagreement about whether a problem involves a particular question. A good test for determining a relevant question is whether you can make a plausible argument for each side, even though you may not be persuaded by the arguments for one side. Be careful of one pitfall. Some issues will appear more directly relevant to your problem than others. Although you will spend the great bulk of your discussion on these issues, never fail to identify a less relevant issue.

In the Brookson case, the large bodies of applicable law are torts and civil procedure. The cases and the excerpt from the legal encyclopedia indicate that several tort rules are potentially applicable. Both Fred and Ellen Brookson may have a cause of action for intentional infliction of emotional distress because Carter may have intended to cause their distress. Both Brooksons may also have a cause of action for battery against Carter, and Fred Brookson may have an additional cause of action for battery against the unidentified demonstrator. The encyclopedia excerpt indicates that the elements of battery are intent to cause unlawful contact, actual contact, causation, and actual damages (where more than nominal damages are sought). All of these elements may be present here. The jurisdictional rules requiring diversity of the parties and an amount in controversy in excess of $10,000 also seem applicable. Although you may later exclude some of these rules from consideration, they are nonetheless legally relevant to this factual situation.

The rule regarding admiralty jurisdiction, however, is not relevant and should be excluded from further consideration. No plausible argument for the application of that rule can be made based on the *Krebs* decision. Although the incident in Brookson's case took place on a wharf over the waters of a river, the incident had nothing to do with maritime commerce. The rule is so far afield that it should be rejected as inapplicable and not even mentioned in the memorandum.

2. Exclude All Questions Outside the Scope of the Problem

Legal memos and briefs should discuss only those questions necessary to resolve the problem presented; they are not the place for unfocused dissertations or answers to questions that were not asked. This is not to say that other questions are unimportant; they are simply outside the scope of the problem.

Two considerations are especially important in determining what legal questions are within the scope of a particular problem. First, be aware of the precise legal questions you are asked to address. Most legal problems that require the writing of an office memo or a brief are accompanied by express instructions that restrict the scope of the legal questions to be considered. Even in the absence of express instructions, the relationship of the parties to the legal problem will exclude some questions from consideration. You should, for example, only discuss questions that concern your client's rights against the named adversary, and not consider questions which pertain to additional parties. Second, the questions which should be identified will vary with the procedural context of the case. Questions which are relevant but not important at a given point in the procedural development of a case should be excluded. For example, potential defenses to the suit would be proper questions in the context of a motion for summary judgment, but would not be proper questions to consider in the context of a motion to dismiss.

In the Brookson case, look for legal questions dealing with the encounter between Fred Brookson and Wendell Carter. The diversity jurisdiction question is clearly within the scope of the memorandum because the instructions specifically direct consideration of this issue. Possible questions concerning a cause of action on behalf of Fred Brookson for battery and intentional infliction of emotional distress are also within the scope of the memorandum. Both of these issues are dictated by the procedural context of the case, which requires you to assess the chances of success if suit is filed. The materials and factual situation suggest a possible cause of action Fred Brookson may have against the unidentified demonstrator. This question, however, is outside the scope of the memo because you are asked only to examine causes of action against Carter. Likewise, Ellen Brookson's possible cause of action against Carter is outside the scope of the memo. Since Fred Brookson is the party for whom the lawsuit is contemplated, your only concern is with possible avenues of relief for him.

3. Exclude "Givens" from Detailed Discussion

A "given" is a legal question with a clear answer. Some questions, even though relevant and within the scope of the problem, are so easily resolved that they are not genuine issues. Since legal documents must be concise, a question should be discussed at no greater length than it deserves. A memorandum or brief should usually mention "givens" if necessary to proceed in a logical fashion or to fully describe the context, but "givens" should not be discussed in detail. Tell the reader in two or three sentences what the rule and relevant facts are and what the result will be. If, however, you are unsure whether a question is a "given," discuss it in detail as you would any issue.

There are three "givens" in the Brookson case. In regard to jurisdiction, the amount in controversy is a "given." The amount in controversy plainly exceeds $10,000 since Fred Brookson's medical expenses alone are $15,000. Your discussion of the diversity jurisdiction issue should make this point but not analyze the matter further. Since there is some question whether the parties are from different states, you should spend your time on that issue. Although Brookson is an Oregon citizen, it is not clear whether Carter is a citizen of Oregon or California, and this uncertainty renders the diversity question an issue.

The battery and intentional infliction of emotional distress questions may be similarly analyzed. Two of the four battery questions are "givens." Carter certainly intended to touch Fred Brookson because he lunged at Brookson with a knife. Fred Brookson's medical expenses also indicate that damages have occurred. There is likely to be no dispute whatsoever regarding the applicability of these two rules or the result. As with the amount-in-controversy question, these two questions should be mentioned but not discussed in detail. The more difficult questions are whether Carter's actions can be linked to the injuries suffered by Brookson after he bumped into the unidentified demonstrator, and whether the placard Brookson held was connected closely enough to Brookson's body that Carter can be held to have touched him when he struck the placard with his knife. More research and analysis are required before these questions can be resolved. In the same vein, it is not clear whether Carter intended to cause Brookson's psychological problems and should thus be held liable for intentional infliction of emotional distress. In each of these questions there is some dispute about the outcome. These questions are the issues in this case and their analysis should be the core of your memo.

4. Separate Issues and Sub-Issues

Some issues can only be resolved by first resolving several smaller included issues known as sub-issues. The best way to identify sub-issues is to outline all the relevant issues in your case. Sub-issues occur when you have several issues related to the application of a broader legal issue, and thus two or more subpoints under any one point in your outline. This usually happens when the application of a legal rule depends on the applicability of several separate elements of that rule. There is no particular magic that separates issues from sub-issues; what is an issue in one case might be a sub-issue in another, depending on your organizational scheme and whether you have eliminated some questions by the rules of relevance, scope, and "givens." The distinction between issues and sub-issues is simply a useful tool for understanding and stating the relationship between different issues in your memorandum or brief.

While sub-issues serve a useful organizational purpose, they should not be fabricated by imposing artificial divisions for the sake of organizational nicety. Sub-issues must be issues in their own right. They must concern questions of law on which there can be some disagreement between the parties. They must also be analytically independent of each other; the resolution of one must not automatically resolve the others.

Keep in mind that issues involve the application of specific legal rules to a factual situation. Issues, therefore, must not be stated in terms of whether your client should win the case or whether a motion for summary judgment should be granted. You must be more specific, focusing on the application of the precise legal rule involved to your situation. The same reasoning applies to sub-issues.

In Brookson's case, diversity jurisdiction depends solely on whether there is sufficient diversity of citizenship. This issue would have been a sub-issue had there been some question whether the amount in controversy exceeded $10,000. The main issue would have been whether there is diversity jurisdiction, and the two sub-issues would have concerned the amount in controversy and diversity of citizenship. Since the amount-in-controversy question is a "given," the remaining sub-issue is incorporated into and becomes the main issue.

The tort of intentional infliction of emotional distress depends on whether Carter intended to inflict such distress on Fred Brookson. Here, too, there seems to be only one issue.

The battery claim, however, involves two sub-issues. Whether Carter touched Brookson and whether the touching proximately caused Brookson's injuries require further analysis. Both are independent issues, and both must be resolved in favor of Brookson for there to be battery. Both are sub-issues under the issue of battery. The intent and damage questions are "givens" and, therefore, cannot properly be considered issues.

This careful screening of the questions that merit analysis in the

Brookson case leaves three tentative issues, with two sub-issues under the third. They should be outlined roughly as follows:

1. Whether there is diversity of citizenship between the parties for federal diversity jurisdiction.

2. Whether Carter intentionally inflicted emotional distress on Fred Brookson.

3. Whether Carter committed battery on Fred Brookson.

   a. Whether Carter unlawfully touched Brookson.

   b. Whether Carter's actions proximately caused Brookson's injuries.

This problem has been cut to its bare legal bones. These issues all merit analysis, and those questions that do not merit analysis have been excluded. Keep in mind that your list of issues will always be somewhat tentative. You may find cases in your jurisdiction that clearly resolve something you had thought to be an issue. You may also come across other cases that open up questions you had thought closed, or raise entirely new questions. Much will depend on the quality of your research. For example, you may have guessed that Brookson has a potential cause of action against Carter for assault—a possibility you would investigate if you were researching this problem.

The following exercises are designed to let you work through these four steps of issue identification.

Exercise 4-A

McKay, who has a reputation as a practical joker, telephoned Green and, as a joke, offered to sell Green his speedboat for $5,000. The boat was worth $8,000. Green, who did not know about McKay's reputation, but who did know the true value of the boat, said, "You can't be serious," and, "You must be crazy." He then told McKay that he needed time to raise the money.

One year earlier McKay and Green had made a $3,000 bet on a football game, which McKay had lost. McKay had never paid this bet and Green had forgotten about it. The day after McKay's initial offer, in furtherance of the joke, McKay telephoned Green, reminded him of the debt, and said, "How about if I transfer the boat to you in payment for the debt I owe you?" Green still wanted time to think it over. Three days after the initial offer, Green telephoned McKay to accept the offer, but McKay was golfing. Green told the secretary to tell McKay that Green had called concerning the boat. The secretary then called the golf course. By that time, McKay was in the clubhouse and was intoxicated. The bartender took the secretary's message to McKay, who then telephoned Green. Immediately after he started talking with Green, McKay passed out in the phone booth. While McKay was unconscious, Green told him, "I accept the offer," and added, "It would be nice if you would throw your old set of golf clubs into the deal." McKay does not remember the conversation and now refuses to sell the boat to Green. Is there an enforceable contract?

The following two cases are from your state:

Derek v. Beir (1965)

Appellant, Morse Beir, was a known eccentric with a reputation for playing practical jokes on his neighbors. One day he approached his neighbor, Bob Derek, whom he disliked. Beir stated, "For five bucks I will build a ten-foot-high wall at my own expense between our lots just so I will never have to look at your ridiculous face again." Derek, who was well aware of Beir's reputation, immediately agreed and paid Beir five dollars. Beir failed to build the wall, and appellee filed this suit for breach of contract. The trial court awarded Derek $3,000 in damages, which represented the cost of building the wall. Beir appealed.

Although the trial court made several errors in this case, we do not have to discuss most of them here because we find the contract unenforceable. The general rule is that a contract is not enforceable unless there is an effective offer. For an offer to be effective, the offeror must intend to make a binding contract. In this state, the test for intent by the offeror is whether a reasonable person in the offeree's shoes would believe that the offeror intended to make a binding contract. We conclude that Derek knew or should have known that Beir was not serious and did not intend to make a contract. Since there was no offer, we do not have to reach the question whether the consideration was so grossly disproportionate that it would shock the conscience of the court to enforce the contract. Reversed.

Anselm v. Kinnet Textiles, Inc. (1960)

Appellant Charles Anselm offered to sell 200 bales of cotton to appellee Kinnet Textiles, Inc. One hundred bales were to be delivered on March 1, and the remaining 100 were to be delivered on April 1. Kinnet sent a messenger to Anselm's office with a written note that stated, "We agree to your offer in all respects, but we will instead take delivery on March 5 and April 5." Since Anselm was out of the office, his secretary accepted the note from the messenger and placed it on Anselm's cluttered desk. Anselm did not see it for several weeks and, in the meantime, committed the cotton to another buyer. Kinnet filed suit for breach of contract. The trial court found that the contract was valid and awarded damages to appellee. We disagree.

A contract is not formed unless there is a valid acceptance. Since we have not adopted the Uniform Commercial Code in this state, the case is governed by common law. Appellant claims there was not a valid acceptance for two reasons. First, appellant claims there was no acceptance because he did not see or read the note. We find the delivery and placement of the acceptance on appellant's desk to be a sufficient communication of the acceptance. Once the offeree has delivered a written acceptance, it would be unreasonable to require the offeree to insure that the acceptance is read. We do, however, agree with appellant that the contract is invalid because the acceptance differs from the offer. The rule in this state is that the acceptance must mirror the offer in every respect. If it varies from the offer, it is considered a counter-offer and not an acceptance. Since the dates for delivery in the acceptance here varied from those in the offer, we find there was no acceptance and thus no enforceable contract. Reversed.

You have also found the following:

Excerpt from Hollaway, *A Treatise on Contract Law* 10 (2d ed. 1953)

No satisfactory definition of contract has ever been formulated. Generally, however, an enforceable contract must contain three elements: (1) an offer, (2) an acceptance, and (3) consideration by both sides. Consideration means that each party must incur a legal detriment—give something of value or promise to do something each is not already obligated to do. As a general rule, any consideration is sufficient, no matter how slight.

1. List the potential issues in the McKay case.

2. Are there any issues you would exclude from analysis because they are "givens"? If so, which ones?

3. Does the problem contain any sub-issues? If so, arrange them under the appropriate issue(s).

Exercise 4-B

Cynthia Mickel, a reporter for the *Star City Banner-Patriot,* was recently assigned to write an investigative series on an organization called Citizens for Law and Order (CLO). She learned from her investigation that CLO is a paramilitary organization whose primary purpose is to arm citizens against "the revolutionary elements in our society." The organization is so secretive that its members refused to discuss it with her or to even acknowledge that they were members. Several former members stated that CLO believes that "the whole country is crawling with communists," that "everybody in power has sold out to the reds," and that only CLO "could buck the red tide." The organization sponsors target-shooting events for its members, publishes a newsletter discussing different kinds of rifles and handguns, and routinely sends anonymous letters to the *Banner-Patriot* accusing certain Star City politicians of being communists.

Mickel recently learned that the Star City Police Department has been investigating CLO for two years. Although the Department has never arrested any CLO members for illegal activities related to their membership, Mickel has reason to believe the police files are extensive, and contain information primarily concerning the structure, activities, and membership of the CLO. She has learned, for example, that the mayor's wife is an officer of CLO, and that the files describe her involvement in detail.

Pursuant to the state Freedom of Information Act, Mickel filed a request with the Police Department seeking all files concerning its CLO investigation. Three days later the Department denied her request, stating in part that "these records are confidential." Two days later, the mayor phoned her, stating that he would sue the newspaper "for every penny it has" if it published a story about CLO. Mickel's editors are reluctant to run the story without corroborating information from the police files. The paper has asked you to determine whether it can obtain the information through a lawsuit against the Police Department.

The state Freedom of Information Act, as amended in 1978, provides:

Sec. 2. As used in this act:

(a) "Person" means an individual, corporation, partnership, firm, organization, or association.

(b) "Governmental body" means—

(i) A state officer, employee, agency, department, division, bureau, board, commission, council, authority, or other body in the executive branch of the state government, but does not include the governor or lieutenant governor, the executive office of the governor or lieutenant governor, or employees thereof.

(ii) An agency, board, commission, or council in the legislative branch of state government.

(iii) A county, city, township, village, intercounty, intercity, or regional governing body, council, school district, special district, municipal corporation, or a board, department, commission, council, or agency thereof.

(c) "Public record" means a writing prepared, owned, used, in the possession of, or retained by a governmental body.

Sec. 3. (a) A person desiring to inspect or receive a copy of a public record may make an oral or written request for a public record to the governmental body.

(b) The governmental body shall grant or deny a request in not more than five business days after the day the request is received.

Sec. 4. If a governmental body denies a request, the requesting person may commence an action in circuit court to compel disclosure of the public records. An action under this section may not be commenced unless the requesting person has allowed the governmental body five business days to respond to the request.

Sec. 5. A governmental body may exempt from disclosure as a public record under this act:

(a) Records of law enforcement agencies that deal with the detection and investigation of crime and the internal records and notations of such law enforcement agencies which are maintained for its internal use in matters related to law enforcement.

(b) Information or records subject to the attorney-client privilege.

(c) Records of any campaign committee, including any

committee that receives monies from a state campaign fund.

(d) Information of a personal nature where the public disclosure of the information would constitute a clearly unwarranted invasion of an individual's privacy. (added in 1978).

The highest appellate court in your state has decided the following case:

Holcombe v. Badger Newspapers, Inc. (1976)

Plaintiff, a rape victim, brought an action for damages for invasion of privacy against defendant newspaper for publishing a factual article about the crime, including her name and address. The trial court dismissed her complaint and we affirm.

The state Freedom of Information Act provides that every citizen has a right to the disclosure of any public record. Although the Act exempts certain public records from disclosure, none of these exceptions pertain to this factual situation. There can be no liability for invasion of privacy at common law when the defendant further discloses information about the plaintiff that is already public. We are sympathetic to plaintiff's problem, but our duty ends when we have construed the statute. The legislature may amend the act, but we cannot.

The federal district court in your state has decided the following case:

Wheeler Publishing Co. v. City of Bad Axe (1975)

The Bad Axe Police Department maintains two kinds of records relevant to this case. One is called an "Offense Report," and it includes information concerning the offense committed, the surrounding circumstances, the witnesses, and the investigating officers. The other is called a "Supplementary Offense Report," and it includes information such as the names of potential informants, officers' speculations about a suspect's guilt, and the results of various laboratory tests. Plaintiff, the owner of the Bad Axe *Daily Telegram,* sought to inspect both kinds of reports for its daily newspaper coverage of crime in the Bad Axe area. The Department refused, claiming that the information fit the "police records" exception to the state's Freedom of Information Act. Plaintiff is challenging the constitutionality of that exception.

We hold the Act unconstitutional under the free speech provision of the First Amendment, but only insofar as it applies to the Offense Report. The press and the public have a constitutional right to information concerning crime and law enforcement activity in the community. In determining the reach of that right in specific situations, however, it is necessary to weigh and balance competing interests. With respect to the Offense Report, the public's right to know about specific crimes is paramount. Access to the Supplementary Offense Report, on the other hand, is not protected under the First Amendment. To open this material to the press and the public might reveal the names of informants and otherwise jeopardize law enforcement activities. The Department must release the Offense Reports, but is entitled to retain the Supplementary Offense Reports.

1. Briefly identify all the possible legal questions in this problem.

2. Is it relevant to this problem that the mayor's wife may be able to sue the *Banner-Patriot* for invasion of privacy? Why?

3. Is it relevant that the Police Department responded to Mickel's request in three days? Why?

4. What "givens" can be eliminated from detailed consideration?

5. Separate the remaining legal questions into issues and sub-issues.

5

Common Law Analysis

THE peculiar way lawyers think has been ridiculed for centuries, and often for good cause. Montaigne wrote of several men who had been executed for a crime, even though the actual culprits were discovered after their trial, because the authorities did not want the public to think the judicial process was imperfect. Charles Dickens devoted a lengthy novel, *Bleak House,* to what he described as the "foggiest and muddiest" place in London, the High Court of Chancery.

Although legal reasoning often seems unreasonable on its face, much analysis reflects honest intellectual differences about what the law means or what direction it should take. Perceived unreasonableness also reflects limitations in the analytical process. There are few judicial opinions whose logic is airtight, whose assumptions cannot be questioned, or whose analysis answers all of the ramifications of the decision. Dissenting opinions often bring these shortcomings (actual and perceived) into sharp relief. Justice Brennan's dissenting opinion in a 1975 United States Supreme Court decision, for example, was strongly critical of the "glaring defect[s]" and "outmoded notions" of the majority opinion.*

All these criticisms notwithstanding, there is a method to legal analysis, and a sensible one. Previous chapters examined some of the basic principles of legal analysis. This chapter will describe and illustrate the method of common law analysis.†

The common law is the body of rules and principles found exclusively

---

*Warth v. Seldin, 422 U.S. 490, 520, 521 (1975) (Brennan, J., dissenting).

†Statutory analysis is described in Chapter 6. Constitutional analysis, a hybrid of common

in judicial decisions. It is not created by legislatures, and it is not found in constitutions; the common law is judge-made law. The development of the common law began many centuries ago in England, when early courts were first called on to resolve disputes. These disputes were resolved according to particular principles derived from earlier decisions. Common law analysis has remained virtually unchanged since that time—judges look to earlier cases for guidance in resolving disputes.

The common law develops cautiously because the principles of precedent and *stare decisis* render it comfortable with the familiar, less comfortable with the unknown. As new cases are decided, legal rules evolve and become more complex. Although many areas of the common law have been translated by legal scholars into "restatements"—statute-like rules with accompanying commentary—the facts and policies of the cases on which these rules are based are still of great importance.

The primary methods of common law analysis are analogy and distinction. Every case involving the possible application of a common law rule involves two basic questions: (1) How are the decided cases similar to my client's case? (2) How are the decided cases different from my client's case? The more analogous these cases are, the more precedent and *stare decisis* dictate the application of their conclusions to the present case. The more distinguishable they are, the more irrelevant they should be.

Common law analysis must be undertaken on several related levels. You must first look at the actual facts of the decided cases and compare them with the facts of your case. You must then examine the reasons and policies stated in the decided cases and see if these reasons and policies apply to your case. Much of this examination will concentrate on why your significant facts are actually significant. You may find that a policy stated in the decided cases is inapplicable because the facts of your case are very different, or you may find that a decided case is applicable to your case for reasons the court did not state. You should always be alert to similarities and differences in both the factual situations and underlying policies.

Analogy and distinction are not simply matters of spotting obvious similarities and differences. A good lawyer will spot threads running through entire lines of cases that the courts themselves may not have made explicit, and use these threads to weave sophisticated arguments for or against the application of these cases.

A sound understanding of both sides of a controversy is the primary goal of common law analysis, or any other legal analysis. Only when you

---

law and statutory analysis, is not specifically addressed in this book. Constitutions, particularly the United States Constitution, are similar to, but far more general than, statutes. Judicial decisions interpreting and applying constitutional provisions are thus highly significant because they create a body of "common law" on the meaning of these provisions. But constitutional provisions, like statutes, must also be understood in light of their language and the intent of their drafters.

fully understand both sides can you accurately assess the strengths and weaknesses of your client's position. Even when particular cases seem to be favorable to your client, you cannot afford to ignore distinctions between those cases and your client's situation. You must be prepared to determine whether the similarities are more important than the differences, and why. If you fail to objectively analyze both sides of the problem, you may mislead your client about the strength of her legal position or be unable to properly state and defend that position. Common law analysis must not be a one-sided process.

The basic rules of common law analysis can best be stated and understood in the context of a specific problem.

*   *   *   *   *

Your client, Arthur Dooley, a tenant in a large apartment building, had several grievances with the building's manager, Otis Fremont. Dooley designed a one-page flyer in which he made a series of inflammatory and untrue statements about Fremont's personal life. He made 200 copies of the flyer at his print shop for distribution to other tenants in the building. On his way back from the print shop, Dooley met Fremont by chance and, after a lengthy conversation, they settled their differences. The pamphlets were not mentioned. Although Dooley intended to destroy the flyers when he returned to his apartment, he was struck by a teenager riding a skateboard and the flyers were scattered by the wind. Many of the flyers were read by other persons, and Fremont filed suit for libel.

Dooley's only defense is that there was no libel because the flyers were not "published." There are two relevant cases. Both are from the highest appellate court of the state:

White v. Ball (1966)

Ball appeals from a libel judgment awarded to White and two other employees of the R&T Construction Company. Ball had hired the company to remodel his home. The judgment was based on a letter written by Ball to the company president shortly after the work was completed, in which Ball falsely accused the employees of stealing a valuable watch.

The sole issue on appeal is whether the letter was intentionally published. As general matter, libel consists of the publication of false statements about a person that humiliate that person or subject him to the loss of social prestige. All that is necessary for publication to occur is the delivery of the defamatory matter in written or other permanent form to any person other than the one libeled. It is receipt by a third person that makes the statements so damaging. Since the president of the company, a third person, received and read the letter, the trial court was correct in finding that there was intent. Affirmed.

Simmons v. Deluxe Plaza Hotel (1968)

The manager of defendant hotel wrote Simmons a letter falsely accusing Simmons of staying in the hotel, failing to pay for the room, and taking several articles from the room. The manager was mistaken as to the culprit's identity, so the letter was false. The letter was addressed to Simmons personally and sent by certified mail.

Simmons's wife signed for the letter at his residence and read it. The question on appeal is whether the trial court correctly ruled that the letter was not intentionally published. The evidence shows the manager considered it possible that some third person might receive the letter, though he did not know Simmons was married. This falls far short of a showing that he was reasonably chargeable with appreciation or knowledge of likelihood that the letter would be opened and read by another. A mere conceivable possibility or chance of such eventuality is not sufficient to constitute intent. Affirmed.

As the cases indicate, libel occurs only where the defendant intends to publish the defamatory material. The issue is whether the "intent to publish" rule should be applied to these facts. The following outline provides a method for analyzing that issue.

1. Determine How the Facts of the Decided Case(s) Support Your Client's Case

Since each case is decided on the basis of a unique factual setting, it is important to understand that setting as clearly as possible. That understanding is gained by identifying similarities and differences between the facts of the decided case(s) and those of your client's case. In each instance, ask yourself how the facts of a case lend support to your client's position. If a decision is favorable to your client's position, you should show that the decision is factually similar. If the decision is unfavorable, you should show that the decision involves different facts. These facts offer clues about the policies involved in the problem, and also begin to suggest the varying usefulness of the different cases to each side.

In *Simmons v. Deluxe Plaza Hotel,* where the court found there was no publication, the defendant wrote a letter to the plaintiff containing false accusations against him. The defendant attempted to insure that the letter would be read only by the plaintiff by addressing it to him personally and sending it by certified mail. Despite these precautions, the plaintiff's wife read the letter. *Simmons* is like the present case because Dooley, like the defendant hotel manager, did not intend to distribute the flyers to third persons after his conversation with Fremont. He intended to destroy the flyers when he returned to his apartment, and it was only by accident that they were released. In any event, he never intended distribution to passers-by, just as the defendant in *Simmons* did not intend plaintiff's wife to read the letter.

In *White v. Ball,* the defendant wrote a third person, a company president, making false accusations against company employees. The court found publication because the president received and read the letter. *White* is different from Dooley's case in that the release of the flyers was not intended and, unlike the defendant in *White,* Dooley did not address his accusations directly to a third person.

This analysis indicates that the interpretation of *White* and *Simmons* most favorable to your client would emphasize the unintentional release of the flyers. You will draw an analogy to *Simmons* and distinguish *White* to support that conclusion.

2. Determine How the Facts of the Decided Case(s) Support Your Opponent's Case

The omission of certain facts in the previous discussion suggests how your opponent will use the decided cases. Identification of the facts supporting your opponent's position requires you to think like he will. Actually construct your opponent's best arguments. Where you think there are similarities, he will try to show differences. Where you find distinctions, he will find analogies.

Thus, in *White v. Ball,* the defendant prepared a false letter, fully intending to send it to a third person. Similarly, Dooley prepared a false flyer with intent to distribute it. In both *White* and the present case, the defamatory material was received and read by third persons.

Preparation with intent to publish is what makes *Simmons v. Deluxe Plaza Hotel* a different case from this one. In *Simmons,* the defendant prepared a letter intending that only the plaintiff see it. The fact that an unintended third person read the letter was not enough for publication. In Dooley's case, although passers-by rather than tenants read the flyer, Dooley intended it for third party distribution when he prepared it.

These cases suggest that your opponent's strongest case would be based on Dooley's preparation and printing of the flyers with intent to distribute them. Unlike you, he would rely on *White* and distinguish *Simmons.*

3. Determine How the Reasons and Policies of the Decided Case(s) Support Your Client's Position

The factual similarities and differences between the decided cases and the present case are significant only to the extent that they are given importance by the reasons and policies of the decided cases. Since the intent issue was of concern in both *White* and *Simmons,* the factual analysis in the present case has focused on the absence or presence of facts which evidence an intent to publish. That analysis has suggested two interpretations, one based on intent at the time of preparation, and the other based on intent at the time of distribution. Neither of the decided cases specifically addresses this issue.

The next level of analysis requires examination of the reasons and policies of the decisions. This examination could show what considerations the courts thought were important to the intent question. Such considerations assist the analysis of the present case because the courts indicate that some principles are more significant than others, even though those courts dealt with different factual settings.

The court in *Simmons* refused to find publication simply on the possibility that someone other than the plaintiff would read the letter. The court's conclusion that defendant "was not reasonably chargeable with appreciation or knowledge of likelihood that the letter would be opened and read by another" suggests that intent at the time of distribution is required for publication. Dooley originally intended to distribute the flyers only after they were printed, but after they were printed he decided not to distribute them at all. At that point, you would reason, the possibility of the accident, just like the possibility of a third person reading the letter in *Simmons,* was speculative.

The court in *White v. Ball* focused on receipt of defamatory material by a third person and the subsequent damage caused to plaintiff's reputation. *White* must be viewed narrowly rather than broadly because, as the court said in *Simmons,* delivery of defamatory material to a third person is not enough. You would conclude that there must be an intent to publish at the time of distribution.

4. Determine How the Reasons and Policies of the Decided Case(s) Support Your Opponent's Position

Your opponent will emphasize reasons that you would subordinate to others, and de-emphasize reasons you believe to be most significant. He may also show that your policy arguments are inapplicable because of the different factual situation presented by this case, and demonstrate why his policy arguments are relevant and more important.

The court in *White v. Ball,* your opponent would argue, shows primary concern for a person's reputation. This concern is illustrated by the court's definition of publication as delivery of defamatory material to a third person, and its observation that receipt by such a person is what makes the defamation damaging. If intent to publish the defamatory material is what made the defendant blameworthy in *White,* then Dooley should also be held blameworthy. By intending to harm Fremont's reputation, and by writing and printing a flyer to do so, Dooley showed that he was prepared to go to great lengths to injure him. Even assuming his change of mind was genuine, your opponent would reason, Dooley set in motion a series of events that resulted in harm to Fremont.

Simmons represents a different case from Dooley's because in *Simmons* there was an unintentional distribution of defamatory material. Dooley, on the other hand, intentionally prepared and printed it for distribution. Persons who print 200 copies of a flyer, and who hold them so carelessly that an accident sets them loose in the wind, are not unintentionally defaming others. If he had not taken his scheme of damaging Fremont's reputation as far as he did, your opponent would conclude, the flyers would not have been distributed.

5. Evaluate the Strength of Your Client's Case

The process of constructing and evaluating arguments runs from very technical levels—comparing facts—to increasingly abstract levels involving basic assumptions and values about the point at which one should be held blameworthy for damage to the reputation of another. Your conclusion should be based on a careful examination and analysis of the facts, policies, and reasons of the decided cases and their application to the present case.

You might conclude that there was publication because the flyers were written and printed for distribution to third persons, and because they were distributed to third persons. This interpretation follows from *White* and *Simmons* and seems to be the most likely outcome here. But you might also conclude that there was no publication because the flyers were distributed when Dooley no longer intended to distribute them, and because they were distributed accidentally to third persons. That conclusion also reasonably follows from *White* and *Simmons.*

Whatever your thoughts are about the strength of your client's case, you must draw a conclusion, and you must be prepared to show that your conclusion is more reasonable than any other. This is the essence of common law analysis. Whether you are writing a brief or an office memo, you cannot simply state the competing considerations or describe the relevant cases. You must scrutinize each consideration, weigh it, and then balance it against other considerations. If you cannot come to a satisfactory conclusion, think about it some more. Reaching a well-reasoned conclusion requires careful reading of the cases and thoughtful analysis. There is always a good reason, if not a definitive one, for preferring one side over another.

Think through the following exercises using these five rules. Although the process may seem overly mechanical, it will become more comfortable as you gain familiarity with it.

Exercise 5-A

Bradley Greenleaf just finished renovating an old house located on a busy street in Porterville. The house, which is now the office for his twelve-person architectural firm, cost $15,000. The renovations, which included retrofitting the house with solar panels, cost an additional $85,000. The solar panels provide heating and cooling for the air and water in the building, but they do not provide electricity. His firm, Greenleaf Associates, which specializes in solar design for residences, uses the building as a model for persons who are interested in constructing or retrofitting homes with solar panels. Its extensive "You can do it" promotional campaign relies heavily on the building for that purpose.

Two large billboards were recently erected on the property just west of the office. They shield the sun's rays from the panels by early afternoon, and force Greenleaf to rely on conventional energy sources. This increases his cost substantially (about $300 per month, he estimates) and makes his promotional appeal less attractive. What good is solar energy, some potential customers ask, if it can be blocked? Greenleaf contacted the owner of the property. The owner apologized for any inconvenience the billboards caused, but refused to remove them because he would lose too much money.

Greenleaf has asked you if he has a basis for a lawsuit against the owner of the other property. You have determined that there are no relevant statutes, easements, or zoning provisions. There is, however, one relevant case from this state:

Horton v. Eicher (1959)

Appellee, who owns 200 acres of growing honeydew melons, hired appellant, a crop duster, to dust his melons with calcium arsenate, an arsenic compound. The compound is toxic to a number of agricultural pests, but it is also toxic to bees. Appellee owned sixty-five hives of bees on a parcel one-half mile from the melons. The bees were important to the pollination of his melons and other plants, and thus contributed to his livelihood. Appellee brought this action for nuisance after the spray from appellant's plane drifted over the hive and killed all of the bees. The trial court awarded $450.00 in damages, and we affirm.

A property owner is entitled to the peaceful enjoyment of his property, free from unreasonable interference from others. The incident unmistakably interfered with appellee's use of his own property. This is a fair result because appellant knew or should have known about the slight breeze blowing toward the hives the day he sprayed, and the toxicity of the compound to bees.

The following case is from another state:

Cassells v. Avery (1958)

Appellant, who owns a large resort hotel on an ocean beach,

brought suit against appellee, a neighboring hotel owner, to prevent the construction of a ten-story addition to appellee's existing hotel. Appellant claims that the addition will cast a shadow on the beach and make it unfit for the use and enjoyment of guests. The trial court refused to enjoin the construction, and we agree.

The doctrine of nuisance does not mean that one must never use property to the injury of a neighbor, but rather that one must not use the property to injure the legal rights of a neighbor. We have been unable to find a case establishing—in the absence of a contractual or statutory obligation—that a landowner has a legal right to the free flow of light. Affirmed.

1. Identify the issue(s) in Greenleaf's case.

2. Is it important that the *Cassells* case is from another state? Explain.

3. How do the facts of each case support Greenleaf's case? How do the facts of the cases taken together support Greenleaf's case?

4. How do the facts of each case support the billboard owner's case? How do the facts of the cases taken together support the billboard owner's case?

5. How do the reasons and policies of each case support Greenleaf's case? How do the reasons and policies of the cases taken together support Greenleaf's case?

6. How do the reasons and policies of each case support the billboard owner's case? How do the reasons and policies of the cases taken together support the billboard owner's case?

7. Evaluate the strength of Greenleaf's position. Should he bring suit? Why?

Exercise 5-B

Fourteen-year-old Andrew Quale was struck by a truck while riding his bicycle. Although his injuries seemed slight, his mother, Mary Quale, took him to the hospital. His sole complaint was a headache. After Mary related the history of the accident, the doctor ordered x-rays. The x-rays did not indicate a skull fracture. The doctor did not examine the back of the boy's head, where there was a red mark, nor did he use many of the other diagnostic procedures normally conducted in such cases. The doctor sent the boy home, and asked his mother to observe him. Andrew died early the next morning. The coroner concluded from an autopsy that the boy died from hemorrhaging due to a basal skull fracture.

Mary Quale has asked you to sue the doctor and the hospital for malpractice. You contacted another doctor for possible use as an expert witness. He told you that there is no doubt that the doctor was negligent. In answer to your question about the likelihood of the boy's survival if there had been proper treatment, he said that the mortality rate for such injuries was about 100 per cent without surgery. He then added, "There certainly is a chance and I can't say exactly what—maybe some place around fifty per cent—that he would have survived with surgery." He cannot give you a more definite answer.

Did the doctor's negligence proximately cause the boy's death? There are two relevant cases in your state:

Moulton v. Ginocchio (1966)

Appellant, who is the administrator for the decedent's estate, brought this action against appellee, a physician, for negligence in treating the decedent's illness. The trial court dismissed the complaint on the ground that the doctor's negligence did not proximately cause her death. We disagree and reverse.

Decedent, a diabetic, went to appellee's hospital with intense abdominal pain, which appellee diagnosed as a "bug" in her stomach. He gave her some drugs for the pain and released her. She died several hours later from massive hemorrhaging caused by an intestinal obstruction. Appellee claims that there is no basis for concluding with certainty that the appellee's negligent diagnosis and treatment caused her death. The law does not require certainty, however; a physician is answerable if he prevents a substantial possibility of survival. Appellant's experts testified categorically and without contradiction that the decedent would have survived had she undergone prompt surgery. Appellant, therefore, satisfied that "substantial possibility" requirement.

Mallard v. Harkins (1969)

Appellant brought suit against appellee, a physician, for appellee's allegedly negligent failure to immediately diagnose and perform surgery to arrest a degenerative disease which has now left appellant paralyzed. The trial court found that appellee breached his duty of reasonable care, but that his actions did not proximately cause appellant's condition. Only the latter ruling has been appealed. We agree with the trial court and affirm.

We held in *Moulton v. Ginocchio* (1966) that a doctor is liable where his negligence "prevents a substantial possibility of survival" for the decedent. In that case, there was certainty that the decedent would have survived. Traditional standards of proximate cause similarly require evidence that the result was more likely than not caused by the act. Appellant does not meet that standard. Appellant's expert witness testified that prompt surgery would have given appellant "a possibility" of recovery, but that he "probably would not have recovered." We refuse, as a matter of public policy, to hold a physician liable on a mere possibility.

1. Identify the issue(s) in Quale's case.

2. Is it significant that both cases are from your state? Explain.

3. How do the facts of each case support Quale's case? How do the facts of the cases taken together support Quale's case?

4. How do the facts of each case support the doctor's case? How do the facts of the cases taken together support the doctor's case?

5. How do the reasons and policies of each case support Quale's case? How do the reasons and policies of the cases taken together support Quale's case?

6. How do the reasons and policies of each case support the doctor's case? How do the reasons and policies of the cases taken together support the doctor's case?

7. Evaluate the strength of Quale's position. Should she bring suit? Why?

6

Statutory Analysis

STATUTORY analysis differs from common law analysis because it focuses on the meaning of legislative pronouncements rather than judicial ones. Legislatures write rules in broad strokes. Since most statutes are enacted to cover categories of future situations, statutory analysis requires a determination of the effect of these broad rules on particular cases. Common law analysis, as you have seen, focuses more on specific situations than on rules. Statutory analysis thus tends to be deductive, while common law analysis tends to be inductive.

Statutory analysis is also different because statutes are less easily modified by courts than are common law principles. The doctrine of separation of powers, under which the legislature writes statutes and courts interpret them, limits courts to ascertaining and carrying out the legislative will. Courts may expand or contract the scope of statutes within the statutory language, but they may not disregard an applicable statute unless it is unconstitutional. Since common law analysis requires courts to look at their own past decisions rather than those of another institution, courts can modify common law rules without encroaching on the prerogatives of another governmental body.

Despite these differences, the primary methods of statutory analysis, like those for common law analysis, are analogy and distinction. Instead of comparing and contrasting specific factual situations, however, statutory analysis requires comparison and contrast of broad factual categories with specific cases. Every case involving the possible application of a

57

statute or statutory provision involves these questions: (1) How are the categories described by the statute similar to my client's situation? (2) How do the categories described by the statute differ from my client's case? The more similar they are, the more the statute or statutory provision should dictate a resolution of the case. The more distinguishable they are, the less relevant the statute or statutory provision should be.

Statutory issues are of two basic kinds. The first is whether the statute covers the situation at all. Statutes impose restrictions on certain people or activities, provide benefits to certain others, or establish procedures for the orderly accomplishment of certain goals. In each case, you should determine the target group or activity for the statute. Statutes frequently have definitional sections that expressly state what persons or activities are covered, and these definitions generally indicate whether the statute is applicable. Once you have determined the statute is applicable, the second issue is what effect application of the statute will have on your client's problem. You must examine the statute again to determine precisely what conduct is commanded, prohibited, or regulated. Determining what conduct is affected requires you to study the statutory language, its definitions, and the relationship between the various sections of the statute.

Statutory analysis can best be described and illustrated by use of a hypothetical problem.

*   *   *   *   *

Until the recent election, members of the Liberal Party held all seven seats on the City Council of Grand View. The Conservatives, who promised in the recent election to significantly reorder the city's budget priorities, now outnumber the Liberals on the Council by four to three. Your client, Joshua Smith, an important member of the Liberal Party, learned that the four Conservative members plan to meet privately within several weeks to write their proposed budget. This budget will then be presented to the full Council. The budget goes into effect once it has been adopted by a majority of the Council. Council meetings require a quorum of five. The Conservatives told Smith that neither he nor any other member of the public would be permitted to attend the meeting.

Is the Conservatives' position lawful under the State Open Meetings Act? That act provides:

> Sec. 1. Purpose. It is vital in a democratic society that public business be performed in an open and public manner so that the citizens shall be advised of the performance of public officials and of the decisions that are made by such officials in formulating and

executing public policy. Toward this end, this chapter is adopted, and shall be construed.

Sec. 2. Definitions. As used in this act:

(a) "Meeting" means the convening of a public body for the purpose of deliberating toward or rendering a decision on a public policy.

(b) "Public body" means any state or local legislative body, including a board, commission, committee, subcommittee, authority, or council, which is empowered by law to exercise governmental or proprietary functions.

Sec. 3. All meetings of a public body shall be open to the public and shall be held in a place available to the general public.

The State Court of Appeals has decided one case concerning this statute:

Times-Journal Co. v. McPhee (1977)

Appellant Times-Journal Co. brought an action seeking declaratory and injunctive relief against McPhee and the other members of the Bedford Board of Education, claiming that they had violated, and planned to continue violating, the state Open Meetings Act by closing a series of "preliminary" and "informal" meetings to the public. The trial court granted defendants' motion to dismiss on the ground that no formal actions were taken at these meetings. Therefore, the court reasoned, they were not "meetings" within the meaning of the act. We reverse.

Section 2(a) defines "meeting" as the convening of a public body "for the purpose of *deliberating toward* or rendering a decision on a public policy" (emphasis supplied). Every step in the decision-making process, including the decision itself, is necessarily part of the deliberation that the legislature intended to affect by enactment of the statute before us. "Preliminary" and "informal" meetings are necessarily part of that deliberative process, especially when the entire Board attends these meetings, as it does here.

Section 3 would require the caucus of the four Conservative Board members to be open if it is a "meeting" and if these members constitute a "public body" within the meaning of section 2. The court in *Times-Journal Co. v. McPhee* emphasized the deliberative nature of the meetings in that case to support its conclusion that they were meetings within the meaning of section 2(a). The same type of deliberation would occur at the caucus of the Conservatives. Whether these four members constitute a "public body" (a term also used in the definition of "meeting") is a more difficult question. It concerns not the effect of the statute but whether the statute applies to this situation. The following rules provide a method for resolving this question.

1. Determine How the Language of the Statute, and the Facts of Any Cases Interpreting That Language, Support Your Client's Position

Statutes should be read and applied according to the plain meaning of their language. As a general matter, courts presume that the legislature meant precisely what it said. This principle insures that the legislature's intent will be carried out even if the court does not agree on its wisdom. Many times, however, the meaning of the language is not plain. Statutory rules often suffer from the same imprecision as common law rules. The word "reasonable," for example, appears as much in statute books as it does in the common law. While such words are often inserted deliberately to insure flexibility in the administration of the law, it is perhaps more often true that what was clear to the policy-minded legislator provides little guidance to an administrator or judge who must apply the statute in a specific factual context.

Statutory analysis also involves the use of previously decided cases. Where courts have interpreted statutes, the statutory rules must be understood generally and also in terms of the specific factual situations in which they have been interpreted. In addition to examining the language of the statute, you must compare and contrast the facts and reasoning of previous cases with those of your case. Where a statutory category is ambiguous, for example, judicial decisions will place certain factual situations in or out of that category. This is most likely to occur in older statutory provisions or more recent enactments that have been the subject of much litigation. By comparing and contrasting the facts of your situation with the facts of these cases, you can better understand whether the statute covers your client's situation.

According to section 2(b), any entity that has the legal authority to exercise governmental or proprietary functions, including those listed, is a "public body." You would argue that the four Conservative members are a public body because they control the Council, an entity that exercises governmental functions. This control exists because they have enough votes to compel adoption of any budget they draft. In that significant sense, their formulation of a budget at a secret meeting would be tantamount to the exercise of a "governmental or proprietary function." They do not need a quorum at this caucus because they can achieve the needed quorum when the full Council meets to consider the budget they have proposed. The *de facto* budget will then become the legal budget. For these reasons, the Conservatives constitute a "local legislative body" under section 2(b), or at least a committee or subcommittee of that body.

Even though the entire board is not present as it was in *Times-Journal Co. v. McPhee*, you would argue that your client's situation is not materially different because the Conservatives have the votes to adopt any budget they choose. In addition, the court in *McPhee* was primarily concerned with the deliberative nature of meetings, rather than with the definition of "public body." The extra weight the court gave to the presence of the entire board at these meetings can be explained by the fact that a meeting with all members present is likely to foster a great deal of deliberation, even if it is "preliminary" or "informal."

2. Determine How the Language of the Statute, and the Facts of Any Cases Interpreting That Language, Support Your Opponent's Position

The same language provides support for the opposite conclusion. Where you try to show how the language of a statute applies to your client's situation, your opponent will try to show that the language of the statute does not. Where you try to analogize cases interpreting the language to support your conclusion, he will show that these cases are inapplicable or that they support his position.

Your opponent would argue that the four Conservative members of the Council are not, by themselves, a local legislative body, since the Council includes several other members. Neither are they a committee or subcommittee in the traditional meaning of those terms. Finally, they cannot exercise any governmental functions at the secret meeting because the Conservative caucus on the Council is still one short of the needed quorum (even if all the other procedural requirements for calling a City Council meeting could be sidestepped). The full Council must still adopt the budget for it to have the force of law, and that Council meeting will be open to the public.

The court in *McPhee*, your opponent would add, seems to require the presence of all the members for there to be a "public body." Since the definition of "meeting" incorporates the term "public body," the court's discussion of the former is highly relevant to the latter. The court concluded that "informal" or "preliminary" meetings were part of the deliberative process in decision making, "especially when the entire board attends these meetings, as it does here." The *McPhee* court requires complete attendance, or at least a quorum, for there to be a "public body."

3. Determine How the Policies of the Statute, and the Policies of Any Cases Interpreting the Statute, Support Your Client's Position

Where the statutory language alone does not decide the matter, statutes should be read and applied to carry out the legislature's intent in enacting them. This intent can be ascertained from two sources—the statute itself and the legislative history. The statute may contain an introductory section or preamble explaining its purpose. The purpose may also be evident from the subject matter and provisions or from amendments to the statute. When the language is unclear, and one interpretation would promote the legislature's intent while the other would not, you should choose the former. If more than one interpretation would carry out the legislature's intent, you should choose the interpretation that does so most fully.

Legislative history offers equally useful and even more detailed guidance on the meaning of statutory provisions. The legislative history of a statute is the published record of the debates, committee reports, early bills, and other materials that shed light upon what the legislature did and why. The materials are not expository. The researcher must discern the legislative purpose by looking at concerns voiced during the legislative hearings and debates, and by comparing the proposed statutory language to the language adopted. Courts make substantial use of legislative history when interpreting and applying federal statutes because it is printed and accessible. While legislative history is valuable, it is not always available. Often, particular statutory provisions are not discussed in these documents. In addition, there is generally very little, if any, legislative history for state statutes because state legislative proceedings are usually not reduced to writing.

Although there is no legislative history for this particular statute, section 1 provides an important statement of the legislature's intent. You would argue that section 1 declares in broad terms the importance of conducting "public business" in an "open and public manner" so that citizens can know what decisions are made and the reasons for these decisions. Section 1 also requires interpretation of the act to effectuate this goal. This purpose was underscored in *McPhee* by the court's conclusion that each step in the decision-making process ought to be made public.

These policies, you would continue, are particularly applicable here because the most important steps in the decision-making process for the budget will be made at the caucus. Whatever form the debate before the full Council takes, much of that debate will be foreclosed because the Conservative members will resolve many of their differences at the caucus. Since the Conservatives will in all likelihood be locked into their positions after the caucus, the debate at the City Council will be more form than substance. As a result, an important piece of "public business," the budget, will not be resolved in the "open and public manner" contemplated by the legislature. Section 1 implies that the legislature believed open meetings to be of greater importance than the privacy of political parties, and that decision should be respected.

4. Determine How the Policies of the Statute, and the Policies of Any Cases Interpreting the Statute, Support Your Opponent's Position

Your opponent will argue for the merits of other policies in the statute, some explicitly stated, some merely implicit in the legislative scheme. He will attempt to show that your policy arguments are inapplicable to the facts of this case, or that they are simply not as important as his.

Your opponent might thus argue that the statutory emphasis on "*public* body" and "*public* business" indicates that the legislature did not intend the Open Meetings Act to reach what is essentially private behavior. The planned caucus is only for members of a private political party. *McPhee* supports this conclusion because the court in that case dealt with meetings of the full Board of Education, not with some faction of the Board. To require that private groups open their meetings to the public because of their conceivable impact on public business would stretch the Act far beyond its intended meaning.

There is, he would add, no guarantee that debate will be stifled or foreclosed at the City Council meeting. The caucus would provide the Conservative members, all of whom are newly elected, with a chance to discuss the budget and arrive at a consensus about how it should be shaped. There is no reason to believe that the four members will vote as a bloc on every single budget issue debated before the City Council, since members may later change their minds or receive new information. Arguments to the contrary are simply speculative.

5. Evaluate the Strength of Your Client's Position

Although the issue can be characterized as a technical one involving the definition of several words, it actually raises some important and competing policy considerations that need to be reconciled. Ultimately, your client probably has a stronger legal position because the caucus, a majority of the Council, is likely to greatly influence, if not dictate, the budget adopted by the City Council. Although there is room for a contrary point of view, the more important point is that you must draw a conclusion and be able to demonstrate that your conclusion is more reasonable than any other. It is not enough merely to list competing considerations; you must scrutinize and evaluate their merits.

This illustration focused on analysis of the first kind of statutory issue—whether the statute applies to the case. Still another question would have been presented, however, if the secret meeting were planned for a conference room that could hold only ten people, because section 3 requires that meetings be held "in a place available to the general public." This second kind of issue, what effect an applicable statute will have on the outcome of your case, would be analyzed in the same way as the first.

Work through the following exercises with the help of these five rules. Try to understand the similarities and differences between common law analysis and statutory analysis, and remember that the process will become easier as you gain familiarity with it.

Exercise 6-A

The Metropolitan Social Welfare League is an organization composed of social workers and welfare recipients that advocates welfare reform. For two years the League has urged the City of Lake Rapids to set aside an eighteen-square-block area on the city's east side for low income housing. That area is now vacant. The League has negotiated with city, state, and federal officials on this matter since ten months ago when the mayor said the proposal "was worth looking into" at a news conference.

The Swift Land Development Corporation applied eight months ago for a zoning amendment to permit the construction of an auto salvage yard on one block of that eighteen-block area. Several other companies are also interested in zoning amendments. The area is now zoned for multiple-family housing. Six months ago, the city denied Swift's proposal. Swift filed suit immediately to force approval of the amendment. Last week, the city attorney stated that he thought the city might be wrong in this case. The mayor has stated several times that, "City Hall represents the people, not narrow special interest groups."

Can the League now intervene as a defendant under State Court Rule 779.1(3)?

> State Court Rule 779.1(3), which is codified in the state statutes, provides:
>
> Anyone shall be permitted to intervene in an action when:
>
> . . . .
>
> (3) Upon timely application when the representation of the applicant's interest is or may be inadequate and the applicant may be bound by a judgment in the action.

The Drafting Committee for the rules made this comment in drafting Rule 779.1(3):

> There may be persons having interests so vital that they ought to

have been made parties in the first place. They must be allowed to intervene. Therefore, the court is given no discretion in this regard.

There is one relevant case in this state:

Halsey v. Village of Elk Mound (1976)

Appellee petitioned the Elk Mound Planning Commission to rezone two adjacent parcels within the village from single-family residential to multiple-family residential. The Commission denied his request, and the Town Council agreed. Appellee brought suit against the village to prevent it from interfering with his proposed use for the parcels. Appellants, persons with homes within 300 feet of the parcels, sought to intervene. The trial court determined that appellants could not intervene because they had not met the requirements of Court Rule 779.1(3). We reverse.

The intervention rule requires (1) timely action by the applicant, (2) possible or actual inadequacy of representation by existing parties, and (3) the possibility that the applicant may be bound by a judgment in the action. There was no unreasonable delay here, since appellants filed their motion to intervene only three weeks after suit was brought. Appellants were not too late to protect their interests. In addition, the rule requires only that existing representation *may* be inadequate. The burden of satisfying this requirement must be minimal. Appellants meet this requirement because the village does not purport to represent the interest of their neighborhood. Finally, we read the term "bound" to mean that, as a practical matter, the appellants' ability to protect their interests may be substantially affected. We do not understand the term in its narrow legal sense as *res judicata*. Since appellants have met all three requirements, they are entitled to intervene.

1. What issue(s) are presented by the League's case?

2. Explain the importance, if any, of the committee comment. Explain the importance, if any, of the *Halsey* case.

3. How does the language of the rule support the League's position? How do the facts of the *Halsey* case support that position?

4. How does the language of the rule support the city's position? How do the facts of the *Halsey* case support that position?

5. How do the policies of the committee comment and the *Halsey* case support the League's position?

6. How do the policies of the committee comment and the *Halsey* case support the city's position?

7. Should the League attempt to intervene under Rule 779.1(3)? Why?

Exercise 6-B

Francine Odegaard was recently elected governor. She received 50.2 per cent of the vote, and her opponent received 49.8 per cent. A state legislative committee set up to monitor the effects of the Election Campaign Finance Act investigated the funding sources of the two candidates and learned that Odegaard's campaign committee received $41,995.00 from her grandfather after the election. This amount was precisely the debt with which her campaign committee ended the general election. Odegaard's natural parents died when she was very young. She was raised by her grandfather, although he never formally adopted her. Her grandfather made no other contributions to her campaign. The committee has drafted a report recommending that she be prosecuted for violating section 31 of the Act. The committee has hired you to review its recommendation.

The Election Campaign Finance Act provides in part:

Sec. 2. This Act is intended to regulate political activity, to regulate campaign financing, and to restrict campaign contributions and expenditures without jeopardizing the ability of candidates for state public office to conduct effective campaigns.

Sec. 31. (a) Except as provided in subsection (b), a person other than a campaign committee shall not make contributions on behalf of the winner of a primary election for the office of governor in excess of $600.00 for any purpose after the date of such primary election.

(b) A contribution from a member of a candidate's immediate family to the campaign committee for that candidate is exempt from the limitation of subsection (a).

(c) As used in subsection (b), "immediate family" means a spouse, parent, brother, sister, son, or daughter.

Sec. 44. A person who violates the provisions of this act is guilty of a misdemeanor and shall be fined not more than $1,000.00.

The highest appellate court in the state has decided the following cases:

Alberts v. Election Commission (1977)

Section 31 of the Election Campaign Finance Act prohibits any person from making contributions "on behalf of the winner of a primary election for the office of governor in excess of $600.00 for any purpose after the date of such primary election." Appellant challenges the validity of a trial court determination that he violated section 31 by contributing $1,500.00 to the unsuccessful candidate for governor in the 1976 general election. He argues that he made the contribution to help retire that candidate's debt from the primary. We affirm.

Section 31 of the Election Campaign Act was designed to reduce, if not eliminate, the improper influence a contributor gains from a large contribution near the end of the campaign. More generally, the act was designed to help improve the integrity, and the appearance of integrity, of our election system. These policy considerations make it particularly important that the phrase, "for any purpose," be read for its full meaning. We hold that the phrase includes payments made for the purpose of reducing primary debts. Affirmed.

Toland v. Election Commission (1976)

Clyde Swanson lost the general election for governor after winning his party's primary election. His son Raymond handled the finances for Clyde's general election campaign. As treasurer, Raymond received funds from various sources, deposited them in his personal checking account, and then wrote checks from that account to pay for campaign expenses. Clyde's largest contribution, a $15,000 check from Alphonse Toland, was processed in this manner. Toland was convicted of a misdemeanor for violating section 31 of the Election Campaign Finance Act. We affirm that conviction.

Section 31 limits contributions to candidates for governor in a general election to $600.00 per person, unless the contributor is a member of the candidate's "immediate family." The immediate family exception is premised on a legislative desire to protect freedom of expression by candidates. In addition, the Act's purpose of reducing the corrupting influence of outside financial sources has much less force when the contributor is from the candidate's immediate family. Although Swanson's son is a member of his "immediate family" under section 31(b), the son was a conduit, rather than a source, of the funds. The important purposes of the Act should not be undermined by such transparent schemes.

1. Identify the issue(s) involved in this case.

2. For each issue, how does the language of the act support the committee's position? How do the facts of the cases support that position?

3. For each issue, how does the language of the act support Odegaard's position? How do the facts of the two cases support that position?

4. For each issue, how do the policies of the act support the committee's position? How do the policies of the cases support that position?

5. For each issue, how do the policies of the act support Odegaard's position? How do the policies of the cases support that position?

6. Do you think Odegaard violated the act? Why?

PART C

THE OFFICE
MEMORANDUM

7

Elements of an
Office Memorandum

A LAWYER'S most important work occurs when he advises a client how to approach a particular situation in light of the applicable law. Sound legal advice may permit a client to reap certain benefits from some situations and avoid exposing himself to liability in others. When a client seeks advice too late, proper counseling can minimize the damage. Even if litigation occurs—for whatever reason—good legal advice can help steer the lawsuit to a fruitful conclusion. For every case that goes to court, however, there are dozens of others that were never litigated, and did not have to be, because someone followed a lawyer's advice.

Legal advice to a client is often based on a formal memorandum of law. The office memorandum is a basic document of legal writing. It is usually written by a clerk or junior attorney for a more experienced attorney to predict what effect application of the relevant law will have on the client's situation. Senior attorneys use memoranda to determine what advice to give a client. Three fundamental principles should guide you in researching, drafting, and writing an office memorandum:

Be objective. The hallmark of a memo is objectivity. Scrupulously examine your own arguments as well as those you anticipate from your opponent. Only then can you honestly assess the strengths and weaknesses of your client's case. Above all else, you must be honest about what the law permits and what it does not; you cannot afford to mislead your senior attorney or your client with wishful thinking or advocacy.

Be thorough. Office memos form the basis for major choices people make about their lives or businesses. Consequently, your best efforts

70

should be spent insuring that these decisions are based on sound analysis. You can only do this if your knowledge of the relevant law is solid and your thinking clear.

3)   *Communicate.* The memo must be organized and written so that your thoughts are clearly presented and precisely stated. All of your effort is for nothing unless the reader understands what you are saying. People do not usually read legal writing for fun, so make the reader's job as easy as you can.

The memorandum is composed of several distinct but related sections. Label each section (except the heading) by underlining or capitalizing its name on a separate line immediately preceding that section. Although there are many variations, the following format for preparing a legal memorandum is widely used. Appendix I contains a sample memorandum using this format, which you should read in conjunction with this chapter.

1. Heading

The Heading is that part of the memorandum which describes who wrote it, to whom it was written, what it is about, and the date. It should look like this:

MEMORANDUM

To: Cheryl Scott

From: Eli Blackburn

Re: Possible abuse of discretion by trial judge in enjoining landfill operation, Dep't of Environmental Resources v. Fredericks, file no. 80-104.

Date: October 3, 1980

The explanation of the subject matter not only identifies the client and the file number but also briefly describes the general legal question. This description helps separate the memo from other memos in the same file and also provides a means for locating the memo later if a similar issue arises concerning different parties.

2. Questions Presented

This section should contain balanced and understandable statements of the legal questions you will answer in the memo. Where there is more than one question, each should be indicated by a symbol (for example, "I," "II," or "A," "B"), and each must contain a description of the relevant legal rule and a summary of the legally significant facts. The formulation of these questions is discussed at length in Chapter 11 (Questions Presented).

3. Brief Answer (Optional)

This section provides a short answer to each of the questions presented in the previous section. A Brief Answer is a conclusion and a brief explanation of the reasons for that conclusion. It is useful because it provides immediate answers to the questions and alerts the reader to your conclusions. This section is optional because it serves essentially the same purpose as the Conclusion section of the memo, although it differs from the Conclusion in length and form.

Since the Brief Answer section immediately follows the Questions Presented section, it should begin with a direct response to each of the questions such as "yes," "no," "probably," or "probably not." Each answer should be self-contained and should be indicated with the same symbol as the question to which it pertains. The answers should not contain citations to cases, regulations, or statutes except when the citations are so determinative of the issue that it would be senseless to exclude them.

*   *   *   *   *

A judge has enjoined your client, Al Fredericks, from operating a landfill on his property because it causes odors and groundwater contamination. The question discussed in your memo is whether the judge abused her discretion in granting the injunction. Consider these Brief Answers:

ANSWER A: No. The judge's ruling was well within her reasonable discretion. Her conclusion that the damage to nearby landowners from odors and groundwater pollution outweighs the harm caused to the defendant by the injunction is amply supported by the record.

ANSWER B: Injunctive relief is only proper where the damage being enjoined outweighs the harm to the defendant caused by the injunction. A trial court's injunction can be reversed on appeal only if the judge abused her discretion. The findings of the trial judge indicate that she did not abuse her discretion.

Answer A answers the question in a single word, "no," and then succinctly explains this conclusion by applying the legal rule to the summarized facts. It is thus far better than Answer B. Answer B fails to answer the question immediately and directly, and its bare statement of the legal rules involved explains nothing. Answer A directly answers and explains the question; Answer B does neither.

4. Statement of Facts

The Statement of Facts is a formal and objective description of the legally significant facts in the problem. The Statement of Facts must be accurate and complete. This section is addressed in Chapter 10 (Statement of Facts: Office Memorandum).

5. Discussion

The Discussion is the heart of the memo and draws on lessons from many of the chapters in this book. The Discussion is divided into segments according to the issues and sub-issues presented by the problem. Each segment should be headed by a restatement of the question presented or by a statement of the thesis for that issue. Each issue must be analyzed independently of the others and must clearly set forth your conclusion on that issue and the reasons that support that conclusion. The organizational rules from Chapter 8 also require you to discuss the applicable law for each issue or sub-issue before analyzing the facts of your situation. Only after stating the arguments that support your conclusion should you refute or minimize the arguments that oppose your position.

Your analysis of each issue or sub-issue should be based on the rules for common law or statutory analysis, which are described in Chapters 5 and 6. These rules require you to explain how the facts and policies of the cases supporting your conclusions are analogous and distinguish the facts and policies of opposing cases. The comparable rules for statutory analysis should be employed if a statute is involved in the case.

Finally, you must plainly communicate your analysis to the reader according to the principles in Chapter 9 (Writing). Erect signposts for your reader with thesis, topic, and transition sentences. Be sure to show all the steps of your analysis, and explain your reasoning in a concise fashion using plain and precise language. The combined lessons of these four chapters should provide a solid foundation for writing the Discussion section of your memo.

6. Conclusion

The Conclusion is a somewhat longer and slightly different version of the Brief Answer. It describes and explains how you resolved the questions presented by the problem. The Conclusion is longer because it contains a more thorough description of the reasoning supporting the ultimate conclusions. The theory is that if a busy reader has very little time, he will read the Brief Answer; if he has a little more time, he will read the Conclusion; if he has enough time, he will read the entire memo. The Conclusion also differs from the Brief Answer in that it is not segmented by issues. As with the Brief Answer, the Conclusion should not include citations except in rare instances.

*   *   *   *   *

Consider these possible Conclusions to a memo on the landfill injunction problem:

ANSWER A: Injunctive relief is proper where the damage being enjoined outweighs the harm to the defendant caused by the injunction. The judge found that the injunction would deprive the defendant of his only source of income, but would substantially reduce odor and groundwater contamination problems for neighboring landowners.

ANSWER B: The judge did not abuse her discretion in granting the injunction because she carefully followed the *Redding v. Stone River Flour Co.* standards for equitable relief. The judge here found that the injunction would deprive the defendant of his only source of income, and that he and his wife would have severe trouble continuing payments for their house and car. The court also found, however, that eighteen neighboring landowners became nauseous from the site's odors and that the wells from which they pumped household water were contaminated with a variety of harmful chemicals. There is sufficient evidence to show she did not abuse her discretion.

ANSWER C: The judge did not abuse her discretion in granting an injunction because she reasonably concluded that the damage being enjoined outweighed the harm to the defendant caused by the injunction. The injunction deprived the defendant of his only source of income, but it substantially reduced odors and groundwater contamination for neighboring landowners. Although her conclusion may be debated, it has ample support in the record.

All three answers cover the same ground, but Answer C is the best. Answer C states a conclusion and then shows how the applicable law and facts, both of which are summarized, justify it. The answer is brief and to the point. Answer A, in contrast, is not an answer at all. It describes the relevant law and the facts, but it does not draw any explicit conclusion from them. Since the purpose of a memo is to predict the likely outcome of a legal dispute, Answer A is useless. Answer B is also deficient. Although Answer B offers a conclusion, it is much too long and detailed. These extra facts should be in your Discussion, but only essential facts belong in your

Conclusion. Another deficiency in Answer B is the reference to the *Redding* rule. Bare case citations communicate very little to the reader because he most likely will have no idea what a case means. Remember, your Conclusion must be self-contained.

The parts of the memorandum used in this chapter also illustrate the most fundamental rule of memorandum writing: above all else, be objective. Since the memorandum concludes that the trial judge properly enjoined the client from operating his landfill, it does not tell the client what he wants to hear. The unfavorable nature of this conclusion indicates that an appeal in this case would cost a great deal of time and trouble with little likelihood of success. The lawyer should thus try to resolve the client's problem in some other way. You must look for everything possible to help your client, but you must be completely honest about what you find.

8

Organization

GOOD organization is fundamental to effective legal writing. No matter how well you have stated the question and the significant facts, how thoughtfully you have analyzed the problem, or how skillfully you have used language, your work will be wasted unless it is organized intelligently. As a lawyer, you will be lucky if you are simply asked to rewrite poorly organized documents. If you are not lucky, you will be ignored or misunderstood.

Poor organization happens more frequently than you might imagine; readers of legal materials often have no idea what the writer is trying to say. Although the failure to effectively communicate ideas can result from many causes, most such failures are caused by the writer's shoddy organization. Even though a perceptive reader may be able to piece together the writer's ideas anyway, extracting these ideas from a disorganized discussion is not the reader's job. A writer is obligated to make his work as accessible as possible.

Just as legal thinking has its own analytical framework, it also has its own organizational requirements. You will find that the material is sufficiently difficult that you cannot simply use a mental checklist of ideas or a few scribbled notes when writing papers. Good organization begins with advance planning, and advance planning requires a detailed outline before you begin writing. Outlining helps you think through the problem and insures against omissions. Outlining is also helpful because it is easier to spot organizational deficiencies in a bare outline than it is when the details of the paper are all in place. While it may seem like extra work at

76

first, outlining is ultimately a time-saving method of organization. Rewriting an outline is easier than rewriting a paper.

Apart from carefully outlining your paper, there are four basic principles of good organization.

1. *Discuss Each Issue Separately*

Where there are two or more issues that merit analysis, you must examine each separately. Discuss and draw a conclusion about one issue before discussing the next. Distinct separation of issues enables the reader to understand what the issues are and sharpens your ability to anticipate the important points of each issue.

Issue separation is especially difficult in three types of situations. First, several issues may be hard to distinguish from one another because they are similar or similar-sounding. Effective organization requires a sound understanding of the relevant law. Second, the same reasons or policy considerations are sometimes needed for several issues because these issues are so closely related. Never ignore points you have already discussed when they are relevant to a subsequent issue. Instead of completely restating a point you have already made, though, you may simply make brief reference to it. Finally, a case may deal with several issues relevant to your problem, requiring you to discuss that case at several points in your paper. Set out the case's holding and underlying *1st* facts pertaining to Issue X when you are discussing Issue X, and discuss the holding and underlying facts pertaining to Issue Y when you are discussing Issue Y. Avoid the temptation to set out all the facts and *1st* holdings of the case in one place; it will only confuse the reader. This is simply a variation of the basic theme—always discuss each issue separately.

*   *   *   *   *

Johnson is charged with assault and robbery in connection with the theft of $300 from the First National Bank. The prosecutor alleges that Johnson pointed a gun at a teller and told him to hand over what money he had. After Johnson's arrest, police learned that his gun was not loaded. Does this fact provide a defense to the charges? There are two relevant cases:

State v. Coronado (1948)

Coronado was convicted of robbery for taking $15 from a small grocery. He appeals on the ground that his "weapon," a pointed finger pressed against the inside of his coat, was not lethal. We think he misses the real issue, and consequently we affirm. Robbery requires that the taking be accomplished by either violence or the threat of immediate harm to the victim. Since Coronado's act reasonably frightened the clerk into giving away the money, he cannot claim it was only a ruse.

State v. Hines (1962)

Hines appeals from her conviction for assault. We affirm. Hines was convicted for placing the eraser end of a pencil against the back of a blind man and threatening to shoot him if he did not turn over his money. He fainted and she fled. She claims that the absence of a real gun frees her from guilt for assault. We disagree. A person is guilty of assault if she intentionally puts another in fear that she may cause him serious bodily injury or death. A genuine handgun is not likely to make much difference to a blind man.

Consider these two discussions:

ANSWER A: Johnson cannot use his unloaded gun as a defense to either assault or robbery. In *State v. Hines,* the court held that the defendant's failure to use a real gun did not free her from guilt for assault where she caused a blind man such fear for his life that he fainted. The defendant had pressed a pencil against her victim's back as if it were a handgun. The court said that reasonable fear for one's safety makes it irrelevant that there is actually nothing to fear. Similarly, in *State v. Coronado,* the court held that a person can be convicted of robbery if the taking occurs because the defendant caused a reasonable fear of immediate harm to the victim. The court reasoned that the defendant's "weapon," a hidden pointed finger, frightened a clerk into turning over the store's money.

Johnson cannot use the fact that his gun was not loaded as a defense to assault because he intentionally put the teller in fear of serious bodily injury or death by pointing his gun at him. Just like the harmless pencil in *Hines,* the unloaded gun was sufficient to cause the victim reasonable fear for his safety. Nor is the unloaded gun a defense to robbery. Since the threat of immediate harm from Johnson's pointed gun prompted the clerk to give him $300, he is like the defendant in *Coronado* who frightened the clerk into surrendering the money.

ANSWER B: Johnson cannot use the fact that his gun was not loaded as a defense to either assault or robbery. As to assault, in *State v. Hines,* the court held that the defendant's failure to use a real gun did not free her from guilt for assault where she had caused a blind man such fear for his life that he fainted. The defendant had pressed a pencil against her victim's back as if it were a handgun. The court indicated that reasonable fear for one's safety makes it irrelevant that there is actually nothing to fear. In this case, Johnson intentionally put the teller in fear of serious bodily injury or death by pointing the gun at him. The teller, who did not know the gun was unloaded, complied with his demand. Just like the harmless pencil in

Hines, the unloaded gun was sufficient to cause the victim reasonable fear for his safety.

Nor is the unloaded gun a <u>defense</u> to <u>robbery</u>. In *State v. Coronado,* the court held that a person can be convicted of robbery if the taking occurs because of a threat of immediate harm to the victim. The court reasoned that the defendant's "weapon," a hidden pointed finger, frightened a clerk into turning over the store's money. Since the threat of immediate harm from Johnson's pointed gun prompted the clerk to give him $300, it similarly does not matter that the gun was unloaded.

Although the description of the cases and analysis of the facts in Answers A and B are identical, Answer B is preferable because it is easier to understand. Answer B shows a distinct separation of issues. It describes the assault case and its application to Johnson's situation in the first paragraph, and the robbery case and its application to Johnson's situation in the second. The transition from the description of the case law to analysis of the facts for each issue is smooth and easy to follow.

Answer A, on the other hand, is organized as follows: assault, robbery, assault, robbery. It explains the law concerning assault, then explains the law concerning robbery. When it relates the facts to the law, Answer A takes the reader back to assault, then back again to robbery. The organizational pattern is jumpy and hard to follow. Answer A imposes an unfair burden on the reader and is ineffective. Organization makes the difference.

2. Discuss Each Sub-Issue Separately

Each issue, as you have discovered, often has several parts or sub-issues. Each sub-issue involves it own rule, and thus its own set of significant facts. You should deal with each sub-issue in sequence, finishing the discussion of one before continuing to the next. Discuss sub-issues as part of the issue they comprise. If Issue A involves two sub-issues and Issue B also involves two sub-issues, discuss each sub-issue under A before going to any part of Issue B. As with issues, clear separation of sub-issues sharpens your presentation, enabling the reader to better understand your position.

*   *   *   *   *

Burns Research Corp., a consulting firm, successfully persuaded the Salem Township Board of Trustees to grant a zoning amendment to reclassify a ninety-seven-acre parcel from agricultural (A) to research office (RO). A local landowner's group, Save Our Heritage Association, is contemplating a lawsuit challenging the amendment on a number of grounds, including spot zoning. The parcel was previously used by a home for delinquent boys, whose founders believed in the therapeutic value of agricultural work. Burns plans to lease most of the land for pasture. The surrounding area is made up of homes on five-acre lots and farms. There are two relevant cases in the state:

Costello v. Plainview Zoning Commission (1965)

Appellant challenges a decision by the Zoning Commission for the City of Plainview changing the classification of a one-half acre lot from RR (single family residential) to C (commercial). Appellants are homeowners and residents of the fourteen-acre RR zone surrounding the lot. The applicant for the zoning change, a trucking company which is an appellee here, sought permission to build a trucking terminal on the lot. Appellants argued unsuccessfully to the trial court that the Commission's decision constituted unlawful spot zoning.

We agree with appellants and reverse. The essence of zoning is the division of a municipality into districts defining present or potential suitable uses for property. Spot zoning is unlawful where a parcel of land is singled out for special treatment for the benefit of the owner and to the detriment of other landowners and the community. The zoning change at issue here constituted special treatment for the trucking company because it affected only the small parcel owned by the company. Rezoning also was detrimental to the landowners and the community because the terminal would lead to a decline in property values. Under these circumstances, the Commission's action was impermissible spot zoning.

Persich v. Pole (1974)

Pole, the owner of an undeveloped seven-acre tract zoned R2 (multiple family residential) successfully persuaded the Medford Zoning Commission to rezone the property to C (commercial). He plans to build a shopping center on the tract, lease the center to various retail stores, and use the remainder of the tract for a parking lot. Persich, a homeowner on adjoining property, sued to enjoin the amendment as spot zoning. The trial court agreed with the Commission and we affirm.

We ruled in Costello v. Plainview Zoning Commission that spot zoning is impermissible "where a parcel of land is singled out for special treatment for the benefit of the owner and to the detriment of other landowners and the community." Pole is not being unfairly benefited here because the rezoning applies to a large block of land, unlike the half-acre rezoning for the trucking company rejected in Costello. In addition, since the record shows the absence of any shopping centers in the area, location of the center on this property will benefit the neighborhood and the city.

Consider these discussions:

ANSWER A: The amendment was not improper spot zoning. "Spot zoning is unlawful where a parcel of land is singled out for special treatment for the benefit of the owner and to the detriment of other landowners and the community." *Costello v. Plainview Zoning Commission.* The amendment is not an unfair benefit to Burns Research Corporation or a detriment to the landowners. The court in *Costello* concluded there was spot zoning where a one-half acre lot located in a large residential area was rezoned commercial to accommodate a trucking terminal. The court said the essence of zoning is division of a municipality into districts, and apparently believed a one-half-acre lot unreasonably small for a district. The court also found that the amendment would lead to lowered property values in the neighborhood.

In *Persich v. Pole,* the court concluded that a zoning commission's decision to rezone an undeveloped seven-acre lot from a residential classification to a commercial one for a shopping center and parking lot was not spot zoning. The tract owner was not "unfairly benefited," the court reasoned, because the property was much larger than one-half acre. The court also found a benefit to the neighborhood because of the absence of any shopping centers in the area.

In this case, there is no unfair benefit to Burns because of the large size of the tract and because the basic use of the property will remain the same. The ninety-seven-acre property is larger than the ten-acre tract in *Persich,* and thus a reasonable size for a zoning district. In addition, there is no unfair burden to the surrounding landowners. Like the landowners in *Persich,* the surrounding landowners in the Burns case will actually benefit because they can lease land formerly owned by the boys' home. Unlike *Costello,* no decline in property values is foreseeable since the essential use of the parcel for agricultural purposes will remain the same.

ANSWER B: The amendment was not improper spot zoning. "Spot zoning is unlawful where a parcel of land is singled out for special treatment for the benefit of the owner and to the detriment of other landowners and the community." *Costello v. Plainview Zoning Commission.* The amendment is not an unfair benefit to Burns Research Corporation or a detriment to the landowners.

The amendment is not an unfair benefit to Burns because of the large size of the tract. The court in *Costello* found an unfair benefit where a half-acre lot owned by a company in a large residential area was rezoned commercial to accommodate a trucking terminal. The court said the essence of zoning is division of a municipality into districts, and apparently believed a one-half-acre lot was unreasonably small for a district. A seven-acre undeveloped residential tract rezoned commercial in *Persich v. Pole,* however, was not too small. Thus, a ninety-seven-acre tract is large enough to be a zoning district.

In addition, there is no detriment to the surrounding landowners. The court in *Persich* found the shopping center to be beneficial to the neighborhood, rather than detrimental, because no other shopping centers were located there. Like the landowners in *Persich,* the surrounding landowners in the Burns case will benefit because they can lease land formerly owned by the boys' home. This case is also different from *Costello* because the trucking terminal in that case would have led to lowered property values in the neighborhood. No such problems are foreseeable here because the essential use of the parcel for agricultural purposes will remain the same.

Answer B is more understandable because it is better organized. The spot zoning issue depends on two sub-issues: (1) whether there is an unfair benefit to the owner, and (2) whether there is a detriment to other landowners and the community. Answer B sets out both the description and analysis of the law for each sub-issue separately, completing the discussion of one before discussing the next. Since both the description and analysis for each sub-issue are stated in the same place, Answer B is far easier to follow than Answer A.

Answer A describes both cases before analyzing either sub-issue and is organized like this: private benefit, neighborhood detriment, private benefit, neighborhood detriment, private benefit, and neighborhood detriment. Such a zig-zag organizational style requires unnecessary effort simply to understand the discussion. This criticism should be familiar to you from the previous discussion on separation of issues. By describing all the law applicable to multiple points first, then trying to analyze the points, the writer risks leaving the reader in hopeless confusion. Stated another way, the sub-issues dictate the organization in Answer B, while the cases dictate the organization in Answer A. The issues and sub-issues, not the cases, should dictate your organization.

3.   For Each Issue or Sub-Issue, Describe the Applicable Law before Applying It to the Factual Situation

Each issue or sub-issue involves the possible application of a legal rule to specific facts. The relevant legal rules, therefore, provide a framework for your analysis and should be stated first. If you state the facts concerning an issue or sub-issue first, without setting out the applicable law, the facts will mean nothing to your reader.

Stating the applicable law first also enables you to be more concise.

The Statement of Facts at the beginning of the memo will give the reader a complete picture of the factual situation. Stating the facts in your Statement of Facts, then stating the facts for a particular issue or sub-issue, then stating the law, and then applying the law to the facts is inherently repetitious. When you write the body of the paper, therefore, avoid simply restating the facts; apply them. Instead of writing again, "Joe drove through a red light," write, "Since Joe drove through a red light, he is liable for . . . ." The facts, in other words, must be analyzed in the discussion, not simply described again.

*   *   *   *   *

Jenkins owns a riparian lot on Fredda Lake, a shallow, thirty-acre pond with no inlets or outlets. McNulty, who also owns a riparian lot on the lake, wants to drain one-third of the lake for water for a small brewery he plans to establish. McNulty's plans would reduce the size of the pond to fourteen acres, making it difficult for Jenkins to use it for fishing or boating. Jenkins, who is your client, wants to know if he can prevent McNulty from carrying out his plans. There is one pertinent case:

Posner v. Fox (1967)

Appellant Posner wants to construct an apartment complex on Lake Minnesota, a 400-acre lake drained by a small stream. He has owned riparian land on the lake for several years. His plans require the diversion of 1,200-acre-feet of water annually. Appellee Fox, who also owns riparian land on the lake, seeks to block the diversion of the water. The trial court found that the proposed diversion would permanently reduce water levels by about three feet and interfere with boating, swimming, and fishing on the lake by Fox and other abutting landowners. The court permanently enjoined the diversion. We affirm. Each riparian owner has certain rights to use the lake for domestic or recreational purposes, but each owner must accommodate the others. Posner's plans would unreasonably interfere with the rights of the other owners.

Consider the following:

ANSWER A: McNulty's proposal can be enjoined because it would constitute an unreasonable interference with Jenkins's use of the lake. McNulty's plans would reduce Fredda Lake from thirty acres to fourteen acres in size. This reduction in size would make it very difficult for Jenkins to fish or boat on the lake. The court in *Posner v. Fox* held that a similar action could be enjoined as an unreasonable use of water. The defendant in that case sought to divert water from a 400-acre lake for a proposed apartment complex, thus permanently reducing water levels by about three feet. The court held that proposal to be an unreasonable use because it interfered with recreational uses of the water by the other riparian landowners along the lake. In McNulty's case, as in *Posner*, the proposed diversion would significantly interfere with the recreational use of the lake. Reducing the size of the lake by more than one-half seems an even more unreasonable encroachment than *Posner's* comparatively slight reduction in water levels. McNulty's proposal can thus be enjoined.

ANSWER B: McNulty's proposal can be enjoined because it would constitute an unreasonable interference with Jenkins's use of the lake. Each riparian owner of land along a lake must not unreasonably interfere with the rights of other riparian owners to use the lake. *Posner v. Fox.* The court in *Posner* held that the defendant could be enjoined from diverting enough water from a 400-acre lake to permanently reduce water levels by about three feet. The court reasoned that the reduction would unreasonably interfere with the rights of other owners to use the lake for recreational purposes. That case is applicable here. McNulty's proposal, which would reduce a thirty-acre pond to fourteen acres in size, would have an even more drastic effect on the lake than the comparatively slight reduction in water levels found in *Posner.* The proposal here, like the proposal in *Posner,* would have a significant adverse impact on fishing and boating by Jenkins and other riparian owners on the lake. McNulty's proposal can thus be enjoined.

———

Answer B is preferable because it describes the *Posner* case prior to analyzing the facts of the McNulty situation. This organizational scheme avoids needless repetition, makes the significance of the stated facts immediately apparent, and gives the analysis greater clarity. Unlike Answer B, Answer A reads like this: facts, applicable law, facts. This organizational scheme is confusing because the reader is incapable of determining the significance of the facts until the legal rules have been stated. This approach is also inherently repetitious because the answer makes a second reference to the facts when they are analyzed later in the discussion. Answer B is more readable, easier to understand, and more concise than Answer A because it is better organized.

4. State the Reasons Supporting Your Conclusion on an Issue or Sub-Issue before Discussing Opposing Arguments

The end result of your thinking on an issue or sub-issue should be a legal conclusion. This conclusion should be the first point expressed in your thesis or topic sentence. After stating the thesis, explain the reasons for it—reasons you may have understood only near the end of your thinking process. The counterarguments, which may have persuaded you at the outset, should be related at the end. It is at this point in the memo, and *only* at this point, that you should discuss why these arguments are not as compelling as the arguments that support your position, and distinguish any important cases you believe are inapplicable. This method of presentation, which should be employed for each issue and sub-issue, makes your discussion easier to follow and also insures that you will draw a conclusion on each point discussed.

This rule does not permit you to intuit a particular result and then marshal justifications for it. This rule, like the others, merely requires you to distinguish your original thinking process from your writing. As other chapters indicate, you should anticipate how your opponent will respond to your conclusions. This process sharpens your understanding of the issues and helps you determine the strength of your case. Your memo will lose direction, however, if it reads "on one hand, but on the other hand, nonetheless, still on the other hand." Do not require the reader to watch a game of intellectual badminton. Writers who adopt a back-and-forth style tend to avoid drawing any conclusions, leaving the reader with only a set of considerations rather than a prediction of the probable legal outcome. This style also makes it difficult to state a precise legal conclusion or the reasons for it when closely related arguments are being discussed.

*   *   *   *   *

Your client, the Wilderness Preservation League, opposes a federal agency's proposed construction of a large hydroelectric dam in a deep western canyon. As required by the 1969 National Environmental Policy Act, the agency has prepared an environmental impact statement (EIS). The Act permits groups such as the League to bring an action in federal district court challenging the adequacy of an EIS. The adequacy of the EIS is one of the three potential issues in this case. Consider the following discussions of that issue:

ANSWER A: The agency's EIS is inadequate under the National Environmental Policy Act. The Act requires that an EIS discuss as fully as possible the environmental effects of, and alternatives to, a project. The EIS in this case discusses the environmental effects of flooding on the wildlife and plants of the canyon, on the river, and on areas that would be affected by subsequent development. It does not, however, give any indication of how long it will take the canyon just upstream from the dam to fill with silt, although it does discuss the siltation issue. This inadequacy is not relevant, though, because courts will not scrutinize an EIS that closely. Since the EIS does not discuss alternatives, however, the agency has violated the Act. The agency did discuss the alternative of "no action," but it did not consider power generation from other sources or whether the power was even needed.

ANSWER B: The agency's EIS is inadequate under the National

Environmental Policy Act. The Act requires that an EIS discuss as fully as possible the environmental effects of, and alternatives to, a project. Since this statement did not fully discuss alternatives, particularly power generation from other sources or the need for the power, the agency has violated the Act. The Act does not absolve an agency which has discussed merely some alternatives, and it is thus irrelevant that the agency did discuss the alternative of "no action." The discussion of environmental effects of flooding, however, is probably adequate because there is full discussion of the wildlife and plants of the canyon, the river, siltation behind the dam, and the areas that would be affected by subsequent development. Although there is no indication of the time necessary for large-scale siltation to occur, the courts do not subject a statement to this kind of close scrutiny.

Answer B is preferable because it is easier to understand. Answer B begins by discussing the alternatives sub-issue as the basis for its thesis. The reason for the conclusion on that sub-issue is explained (no full consideration of alternatives), and then the counterargument (discussion of "no action") is refuted. Finally, Answer B draws a conclusion as to the environmental effects sub-issue, explains the basis for that judgment, and dismisses the counterargument. The procedure remains the same even though the client loses one of these sub-issues and wins the other.

Answer A considers the alternatives and environmental effects sub-issues separately, but the discussion of each is muddled by its back-and-forth style. On one hand, it says, these effects have been considered. On the other hand, one effect has not been considered. Answer A concludes that the failure to consider that effect is probably not too important. This style is extremely awkward—a zig-zag path is taken where a straight line should have been followed. The same style is used with the alternatives sub-issue.

There is another basic flaw in Answer A. Since the alternatives sub-issue determines the inadequacy of the EIS in this case, that sub-issue should have been discussed before the sub-issue of environmental effects. Always remember, the points supporting your conclusion, not necessarily those supporting your client's case, should be discussed first.

The following exercises should help you learn to apply these rules.

Exercise 8-A

Several months ago, Colonel Augustus P. Ferguson, who won several medals for bravery in the First World War, died at age eighty-seven in the crash of a private plane. His only surviving child is Augustus, Jr. In 1928, the Colonel and his wife executed wills leaving all their property to each other, or in the event the spouse had previously died, in equal shares to their surviving children. His wife passed away in 1977. Shortly after her death, the Colonel became involved with Arizona Properties, Inc., a land development company. He was vice-president of the company at his death. Before he died, he revoked his 1928 will and executed a new will giving his entire $1.3 million estate to Arizona Properties.

Augustus, Jr., has asked your senior attorney to challenge the validity of the second will in probate court. The law in this state reinstates the previous will if the latter will is invalid. Junior stated that the Colonel's new attorney, also general counsel for Arizona Properties, drafted the second will. This attorney and the Colonel were both avid fishermen and went fishing together two or three weekends each month. The attorney resigned as general counsel a year ago. Junior also said that the corporation financed trips for the Colonel, "allegedly for purposes of learning foreign land development strategies," to Hong Kong, Rio de Janeiro, and Cairo. These trips occurred before he revoked the first will. Junior admitted that his father, from whom he was estranged since the death of his mother, "was not at all senile." You are to write an office memo ascertaining the validity of the second will.

There are two relevant cases in this state:

In re Estate of Steffans (1962)

This case involves the validity of the will of Maxine Steffans, a real estate broker, who left her entire $385,000 estate to her paperboy for eight years, Rodney Prentice. This court has recently required those challenging a will for undue influence to show (1) susceptibility to undue influence, (2) opportunity to influence, (3) disposition to influence, and (4) coveted result. The court below concluded that no such influence occurred, and we agree.

Mr. Prentice testified without contradiction, and the trial court found as fact, that Steffans spoke to Prentice only when he came to collect his biweekly payment for the paper, and that she frequently paid him by putting a small envelope under her doormat to avoid this contact. A neighbor also testified that Steffans, who had a reputation as eccentric, told her that she, Steffans, was willing Prentice her entire estate because he brought the paper on time. Under these circumstances, the claim of undue influence is speculative at best, particularly when the neighbor did not pass this information on to Prentice or anyone else.

In re Will of Kendall (1969)

Harriet Kendall's first will, executed when she was fifty-two, left her entire estate to her husband, Ralph. She entered a nursing home in 1965, when she was eighty-one. Shortly thereafter, she called an attorney to ask some questions about her will. Harriet was bedridden at the time, unable to carry on a conversation for more than several minutes, and prone to forgetfulness.

The attorney made his first visit to the nursing home with Harriet's sister, Mabel. Mabel suggested that she think about writing a new will. On their second visit, about one week later, the attorney and Mabel brought a new will for Harriet to sign. Although she was too weak to sit up to sign it, she was able to mark it with an "X" after Mabel propped her up with some pillows. When Harriet died in early 1966, her husband learned that the second will left her estate to Mabel's only son, Edmund. He also learned that the attorney who drafted the second will was not Harriet's personal attorney, but rather was Mabel's attorney. The trial court nonetheless admitted the second will to probate. We reverse.

There are two tests for determining whether there was undue influence in the execution of a will. The first test, described in *In re Estate of Steffans* (1962), need not be considered here because we find the trial court erred under the second test. Undue influence can occur when there is a confidential relationship between the testator and the one alleged to have exercised undue influence, and there are suspicious circumstances surrounding the making of the will. The existence of a confidential relationship depends on the ease with which the confidant controlled or influenced the drafting of the will. Suspicious circumstances exist when there is a sudden and unexplained change in the attitude of the testator, activity by the beneficiary in procuring the drafting and execution of the will, or similar circumstances. The activity of the attorney and the beneficiary's mother in procuring a will from an elderly woman in this situation meets both requirements.

1. What issue(s) would you discuss in this memorandum?

2. Are two or more sub-issues included under any of the issue(s)? If so, state them.

3. State all plausible arguments for and against your client's position on each issue or sub-issue as precisely as possible.

4. Using your answers to question 3, draw a conclusion about a probate judge's likely decision on each issue or sub-issue. What arguments support each conclusion? What arguments do not?

5. Outline your analysis of the problem as if you were preparing to draft the Discussion in a memorandum.

Exercise 8-B

All-Rite Industries, Inc. operates a coal-fired powerhouse to generate steam and electricity at its factory in Junction City. The powerhouse has a capacity of 500,000 pounds of steam per hour, and burns coal containing 0.9 per cent to 1.2 per cent sulfur content by weight. All-Rite manufactures chemicals, inks, and dyes at this factory for a variety of commercial products. The short smokestack from the powerhouse emits about 500 pounds of sulfur dioxide per hour.

Farmers downwind of the powerhouse have complained about sulfur dioxide emissions for several years. They can show that sulfur dioxide settles on their alfalfa fields under certain atmospheric conditions, whitening the leaves and reducing the value of the crop by at least five per cent. The tax assessor has told several of these farmers that the value of their property is $500 to $2,500 lower because of the sulfur dioxide emissions. A physician for several of the farmers attributes their above-average number of respiratory ailments to inhalation of sulfur dioxide.

All-Rite has ignored these complaints. A spokesman for the company states that the factory employs 590 persons and provides millions of dollars of income for the community. By contrast, he says, the farmers' claims are insignificant. The Junction City *Ledger-Gazette* refuses to print letters from the farmers complaining about sulfur dioxide emissions, and regularly praises the company in editorials for its "good work and solid contributions to our economy." An article published six months ago in the paper cited the sulfur content of the coal burned at the powerhouse and pointed out that lower sulfur coal releases less sulfur dioxide when burned than higher sulfur coal. "When you compare that with the high-sulfur coal used in other states," the paper said, "it is clear that top management at All-Rite is dedicated to the environment."

The farmers have retained your firm to determine whether they have any causes of action against the company, and your senior attorney has asked you to draft a memorandum on the matter.

The state Air Quality Act provides in part:

> Sec. 11. The Department of the Environment shall promulgate standards for classes of industries sufficient to assure the highest practicable degree of protection for public health and welfare.
>
> Sec. 14. Any person may bring an action in the appropriate trial court to enforce the provisions of this Act and the regulations promulgated pursuant to it.

The regulation in the state Administrative Code promulgated by the Department of the Environment provides in part:

> Sec. 405.221(a). It is unlawful for a powerhouse that has a capacity of more than 500,000 pounds of steam per hour to burn fuel that exceeds 1.0% sulfur content by weight.

The following are three relevant cases from your state:

Neely v. Hoff Theatre Co. (1970)

Appellee Hoff Theatre Co. operates an outdoor motion picture theatre on a large lot adjoining the home of appellant Ervin Neely. Neely brought suit against appellee for trespass to land, claiming that light from the theatre and the automobiles of its patrons constituted a physical invasion of his land. The trial court granted summary judgment for the appellee, and we affirm. Trespass to land requires a physical invasion—the presence of some tangible object on another's property. Appellant argues that light is a physical invasion because he can see the presence of light on his property. We think this argument goes too far. If appellant found the light objectionable, he should have brought his action in nuisance, not in trespass.

Peters v. Hancock (1921)

Peters brought action against Hancock in nuisance to enjoin Hancock from operating her saloon, located on a parcel of land adjoining Peters's home. Peters alleged in his complaint that patrons of the saloon "severely disturb plaintiff's sensibilities and sleep by loitering on the street outside plaintiff's house, and by occasionally using loud and abusive language." The trial judge granted judgment for plaintiff. This court hesitates to reverse the judgment of the learned trial judge, but the allegations in the complaint do not constitute nuisance. Nuisance requires an unreasonable interference with the use or enjoyment of the plaintiff's land. Defendant should exercise what control she can over her patrons, but we do not think their occasional loudness or rudeness is "unreasonable" under the circumstances. Reversed.

Jacobs v. Metzger (1934)

This action arose when defendant's motor vehicle left a one-lane dirt road to avoid colliding with another motor vehicle speeding from the opposite direction. Defendant's car stopped in plaintiff's front yard. Plaintiff won damages for trespass in the trial court. We reverse. Although there clearly was a physical invasion of plaintiff's land by the defendant and his automobile, the defendant was privileged by necessity. The defendant should not be penalized for attempting to save his life from a speeding car.

1. List the issue(s) you would discuss in this memorandum.

2. Are two or more sub-issues included under any of the issues? If so, state them.

3. Draw a conclusion about a judge's likely decision on each issue and sub-issue. What arguments support each conclusion? What arguments do not?

4. Outline your analysis of the problem as if you were preparing to draft the Discussion in a memorandum.

9

Writing

ALMOST everything you need to know about writing can be summarized in one principle: write to communicate. Since memos are written to predict legal outcomes, you will impress the reader most with good organization, thoughtful analysis, and clear writing, rather than with rhetorical flourishes, knowledge of Latin, or vocabulary. Every last comma in your writing should be inspected, then examined again, to further that principle. Anything you write that interferes with the communication of your thoughts, no matter how good it sounds, is wrong.

Although the law contains very little that cannot be explained to a lay person, most nonlawyers are confused and mystified by legal writing. They believe—too often with good reason—that legal writing consists of lengthy sentences, unintelligible phrases, plenty of legal sounding words, and a careful blend of the pompous and the dull. This style results from misplaced professional pride, professional insecurity, sloppy thinking, the need to impress clients, habit, and blind repetition of previous bad legal writing. As Professor Wydick comments, "We lawyers cannot write plain English."* Legal writing, however, does not have to be this way. The law is a literary profession; legal writing should and often does approach the level of good literature. Many judicial opinions, for example, are

---

*R. WYDICK, PLAIN ENGLISH FOR LAWYERS 3 (1979). An earlier version of this book is Wydick, *Plain English for Lawyers*, 66 CALIF. L. REV. 727 (1978). *See also*, W. STRUNK, JR. & E. WHITE, THE ELEMENTS OF STYLE (3d ed. 1979). These are useful supplements to the rules described in this chapter.

remembered not only for their ideas but for the way in which they are expressed.

This chapter should provide a sound foundation for developing a good legal writing style. It devotes very little attention to the most basic writing skills, such as grammar, usage, sentence structure, or paragraphing because these subjects are addressed in detail in basic grammar texts. The chapter examines, instead, some broader principles of written expression. It gives an overview of the writing process and then states a few rules necessary for effective legal writing.

An office memo (or any legal document) should develop in three steps: prewriting, writing, and rewriting. Long before drafting a memo, think about what you are going to say. This is prewriting. Part of that, as previously emphasized, is outlining your thoughts. You should spend some time, too, thinking about the beginning lines of your discussion, your choice of language, and some of the finer points of your paper. Effective writing results from clear thinking, and clear thinking takes time. If you "blank out" when you begin drafting, chances are good you have not given the problem enough thought.

The actual drafting of your memo will be much simpler after prewriting. Although different people will approach their first draft in different ways, two guidelines apply to all styles. First, include everything you want to say even if you are not sure it belongs in the final product. It is easier to edit what you later determine to be unnecessary than to add something. Second, anticipate substantial revisions in later drafts. The first draft should be written to give general shape and direction to the memo, not to fine tune its language or grammar. Perfection cannot be achieved in the first or second draft, and writing will be easier if you do not try. When you finish the draft, set it aside for a few days.

Rewriting may be the most painful part of the process because it requires critical evaluation of your own work. After you have let the paper rest, read it carefully. You will often find that the organizational scheme is not working quite the way you intended, that the discussion is unclear at points, or that you have a sentence ten lines long. If you do not see any such problems, you are not looking at the paper critically enough. Although it is difficult, you must separate the intensely personal effort required to write from the product. The development of your writing ability can be partially measured by the readiness with which you take a scissors to your draft and reorganize it, toss away or insert entire pages, or rewrite paragraphs or sentences. Several rewrites may be necessary before you arrive at a satisfactory working draft. After you have roughed out a solid working draft, refine and polish it until your ideas are clear and focused. Economist John Kenneth Galbraith wrote recently that it takes him four or five drafts to get the right note of spontaneity.

Prewriting, writing, and rewriting take time. Those who indulge in the common undergraduate luxury of cranking out an assignment the night before it is due will most likely do poorly. The law demands precision of its practitioners and penalizes those whose work is rushed and sloppy.

The remainder of this chapter explains and illustrates some fundamental rules of effective legal writing. While these rules are not an all-inclusive list or the final word on good legal writing, they are a starting point for the development of effective communication skills.

1.   Tell Your Reader Where You Are Going

Clearly and carefully guide the reader through your paper. This is especially important when discussing multiple issues, each of which may have several sub-issues. Thinking through a legal problem is like hacking through a dense jungle. You often have little idea where you are or where you are going; you may backtrack, go in circles, or make long detours because you started in the wrong place or reached an impossible obstacle. While this is a necessary part of thinking, it is a poor way to write. Do not take your reader on such a confused and twisted journey. When you put your thoughts on paper, pave a superhighway straight to your conclusions. Take the reader only where necessary, and erect clear signposts. Remember that you are far more familiar with the area of law than the reader. You can erect signposts in three ways:

a. Use Thesis Sentences   The thesis sentence is that sentence in the first or second paragraph of any formal paper which states its basic conclusion. It gives the reader a framework for reading and understanding the paper. Similarly, an office memo must begin with a statement of your basic conclusions; the rest of the Discussion should explain and support them. You should have a thesis sentence at the outset of the Discussion, and a thesis sentence for each issue and sub-issue. Clues about your direction will be provided, in part, by the Questions Presented, Brief Answer, and Conclusion sections of your memo, but the Discussion itself should be an independent, coherent whole.

*   *   *   *   *

Your client, Alice Woodford, has been indicted for extortion and grand theft. The legal questions for your memo are whether she violated the two laws. Which of the following introductions to the discussion is preferable?

ANSWER A: In *Porter v. Falk,* the court held that a defendant could not be guilty of extortion simply because he had engaged in "hard bargaining" prior to entering into an otherwise lawful contract . . . .

ANSWER B: Woodford did not commit extortion, but she is guilty of grand theft. As to extortion, in *Porter v. Falk,* the court held that a defendant could not be guilty of extortion simply because he had engaged in "hard bargaining" prior to entering into an otherwise lawful contract . . . .

Answer B is preferable because it states how the writer resolved each issue before beginning the Discussion. The thesis sentence in Answer B gives the reader direction. Answer A, in contrast, sends the reader into the middle of the Discussion without giving any clues about the context. The reader should not have to guess where you are or where you are proceeding.

   b. Use Topic Sentences   A topic sentence is a thesis sentence for a paragraph. It summarizes the basic point of a paragraph, and is best stated in the first, or occasionally second, sentence of a paragraph. Like a thesis sentence, a topic sentence helps give direction to your writing.

*   *   *   *   *

   Your client, Cindy Ortez, was recently discharged from her job at Packey's Toys, Inc., for filing an antitrust complaint against her employer. As a general rule, an employer can discharge an at-will employee (one who is employed for an unspecified time period) at any time for any reason. There are certain exceptions to this rule, one of which occurs when the employee's discharge violates public policy. Several cases illustrate what sorts of discharges violate public policy. Consider the following excerpts from discussions of whether public policy has been violated in Ortez's case:

ANSWER A: . . . and upon his failure to do so he was discharged. The court held this to constitute a wrongful discharge because of policy considerations concerning the necessity of truthful testimony and the fact that perjury is a criminal offense.

   Public policy can also be violated when an employer discharges an employee for exercising a statutorily conferred right. In *Frampton v. Central Indiana Gas Co.,* an employee filed a workmen's compensation claim for injuries she received in the course of her employment. She was promptly fired. The court held this to be a wrongful discharge. In arriving at its conclusion, the court drew an analogy to retaliatory eviction under the state's landlord-tenant law. The court also determined that the discharge was contrary to the purposes of the workmen's compensation statute . . . .

ANSWER B: . . . and upon his failure to do so he was discharged. The court held this to constitute a wrongful discharge because of public policy considerations concerning the necessity of truthful testimony and the fact that perjury is a criminal offense.

In *Frampton v. Central Indiana Gas Co.,* an employee filed a workmen's compensation claim for injuries she received in the course of her employment. She was promptly fired. The court held this to be a wrongful discharge. In arriving at its conclusion, the court drew an analogy to retaliatory eviction under the state's landlord-tenant law. The court also determined that the discharge was contrary to the purposes of the workmen's compensation statute. The court reasoned that public policy is violated when an employer discharges an employee for exercising a statutorily conferred right . . . .

Both answers cover the same ground, but Answer A is the clearest and most direct. Not only does Answer A state the subject of the paragraph, it also indicates how that paragraph fits into the rest of the Discussion. All of this happens before the description of the *Frampton* case begins. Answer A gives the reader adequate guidance concerning the direction of the Discussion, and represents a good use of the topic sentence.

Answer B is less satisfactory because it is less direct. It begins the first full paragraph with a discussion of the *Frampton* case, without affording the reader any clues about the subject of the paragraph, or why *Frampton* is being discussed. As a result, the argument leading to the conclusion is harder to follow because it is less obviously focused. Since most people read legal documents only because they are required to, you should make the reader's job as easy as possible.

   c. Use Transitions   Transitions inform the reader that you have completed discussion of one point and are now proceeding to the next. Proper use of transitions allows the reader to immediately understand a change in subject. The reader can be confused by a discussion that treats a second and separate point as a continuation of the first point.

Transitions may be made in many ways. Often the simple insertion of a word like "however" or "though" will be sufficient. Enumeration of points (e.g., first, second, finally) is also acceptable. Sometimes you will want to use one or more sentences to indicate your shift of topic. Whatever alerts your reader to a change from one point to the next will suffice.

There is an important relationship between topic and thesis sentences on one hand and transitions on the other. The more clearly your point is stated, the more aware your reader will be that you are moving to the next point. Often the need for a transition can be eliminated by effective use of a topic or thesis sentence.

* * * * *

The State Utilities Commission has just denied a rate increase to the Flint Edison Company, a major utility. The company is challenging that decision in federal court. Your client is a citizens' group in the company's service area, and it would like to intervene in the case. Assume that Congress has passed an Energy Intervention Act, permitting particular groups to intervene in rate cases under specified circumstances. Rule 24 of the Federal Rules of Civil Procedure provides two methods of intervention. One method is applicable when a statute provides a conditional or unconditional right to intervene. Consider the following (edited) discussions of that method:

ANSWER A: Rule 24(a) permits intervention of right when a federal statute confers an unconditional right to intervene. The Intervention Act does not give an unconditional right to intervene because the right is limited to certain parties and certain circumstances. The group, therefore, may not intervene of right. Rule 24(b) allows permissive intervention when a federal statute grants a conditional right to intervene, as this one does . . . .

ANSWER B: Rule 24(a) permits intervention of right when a federal statute confers an unconditional right to intervene. The Intervention Act does not give an unconditional right to intervene because the right is limited to certain parties and certain circumstances. The group, therefore, may not intervene of right. They should, however, be able to obtain permissive intervention. Rule 24(b) allows such intervention when a federal statute grants a conditional right to intervene, as this one does . . . .

The only difference between Answer A and Answer B is the presence of this sentence in Answer B: "They should, however, be able to obtain permissive intervention." This sentence alerts the reader to the writer's shift to the permissive intervention discussion. Since the sentence also draws a conclusion, it is a particularly concise transition. Answer A's failure to use an effective transition obscures its discussion of permissive intervention. The reader of Answer A could determine that the writer has moved on to something else, but he might just as easily miss the shift.

2. Show All the Steps of Your Analysis

Memos must fully explain your conclusions. Since memos are written for lawyers, it is safe to assume that the reader will have a basic understanding of law and legal process. It is not safe, however, to assume that the reader understands the particular area of law, or to assume that he will know what you are talking about and fill in gaps in your memo. It is not enough that you state a particular result will occur; you must identify the analytical steps leading to that result. Lay out all important steps of your thought process on paper. The reader will thus be able to evaluate the soundness of your conclusions and act accordingly. Unfortunately, many writers understand their subject so well that they telescope several analytical steps into one, make unexplained assumptions, fail to define important terms, and in many other ways obscure their thinking from the reader.

* * * * *

Section 1331(a) of the Judicial Code permits federal district court jurisdiction of civil actions against parties other than the United States where the amount in controversy exceeds $10,000, not counting interest and costs. Approximately 300 persons, each alleging $100 in damages, wish to bring a class action against a private party in federal court. Does the court have jurisdiction? Consider the following:

ANSWER A: Federal jurisdiction is not possible. Section 1331(a) of the Judicial Code requires that the amount in controversy exceed $10,000. Although the claims in our case exceed $10,000, the *Zahn* aggregation rule means this case should not be filed in federal court.

ANSWER B: Federal jurisdiction is not possible. Section 1331(a) of the Judicial Code requires, as a condition of federal jurisdiction in civil suits against private parties, that the amount in controversy exceed $10,000. In *Zahn v. International Paper Co.*, the court held that multiple plaintiffs with distinct claims must each satisfy this jurisdictional requirement, even if the sum of their individual claims exceeds $10,000. Our case is like *Zahn* in that none of the plaintiffs has an individual claim exceeding $10,000, and thus this case should not be filed in federal court.

Answer B is better because it contains a more complete and understandable discussion. Answer B describes the relevant case and explains how that case applies to this one. Answer B is not only easier to read, it gives the reader greater confidence in its conclusion because it allows evaluation of its logical soundness. Answer A is weak because it only refers to the relevant case and does not fully explain the law.

3.   Describe the Context

The importance of a legal issue or sub-issue to the resolution of a problem is not always apparent. When this is the case, you must explain how the issue or sub-issue you are discussing fits into the factual situation and how it is meaningful to the rights and responsibilities of those involved. Where the problem involves a single subsection of a highly complicated statute, you should at least outline the statute. Where there can be genuine controversy about only one of four possible sub-issues, you should nonetheless briefly describe and resolve the other three. Failure to adequately present the context may leave a reader guessing about the relevance of an issue or sub-issue you raise.

*   *   *   *   *

Ann White, an elderly woman, was detained by the clerk of a department store in which she was shopping because the clerk suspected that White had stolen several items from the store. The clerk grabbed White by the wrist as she was leaving the store, quietly saying, "OK, come with me, lady." The clerk then led her by her wrist back to the manager's office, told her not to move, offered her a cup of coffee, and propped a chair against the outside of the door to prevent her escape while he looked for the manager. When the clerk and the manager returned a few minutes later, they found that she had not stolen anything, even though her physical description closely fit that of a woman who had in previous weeks taken several items from the store.

State Compiled Laws § 32.01 provides:

> A merchant's employee who has reasonable grounds to believe that goods have been unlawfully taken by a person may, for the purpose of attempting to effect a recovery of said goods, take the person into custody and detain him in a reasonable manner for a reasonable length of time. Such action does not render said merchant's employee civilly or criminally liable for false imprisonment.

Consider these two ways of discussing the liability of the store for false imprisonment:

ANSWER A: The store is liable for White's false imprisonment because it did not detain her in a reasonable manner. State Compiled Laws § 32.01 permits a merchant's employee to detain a person for the purpose of recovering stolen goods, but only if he does so in a reasonable manner. The clerk in this case grabbed the wrist of an elderly woman who was leaving the store, led her by the wrist to the manager's office, and then physically restrained her there. The clerk's quiet voice and offer of a cup of coffee do not change his excessive use of force.

ANSWER B: The store falsely imprisoned White and is not relieved of liability by state statute because the store's clerk detained her in an unreasonable manner. A person is liable for false imprisonment whenever he intentionally restrains another person against that person's will. There was false imprisonment here because the clerk prevented White from leaving the store and put her in the manager's office, all against her will. The statutory defense of State Compiled Laws § 32.01 does not absolve the store of liability. That statute creates a defense to false imprisonment for a merchant's employee who detains a person for the purpose of recovering stolen goods where the employee has reasonable grounds to believe the person unlawfully took the goods, and where he restrains the person in a reasonable manner for a reasonable length of time. The clerk had reasonable grounds to suspect White because she matched the description of an elderly shoplifter. In addition, the detention period of two or three minutes is a reasonable length of time. The clerk nevertheless failed to detain White in a reasonable manner. He grabbed the wrist of an elderly woman who was leaving the store, led her by the wrist to the manager's office, and physically restrained her there. The clerk's quiet voice and offer of a cup of coffee do not diminish his excessive use of force.

———

Answer B is preferable because it describes the statute as a defense to the common law tort of false imprisonment, shows that false imprisonment has been committed here, and completely explains the application of each element of the statute—reasonable grounds, reasonable manner, and reasonable time—to White's situation. Answer A conveys none of these ideas, simply assuming that the reader will know. Answer A tries to economize by focusing only on the issue supporting its conclusion, and thus fails to give the reader a complete and balanced picture. Answer A also creates the false impression that unreasonable manner is necessary for false imprisonment.

4. Be Precise and Clear

Effective communication is directly related to the care with which words are chosen and sentences and paragraphs are structured. The late T.M. Bernstein of *The New York Times* once said: "If writing must be a precise form of communication, it should be treated like a precision instrument. It should be sharpened, and it should not be used carelessly." Bernstein's statement is perhaps more true of legal writing than of journalism. Legal terms have particular meanings, and the difference between similar sounding words can be enormous. Moreover, since most office memos are written on narrowly defined problems, you must use language that fits their narrow focus as closely as possible. As you write and rewrite the memo, ask yourself if the words, phrases, and sentences convey precisely the meaning you intend. If you have difficulty phrasing a particular point, reread the relevant law and think about it further. These four guidelines should help to achieve clarity and precision:

a. Be Precise about the Facts   Legal conclusions will often depend on the interpretation of the legally significant facts. Your analysis will be strengthened by the precision with which you use facts, both in the Statement of Facts and in the Discussion. Precise use of the facts also fosters greater clarity in your presentation, rendering it more understandable to the reader.

*   *   *   *   *

Your client has filed a compensation claim pursuant to a statute designed to help disabled miners. Only specified disabilities are covered under the statute. Consider the following ways of describing his disability:

ANSWER A: Lockhart is ill because of the dirty air inside the mine where he worked for part of his life.

ANSWER B: Lockhart suffers from pneumoconiosis, or black lung, caused by inhalation of coal dust in the underground mine where he worked for twenty-two years.

Answer A tells the reader that Lockhart is ill from the mine, but Answer B identifies the disease and the reason. You can gloss over insignificant facts but you should always be precise about legally significant facts. Answer B, in addition, gives the popular name for the disease to explain a technical term that the reader may not otherwise understand. Never raise an obvious question in your reader's mind, such as the meaning of a technical term, without answering it immediately.

b. Be Precise about the Law   Many legal words are terms of art and have specific meanings. The difference between words such as "homicide" and "murder," for example, is substantial. Imprecise usage of these and other legal terms can convey a meaning totally different from what you intend.

*   *   *   *   *

Consider the following ways of describing a jury verdict:

ANSWER A: The jury found the defendant guilty of assault with intent to kill but acquitted him of manslaughter.

ANSWER B: The jury found the defendant guilty of attempting to kill but innocent of succeeding.

Answer A is preferable because it precisely identifies the charges on which the defendant was tried and precisely states the jury's verdict.

Answer B is too informal and imprecise. Assault with intent to kill, for example, is a specific variety of assault, and the reference to it in Answer A conveys more information than the vague and misleading phrase, "attempting to kill."

   c. Blend Precision with Simplicity   At the same time you strive for precision, be careful to preserve the clarity of the presentation. Avoid jargon, legalese (said defendant, to-wit, wheretofore), Latin phrases, lengthy sentences, long paragraphs, and long words wherever possible. Persons untrained in law should be able to read and understand the memo.

*   *   *   *   *

Consider these descriptions of a city ordinance:

ANSWER A: The ordinance forbids, *inter alia,* inhalation and exhalation of the fumes of a lighted cannabis sativa instrument.

ANSWER B: Among other things, the ordinance forbids marijuana smoking.

   Answer B is better because it is clear and pointed; there can be little doubt about its meaning. Answer A has far more words, but it probably conveys less information to the average reader. The Latin name for marijuana may make the writer seem more learned, but this is of no value if the reader does not know what is being said. Similarly, the definition of smoking in Answer A, while technically correct, does not convey anything more than the word, "smoking." Answer A also is obscured by the use of legal jargon. The Latin phrase for "among other things," *inter alia,* is one of many you will encounter in law; substitute an English translation whenever possible.

   d. Use Active Voice   Active voice (where the verb in a sentence states an action performed by the subject, rather than upon it, as in a passive voice) improves the clarity and forcefulness of your presentation. Active voice is immediate and direct, leaves no ambiguity about who is doing what, and requires fewer words. Passive voice, by contrast, is detached and often feeble. Writers who use passive voice also tend to omit the subject.

*   *   *   *   *

Consider these statements:

ANSWER A: The department shall disclose all relevant information to the requesting party.

ANSWER B: All relevant information shall be disclosed to the requesting party.

———

Answer A is more forceful and clear than Answer B because the verb (shall disclose) states an action to be performed by the subject (department), rather than upon it (information shall be disclosed). Answer A, unlike its counterpart, also states who will disclose the information. If Answer B is corrected to read, "All relevant information shall be disclosed to the requesting party by the department," it is still less forceful than Answer A and slightly longer. Although passive voice is sensible on occasion—to emphasize "all relevant information," for example—you should generally avoid using it.

5. Summarize the Law Whenever Necessary

When writing about issues that involve only a handful of relevant cases, you should describe and analyze each case in some detail. Many legal problems, however, involve more relevant cases than you can reasonably describe or analyze. In such situations, you must summarize the general legal principles involved in these cases and then describe several representative cases to illustrate your point. In selecting the representative cases, you may choose to examine in detail the few leading cases in an area since these cases are followed by many other courts and are likely to contain a detailed explanation of the court's decision. Another approach is to examine the cases whose factual situations are most analogous or most different. Although there are many legitimate ways to summarize the law, you must do so objectively. Avoid the temptation to oversimplify or slant your summary so that it favors your client's position.

* * * * *

Your client, Susan Wennerberg, was seriously injured while skiing near a small town with a private hospital. Although she had heard many times that this hospital treated injuries, she was refused emergency treatment. She wants to know if she can successfully sue the private hospital for the aggravation of her injury which occurred during the drive to the public hospital. Consider the following ways of describing the relevant law:

ANSWER A: Traditionally, a private hospital has had the right to select those persons who could enjoy its benefits. Private hospitals have been able to lawfully reject emergency patients because they had policies of not accepting members of certain health insurance plans, *O'Neill v. Montefiore Hospital,* or persons with contagious diseases. *Birmingham*

Baptist Hospital v. Crews. This right was so well-established that the *Crews* court said a private hospital needs no reason at all to refuse service to a particular emergency patient.

The principal exception to this right to refuse treatment now occurs when there is an unmistakable emergency and the patient has relied on the well-established custom of the hospital to render aid in such cases. In the leading case for this exception, *Wilmington General Hospital v. Manlove,* a private hospital refused emergency treatment to plaintiffs' four-month-old infant, who had a sore throat, diarrhea, and a 102-degree temperature. The nurse explained that the hospital could not give treatment because the baby was under a physician's care. The baby died of pneumonia several hours later. In affirming the trial court's denial of the hospital's motion for summary judgment, the court stressed the importance of the time lost in fruitless attempts to obtain medical aid . . . .

ANSWER B: Traditionally, a private hospital has had the right to select those persons who could enjoy its benefits. In *Birmingham Baptist Hospital v. Crews,* the parents of a two-and-one-half-year-old girl suffering from diptheria brought her to the defendant hospital, where she was diagnosed and treated with antitoxin. The hospital staff told the parents that the hospital did not accept patients with contagious diseases, and refused to allow her to stay. She died within five minutes of returning home. In deciding that the hospital was not liable for the child's death, the court reasoned that a private hospital can lawfully refuse service to emergency patients, and that preliminary treatment should not prejudice that right of refusal.

In *O'Neill v. Montefiore Hospital,* a private hospital refused admission to a man who complained of heart attack symptoms because he was a member of a certain health insurance plan. The man subsequently died. Although there was some question whether the hospital undertook to aid the man by certain other actions, the court held that the hospital had no obligation to treat him in the first place.

The principal exception to this right of refusal now occurs when there is an unmistakable emergency and the patient has relied on the well-established custom of the hospital to render aid in such cases. In the leading case for that exception, *Wilmington General Hospital v. Manlove,* a private hospital refused emergency treatment to plaintiffs' four-month-old infant, who had a sore throat, diarrhea, and a 102-degree temperature. The nurse explained that the hospital could not give treatment because the baby was under a physician's care. The baby died of pneumonia several hours later. In affirming the trial court's denial of the hospital's motion for summary judgment, the court stressed the importance of the time lost in fruitless attempts to obtain medical aid . . . .

Answer A is preferable because it gets to the point more quickly and clearly than Answer B. Answer A summarizes the absolute-right-of-refusal cases to provide the context for a lengthy discussion of *Manlove*. Since *Manlove* is the leading case on the exception to the rule, it deserves detailed consideration and the reader's focused attention. Answer B, however, describes in detail cases that do not need to be explained at this point, if at all. Writers who devote a paragraph to describing each of several cases in succession tend to produce rambling documents with little analysis of the issues, and Answer B manifests this tendency. You can write more clearly and briefly by summarizing the relevant law in appropriate circumstances.

6. Be Concise

One of Professor Strunk's favorite maxims, according to E.B. White, was, "Omit needless words." Strunk wrote, "This requires not that the writer make all his sentences short, or that he avoid all detail and treat his subjects only in outline, but that every word tell."* Every part of your memo, every word in each sentence, should be there for a reason. If not, delete it; excess language clouds your thinking and the reader's understanding. Needless words result from repetition, fuzzy writing, use of a long phrase when a short phrase or single word will do, poor use of clauses, and other errors. Edit your writing so every word tells.

* * * * *

Consider the following discussions of standing to sue under federal law:

ANSWER A: The essence of the federal standing requirement is the presence of injury in fact. Although for purposes of standing the alleged injury to the plaintiff need not be significant, it cannot be abstract. The plaintiff must allege actual injury in fact, and one which is directly affecting it or its members.

ANSWER B: The essence of the federal standing requirement is actual injury, or injury in fact. The alleged injury to the plaintiff or its members need not be significant, but it cannot be abstract.

Answer B is easier to read and understand because each word is necessary to complete the thought. The reader is not forced to waste time

---

*W. STRUNK, JR. & E. WHITE, THE ELEMENTS OF STYLE 17 (3d ed. 1979).

extracting the writer's ideas from a barrage of needless words. Both answers say the same thing, but Answer A says the same thing several times. Wordiness is not always so obvious, however.

* * * * *

The fourth amendment's prohibition against warrantless or unreasonable searches and seizures is commonly enforced through a judicially created exclusionary rule, which bars the use of illegally obtained evidence in criminal proceedings. Consider these discussions of the purposes of the exclusionary rule:

ANSWER A: It was observed in *United States v. Calandra* that the exclusionary rule is designed as a safeguard to fourth amendment rights through its general deterrent effect on unlawful police conduct, rather than as a personal constitutional right of the aggrieved. Another consideration for applying the rule is the integrity of the courts; that is, unlawful searches should find no approval in the courts. The courts have recently recognized that the tests for judicial integrity and deterrence are much the same. The idea is that if police are deterred from committing an illegal search by exclusion of evidence, the courts are not condoning this behavior. *Calandra* states that the primary purpose, if not the sole purpose, of the exclusionary rule is deterrence of future unlawful conduct. This has been the understanding in subsequent cases, including *United States v. Janis,* which stated that the emphasis on deterrence has been made quite clear in recent decisions.

ANSWER B: The Court in *United States v. Calandra* said that the exclusionary rule serves to safeguard fourth amendment rights through its general deterrent effect on unlawful searches, rather than as a constitutional right in itself. Another rationale for applying the rule, preserving the integrity of the courts, is no longer an independent justification. The Court in *United States v. Janis* stated that the tests for judicial integrity and deterrence are the same. The Court reasoned that the judiciary is not condoning unconstitutional behavior if police are deterred from committing an illegal search by exclusion of evidence.

Answer B is preferable because it is shorter, more focused, and not repetitious. Answer B clearly states that the judicial integrity rule is no longer significant, and then explains why. Answer A is repetitious, less direct about the current role of the judicial integrity rationale, and less precise. As a result of these defects, Answer A is much longer than necessary. Imprecise writing fosters wordiness because more language is needed to achieve the necessary clarity. Although Answer A suffers from other difficulties, such as its use of passive voice, its most obvious failure is disregard of the cardinal rule—make every word tell.

The exercises that follow are intended to give you practice spotting and correcting the errors described in these rules.

Exercise 9-A

Draft a Discussion for a memorandum based on your answer to question 5 in Exercise 8-A (pp. 86–88) using the rules described in this chapter.

Exercise 9-B

Draft a Discussion for a memorandum based on your answer to question 5 in Exercise 8-B (pp. 88–90) using the rules described in this chapter.

10

Statement of Facts: Office Memorandum

THE traditional organizational pattern for memos requires a separate section for stating the facts of the case. The purpose of this statement is to give the reader a clear picture of the legal problem at issue and to indicate what facts are important to its resolution.

Every legal problem involves the interplay of numerous facts, only some of which are relevant to its analysis. Whether you acquire these facts from interviews with clients or witnesses, from examination of documents, or from a memo from a senior partner, you will invariably accumulate more facts than necessary. These facts also tend to be disorganized and scattered through different interview notes and documents. You must pare excess facts away, leaving only those facts necessary to the understanding and resolution of the legal issues presented. You must then arrange these remaining facts in an intelligible, accurate, and coherent fashion. The basic rules for selecting and appropriately stating the facts of your case can best be understood in the context of a specific problem.

* * * * *

You represent Clara Finch in a land dispute. An interview with her and a subsequent investigation have revealed the following facts, stated in the order you learned them:

In 1941, Brauzakas purchased a forty-acre tract of land on the north side of County Highway Q, which runs east and west. Finch purchased

107

five acres of this tract from Brauzakas in 1973, and built her home on this parcel. Finch's primary means of access to her home is by a dirt road running from the highway through Amodio's (formerly Brauzakas's) property. Brauzakas sold the remainder of his land (thirty-five acres) to Amodio in 1975. Amodio has recently felled several large trees across the road through his property to prevent Finch from using the road. Finch's lot adjoins the Amodio property on its north side. There is no reference to Finch's use of the road in Amodio's deed to the property, and there is no recorded easement. Finch is an eighty-year-old widow living on a meager pension. Finch has another access to her house by a dirt road leading from another highway, but that route takes her thirty miles and forty-five minutes out of her way. Amodio is a wealthy banker who bought the Brauzakas property on speculation that land prices would continue to increase. Amodio has stated several times that he blocked the road because he does not like Finch. Brauzakas and Finch had only an oral agreement that she could use his road as long as he owned the land.

There are two relevant appellate decisions in your state:

Carson v. Dow (1934)

Appellant Carson brought this action for injunctive relief against Dow, claiming that he had an express easement to run a natural gas pipeline across Dow's property, and that Dow refused him access. There is no recorded easement. The trial court held that there was no express easement because of the absence of any language about the alleged easement in Dow's deed to the property, or in any other written agreement. We agree. Absent some written contractual agreement, there can be no express easement.

Watzke v. Lovett (1954)

Watzke purchased a tract of land from Lovett. The tract is located on the shore of a lake and is surrounded on the remaining sides by property owned by Lovett. The only means of access to Watzke's property is by a road that crosses Lovett's property and connects to a public road. Lovett has recently blocked the road, claiming that Watzke has no right to use it. Watzke conceded to the trial court that there is no written agreement creating an easement across Lovett's property, but argued that the court should imply an easement out of necessity. The trial court refused. We reverse.

When a parcel of land is owned by one person, and that person transfers part of that parcel to another person, access to the transferred part cannot be denied if the only means of access is through the remaining part of the original parcel. A showing of strict necessity is required before such an easement will be implied. The landlocked nature of appellant's property satisfies that requirement in this case. Watzke has an implied easement to use the road over Lovett's property.

Certain facts have special significance in light of these two cases. The following is a procedure for selecting and stating them.

1. Identify the Legally Significant Facts

The legally significant facts are those which will affect the legal outcome of your client's case. Chapter 2 explained that some facts of a judicial opinion are more important than others. The most important facts are those the court used in deciding whether or not to apply particular legal rules to the case it was deciding. Writing a legal memo reverses this perspective. Instead of looking backward to determine what facts a court thought were important, you look forward to predict what facts in your client's case a court is likely to believe significant. These facts can only be determined after you have ascertained the relevant rules involved and the corresponding issues presented for determination.

Isolating the legally significant facts is largely a process of elimination. The myriad of facts presented in a legal problem must be sifted and pared until only those facts necessary to the resolution of the legal issues remain. All significant facts should be identified regardless of whether they hurt or help your client's position. This will allow a clearer analysis and a greater understanding of the problem because it focuses the reader's and writer's attention exclusively on those facts that matter.

Where the legal rules are sharp and unmistakable you will need to identify relatively few significant facts. The ambiguity of many legal rules, however, means that the legal significance of some facts will depend on how the rule is interpreted. These borderline facts should be included if the interpretation requiring them is plausible.

Conversely, emotional facts should be omitted unless these facts have independent legal significance. Emotional facts are those facts that appeal to a judge's sympathies and sense of justice, influencing the outcome even though they may not be legally significant. These facts will become important and appropriate when you are advocating a position to a court, but they have no place in an office memorandum. The value of these facts is speculative because a court may ignore them. Since a court must consider legally significant facts, however, such facts are the best guide to the likely legal outcome.

The cases indicate that Finch might raise two possible legal objections. She could claim that she has an express easement or that she has an implied easement by necessity. Regarding the first issue, the *Carson* court held that an express easement must be created in either a written agreement or in the deed to the property across which the easement runs. It is thus legally significant that there is no provision in Amodio's deed permitting Finch to use the road across Amodio's property and that there is no recorded easement. These facts will make it difficult for Finch to claim an express easement, but must nonetheless be included in the Statement of Facts.

Finch could also claim that she has an implied easement by necessity, and this question involves a somewhat different set of legally significant facts. The court in *Watzke v. Lovett* held that where the only means of access to a person's property is through the property of the person who originally transferred the land, the person requiring the access is entitled to an implied easement by necessity. In Finch's case, it is legally significant that there is a road across the Amodio/Brauzakas property which Finch uses to get to her home, that there is another route to Finch's house, and that Brauzakas sold part of his property to Finch and the remainder to Amodio.

Although the significance of many facts will be immediately apparent, the significance of others will depend on how the legal rules are interpreted. For example, the *Watzke* court indicated that an easement will be implied only out of strict necessity. As a result, the existence of the second road may work to Finch's disadvantage. It may thus be significant that Finch is eighty years old and that the other road would take her thirty miles and forty-five minutes out of her way (facts which may have appeared at first to be emotional ones) since these facts tend to show that Finch's use of Amodio's road is more of necessity than convenience. These facts should be included in a Statement of Facts because they may have a bearing on the strict necessity rule, even though there was no other access in *Watzke*. Facts should not be ruled out hastily.

This problem includes a number of emotionally significant facts you should exclude from analysis, particularly those which make it appear that the wealthy banker Amodio is spitefully imposing a hardship on the poor widow Finch. Although these facts may greatly influence how a judge perceives the fairness of the situation, they have nothing to do with either of the legal rules concerning easements. Similarly, it is not significant that Amodio bought the property on speculation. Identify only those facts relevant to the possible application of a legal rule.

2.   Identify Key Background Facts

Legally significant facts tell part of the story, but these facts standing alone may not tell the whole story. Background facts are often needed to make the factual situation sensible and to put the legally significant facts in context. Include these facts in your Statement of Facts, but include only enough to help the reader understand the problem without providing so many that you clutter his mind.

In Finch's case, for example, it will probably help the reader to state that Brauzakas's parcel was forty acres in size, that Finch's lot is five acres, and that Amodio's property is thirty-five acres. This information provides further background for the implied-easement question by clarifying Brauzakas's original ownership and subsequent division of the property. The dates on which Finch and Amodio bought their property from Brauzakas may have some additional value in this regard, although the date on which Brauzakas purchased the land does not. In addition, it is useful to state that Brauzakas and Finch had an oral agreement because this fact highlights the absence of a written agreement. The name of the highway, however, is probably not useful here. Nor is it helpful to state that Amodio blocked the access by felling several trees; the statement that he blocked the access will do. Use background facts only as necessary.

3. Organize the Facts Intelligibly

The statement of legally significant and key background facts should be a complete and coherent story of your client's situation. Any organizational scheme that achieves this goal is acceptable, but the most sensible and convenient method of organization is to relate the facts in chronological order. Chronological order is easy for the reader to understand because it is the usual way a story is related; it is convenient for the writer because the facts are stated as they occurred. Although facts may be organized in a number of ways, they should never be organized according to issues, even though the issues are analyzed separately in the discussion. Such segmentation invariably results in repetitious and disjointed factual statements.

The Statement of Facts for this problem should begin with Finch's purchase of her property from Brauzakas and their oral agreement permitting her to use the dirt road across his tract for access. This is the chronological beginning of the problem and sets the stage for the events that follow. You should then state that Brauzakas sold the rest of his land to Amodio. Amodio's deed for the property contains no reference to the access, and there is no recorded easement. Recently, you would continue, Amodio has blocked the access to prevent Finch from using it. You should then add that Finch is eighty and that, while there is another access to her house, this alternative route takes her thirty miles and forty-five minutes out of her way. This last statement is difficult to locate chronologically, but it fits at this point because it suggests the possible consequences of the blocked access. A statement drafted along these lines would be easy for the reader to understand.

4. Describe the Facts Accurately and Objectively

The purpose of the Statement of Facts is to relate the facts accurately and objectively. The legally significant facts should be described precisely because they are crucial to the outcome. Any attempt to paraphrase these facts might cause an inadvertent change in meaning, which could alter your analysis. It is improper and misleading, for example, to say that Brauzakas and Finch had an agreement concerning her use of the dirt road, since it matters whether that agreement is oral or written. It is also improper to simply state that Finch has another access to her property, since her age and the circuitous route involved are relevant to the legal rule concerning implied easements by necessity. These are legally significant facts, and you must describe them precisely. Although you can often summarize background facts without misleading the reader, you should do so as accurately as possible.

In addition to precisely relating the facts, you must describe the facts rather than evaluate, analyze, or argue with them. It is one thing to say that Amodio blocked the access, but quite another to say that Amodio wrongfully blocked it. The latter is an evaluative statement that belongs only in your discussion or conclusion. Similarly, it is one thing to state that the other route takes her thirty miles and forty-five minutes out of her way, but another to state that the other route is impossibly difficult for a person of her age. The Statement of Facts should objectively state the facts; you can argue and analyze in your discussion.

*   *   *   *   *

Consider these possible factual statements for this problem:

ANSWER A: Finch is an eighty-year-old widow living on a meager pension. She has a house on a small tract separated from the highway by property owned by Amodio, a wealthy banker, who bought the land from the previous owner on speculation that prices would increase. The previous owner had long permitted Finch to use the dirt road through the property, but Amodio has refused access out of dislike for Finch. Although there is another road that Finch could use, it takes her thirty miles and forty-five minutes out of her way.

ANSWER B: Finch's land is separated from the highway by Amodio's land. Finch had a deal with the previous owner that she could use an old road through the tract for access to her five-acre lot. Amodio, whose property is thirty-five acres in size, has blocked Finch's access to her property. There was no mention of Finch's easement in the agreement, and the easement is not recorded.

There is another road Finch could use, but that route takes her a considerable distance out of her way, and she is eighty years old. Both Amodio and Finch bought their land from the same person. She bought five of his forty acres in 1973; Amodio bought the remaining thirty-five acres in 1975.

ANSWER C: Brauzakas, who owned a forty-acre tract, sold Finch five acres of that tract in 1973. Finch then built her home on this land. They orally agreed that Finch could use an old road through his property for access to her home, since her lot was separated from the highway by the remaining part of his tract. In 1975, Brauzakas sold this thirty-five acre tract to Amodio. There is no reference to Finch's use of the road in Amodio's deed to the property, and there is no recorded easement. Amodio has now blocked the dirt road across his property. Finch, who is eighty, has access to her house through a dirt road leading from another highway. That route takes her thirty miles and forty-five minutes out of her way.

Answer C is the best of the three answers because it is a neutral and accurate description of the facts and is stated in chronological order. Answer C contains the legally significant facts for both issues and also includes just enough background facts for the reader to understand the problem.

Answer A is defective primarily because it is so biased. The income or motives of the parties involved are not legally relevant. Answer A also omits legally significant facts, such as the absence of a reference to an easement in Amodio's deed, a written agreement, or a separate recorded easement.

Answer B is disjointed and paraphrases several legally significant facts. Answer B tries to separate the facts for each issue into separate paragraphs, making it both muddled and repetitious. The answer's use of "land," "deal," and "considerable distance," instead of more precise statements of the legally significant facts, creates unnecessary ambiguity and perhaps changes the meaning of the statement. Answer B also draws a legal conclusion by describing the road as an easement. That conclusion should be reached in the discussion, if at all, but it is inappropriate in the facts.

The following exercises let you practice identifying and describing facts of particular problems.

Exercise 10-A

Farley, tired of country life and wanting to get a fresh start, recently moved to a large city from his parents' melon farm, where he had lived for twenty-two years. When Farley arrived in the city, he spent several days trying to find an apartment that suited his needs. Living in hotels was quickly consuming his meager savings.

Finally, Farley saw an ad in the paper:

New, beautiful, spacious, one-bedroom apartment; recently redecorated; extremely clean; nice neighborhood; walking distance to university; immed. occupancy; no pets. $95 per mo. Resistance Realty Co. 591-1001.

Farley called the ad number and talked to a rental agent who confirmed all the statements in the ad and told Farley the place was perfect for his needs. The agent further told Farley that several people were interested in the apartment and that Farley should sign the lease at the realty office and then go see the apartment. Taking the agent at his word, Farley went to the realty company, paid a $500 security deposit, and signed the lease. Farley then went to look at his new apartment and received the shock of his life. The neighborhood was the worst one in town. There were two winos asleep on his front steps and several of the apartment windows were broken. The toilet did not work and there was no hot water. Two rats were sitting on the sofa, roaches were all over, and there were large holes in the walls. Dirt and grime covered the floors and walls. Farley went out to his car to leave and found that all of his hubcaps had been stolen. He went back to Resistance and demanded that the agent tear up the lease and refund his money. The agent refused, saying, "A deal is a deal."

Rule of Law: Every sale of a leasehold estate carries with it an implied covenant that the leased property is fit for human habitation. A lease is unenforceable if the covenant is breached.

Issue: Whether the leased apartment was so unfit for human habitation that Resistance Realty breached the covenant of habitability?

Assume the above rule of law and issue are the only ones applicable to Farley's case.

1. List the legally significant facts.

2. Does it matter that Farley's hubcaps were stolen? Why?

3. List any key background facts.

4. Draft a Statement of Facts based on your answers to the previous questions. Is it objective and understandable?

Exercise 10-B

This exercise is based on the facts and cases from Exercise 8-B on pp. 88–90.

1. List the legally significant facts for this problem.

2. List any key background facts.

3. Draft the Statement of Facts for this memorandum based on your answers to questions 1 and 2. Is it objective and understandable?

11

Questions **Presented**

A BASIC principle of legal education and legal practice is that you only receive answers to the questions you ask. The exactness of the question determines the precision and usefulness of the answer.

An office memo usually contains a section where the questions presented in the problem are stated. This section begins the memo and alerts the reader to the precise issues addressed. It is, therefore, important to frame the questions in this section as precisely as possible. A question framed too broadly or too narrowly will mislead the reader about the scope or focus of your analysis and make your discussion less effective.

Properly framing a legal question is a two-step process requiring you to combine the lessons from Chapters 4 and 10. First, you must precisely identify the legal rules that might apply to your problem. Second, identify the legally significant facts—the facts that determine whether a particular rule applies to the situation.

The formula for framing a question is simple: does the relevant law apply to the significant facts? Both the law and the facts should be contained in a concise, one-sentence question.* Generally, the legal rule should precede the facts. The question should be precise and complete.

---

*Although the Questions Presented section is often the last section drafted, it has its origins in the beginning of your research and analysis. As you work through a problem, your understanding of the rules and the legally significant facts will become more refined and complete. This section, therefore, is the common thread that runs through your entire memo—the link between your initial work and the final product.

When you have formulated the statement of the question by combining the relevant law with the significant facts, check to be sure it conforms to the following two additional rules:

1. Be Understandable

Your questions should be as precise and complete as possible without being so complex that your reader cannot understand the issues. Sometimes a problem will contain so many facts relevant to a single issue that including them would make your question unreadably long and awkward. When this occurs, examine your significant facts and choose only those most relevant to the determination of the issue. You may also be able to summarize or condense a group of closely related facts, although you should do so only with great care. Whenever you generalize about the facts, you risk distorting them or making the issue seem much broader than it really is. At the same time, be careful not to frame the question too broadly for the sake of readability. When in doubt, err on the side of being specific and awkward.

2. Be Objective

Remember, an office memo should predict what a court is likely to do with a particular problem. Therefore, you must avoid advocating or anticipating a certain result. Include the significant facts favoring each side of the case. If you paraphrase facts to make the question more readable, do so objectively. You should also state the law objectively rather than take a partisan interpretation. If the legal rule has several reasonable interpretations, state the rule so that you can discuss all of these interpretations. Where the interpretations differ greatly, present separate questions for each.

*   *   *   *   *

Your client, Vosberg, is a frail, thirteen-year-old boy who is chronically ill. Starsky is a seventeen-year-old girl Vosberg and others know to be a neighborhood bully. She is constantly picking fights and has been found guilty of several misdemeanors in juvenile court. Two weeks ago, Starsky confronted Vosberg while he was on his way to a violin recital. She told Vosberg to put his nose against a nearby telephone pole. Vosberg complied. Starsky instructed Vosberg not to move until she gave him permission, and then walked away. At no point did Starsky explicitly threaten Vosberg, touch him, or prevent him from continuing down the sidewalk. Vosberg remained at the pole for two hours and then ran home. He missed the recital and has suffered severe emotional problems as a result of the occurrence. Vosberg's parents want to know if they can sue Starsky.

Your research has revealed only one relevant case:

Palmer v. Woodward (1960)

After making several purchases in Schwenson's department store, appellant Palmer left. He began to walk down the sidewalk when a store detective, appellee Woodward, ran from the store and yelled, "Stop!" Palmer stopped. Woodward approached Palmer, stood in his way, and put his hand on Palmer's chest. After telling Palmer he had to go back and see the store manager, Woodward gently grasped Palmer's elbow and led him back into the store. Palmer, sixty-eight, has failing health and a heart condition. He did not resist. As a result of the incident, Palmer suffered a mild heart attack and severe emotional distress.

Palmer filed suit for false imprisonment. The trial court dismissed Palmer's complaint, holding that restraint, a necessary element of false imprisonment, had not occurred. The trial court reasoned that Palmer voluntarily complied with Woodward's demands because he did not resist or make any attempt to free himself. We disagree.

The trial court correctly stated that false imprisonment requires the defendant to actually confine or restrain the plaintiff. The restraint must be obvious, and the plaintiff must be aware that he is being restrained. But the restraint does not have to be forceful; threats, express or implied, can be sufficient. In this case, the appellant is a frail, elderly man. The appellee is a six-foot, five-inch, 220-pound, semiprofessional football player who works part time as a store detective. Blocking another person's way is restraint where the aggressive person is obviously stronger, as he was here. In addition, the appellee touched the appellant by taking his arm and guiding him into the store. We hold that under the facts of this case, particularly the great disparity of physical strength, there was sufficient restraint. Reversed.

Consider the following attempts to state the question:

ANSWER A: Whether Vosberg can recover damages for false imprisonment?

ANSWER B: Whether Vosberg was sufficiently restrained to support a cause of action for false imprisonment?

ANSWER C: Whether the apparent strength of Vosberg and Starsky was so unequal that Vosberg can recover damages for emotional distress?

ANSWER D: Whether sufficient restraint to support an action for false imprisonment exists when a seventeen-year-old juvenile delinquent with a police record and a reputation as a bully instructs a frail, chronically ill, thirteen-year-old boy who plays violin to remain in one place?

ANSWER E: Whether instructions to put his nose against a phone pole and remain there until told otherwise given by a seventeen-year-old girl delinquent who has been convicted several times, and who has a reputation as a bully and a fighter, to a frail, chronically ill, thirteen-year-old boy on his way to a violin recital, but where the girl never touches the boy or blocks his path and walks away immediately after the boy complies with the instructions, and the boy does not move from the pole for two hours, constitute sufficient restraint to support an action for false imprisonment, where the boy missed the recital and suffered severe emotional problems as a result?

ANSWER F: Whether restraint sufficient to support an action for false imprisonment exists when a seventeen-year-old girl known as a juvenile delinquent and bully instructs a frail thirteen-year-old boy to remain in one place, and he does so for two hours after she has walked away even though the girl neither touched him nor blocked his path?

———

The *Palmer* case indicates that your problem concerns what type of force, if any, is required to satisfy the restraint element of false imprisonment. Answer F presents the best way to state that question. Answer F correctly identifies the relevant law, includes the facts of the problem that a court is likely to find legally significant, and presents the law before the facts. The question is not unduly narrow, nor is it overly broad. It is readable and objectively stated. Answer F clearly identifies the precise legal question presented for determination.

Answer A, by contrast, is useless. The question is too broad and makes no attempt to pinpoint the legal rule or the legally significant facts. The writer might just as well have stated the question: "Whether the law has been violated?"

Answer B does pinpoint the legal question of restraint, but it fails to place that question in context because it omits the significant facts that will provide the basis for its resolution. A question framed this way is too unfocused to be of any value.

Answer C is wrong for several reasons. Unlike Answers A and B, which are too broad, the legal issue here is too narrow. By limiting the legal question to whether the strength of the parties is unequal, it fails to consider other factors that contribute to restraint. In addition, the mention of damages for emotional distress mistakes the real issue. Whether the plaintiff can recover damages for emotional distress is a different question from whether there has been restraint. In this respect, Answer C illustrates an important reason to state the question properly; if you ask the wrong question, you are unlikely to receive the right answer.

Even if your discussion covers the right issue, you have seriously misled the reader about the direction of the memo. Finally, Answer C, like Answers A and B, fails to include the significant facts of the case.

Answer D is incorrect because it is not objective. The question fools the reader about the strength of the client's case because the facts included are relevant to only one side of the question. Answer D fails to note that Starsky did not touch Vosberg or block his path. The answer also includes some irrelevant facts, such as Vosberg's being a violinist. Whenever you state a question, you must include those facts that hurt your case as well as those that help it.

Answer E is no doubt complete enough. It includes all the significant facts, and properly states the issue of law. It is so complete, however, that it is awkward and unreadable. Answer E does not sort out those facts most relevant to the determination of the issue. Answer E also includes several facts that are not legally significant, such as those concerning the violin recital and phone pole. While you may want to include some background facts in the factual statement, do not include them when you frame questions.

As you complete the following exercises, remember that your Questions Presented must combine the relevant law with the significant facts. The Questions Presented form the basis for the rest of the memorandum, and you should focus them as tightly as possible.

Exercise 11-A

Flower Hughes, a twenty-two-year-old law student who also holds a graduate degree in business and accounting, recently inherited $200,000 from a rich uncle. To celebrate her good fortune, Hughes decided to have a few drinks at the Blue Goose Inn, a local tavern. Hughes arrived at noon and had several drinks during the course of the afternoon. Soon after her arrival (about three drinks later), she explained to Ron Zoeller, the bartender and sole owner of the Inn, how much she wanted to invest her inheritance in some enterprise that would yield a high return.

Zoeller began telling her what a fine business he had in the Blue Goose, and how he was getting old and would like to sell it. He told Hughes that the net worth of the Goose was $200,000 and that she could expect to make a $20,000 net profit each year. He admitted that he had only made $12,000 each year for the three years he had owned the place, but assured Hughes that revitalization of the inner city and proposed construction would probably double or triple the Inn's profits in no time. The net worth of the Goose was really only $160,000. Zoeller went to the back room and produced a ledger book that he said contained his business records. The entries in the book were obviously altered to reflect the figures he had quoted to Hughes. (He had originally altered them for tax and insurance purposes.) Hughes examined the book briefly and expressed some concern about the validity of the figures. Zoeller replied: "Sure there might be some mistakes, I'm not very good with figures." He added, "What good are figures anyway? A good businessman trusts his instincts above all else." Zoeller then offered to sell Hughes the tavern for $190,000. Hughes smiled and said she would think it over.

At about 5 p.m., several of Hughes's friends joined her in the tavern. Hughes continued drinking until 1 a.m., when Zoeller leaned over the bar and said, "Tell you what, since you're such a nice kid, I'll sell you the whole place for $175,000. It's a real steal." Hughes, who was slightly intoxicated by this time, could not hear Zoeller over the noise in the tavern, and asked him to write his statement down. Zoeller then wrote his exact statement on one of the bar's napkins, which had Blue Goose Inn printed on it. Hughes laughed and said, "Sure, why not? It'll be a good time."

The next day Hughes remembered the conversation and went to Zoeller and said she hoped he was only joking around. Zoeller said he was serious and that he intended to hold Hughes to the contract. He also told Hughes that a customer who had been sitting next to Hughes at the bar was toying with his new cassette recorder at the time. The customer had accidentally recorded the entire conversation, Zoeller said, and was willing to lend him the tape. He also named several other witnesses who heard the conversation and who would confirm the agreement if necessary.

Hughes has come to you for assistance. After some research and thought on the matter, you have discovered the following statute and cases from your state:

State Rev. Laws § 60.1(4) *Statute of Frauds*
No action shall be brought against any person . . . (4) upon any contract for the sale of lands, tenements, or hereditaments, or any other interest concerning them . . . unless the agreement upon which said action shall be brought, or some memorandum or note thereof, shall be in writing, and signed by the person to be charged therewith, or some other person thereunto by him lawfully authorized.

Treacher v. Plums (1932)
Appellant Treacher entered into an oral contract with appellee Plums whereby Treacher purported to sell Plums a ten-acre tract of farm land for Plums's son. Treacher proposed the deal at 10 a.m. and Plums immediately agreed. Since Plums was illiterate, they did not reduce the agreement to writing. Instead, they immediately proceeded to the church, and they both stated the terms of the agreement in front of the minister and two witnesses. Later that day, Plums wanted to be let out of the deal. Treacher refused and filed suit. The trial court found that the state Statute of Frauds rendered the agreement of no effect. We agree.

The orginal Statute of Frauds was enacted in England in the seventeenth century. The statute in our state is modeled after the English one. Since its enactment, it has been interpreted extensively by the courts. Case law has now clearly established that the statute requires contracts for the sale of land to be in writing. The writing must state with reasonable certainty and accuracy: (1) the parties to the contract, (2) the subject matter to which the contract relates, and (3) the terms and conditions of all promises constituting the contract and by whom and to whom the promises are made. In this case, there is no question that the terms of the contract, the subject matter, and the parties were all described with the requisite certainty. The exact location and size of the property, the purchase price, the conditions of payment, and the names of both parties were all stated. The fact remains, however, that there was no writing. We have recognized two purposes served by the statute. One is evidentiary—the statute insures there will be proof of the agreement. The second is cautionary—reducing the agreement to writing requires the parties to carefully think through the proposed transaction and make sure they are serious about going through with the deal. Even if we were at liberty to disregard the statute, in this case we find that the second purpose was not fulfilled. Affirmed.

Divine v. Zarwakov (1964)

Appellant Carla Divine brought suit seeking rescission of her contract with Zarwakov's School of Ballet. Divine, who has a sixth-grade education and is twenty-five years old, always dreamed of becoming a great dancer. She began taking lessons in classical ballet at appellee's dance school in response to a special introductory offer of ten lessons for thirty dollars. During this time she was repeatedly told that she was a natural dancer, and that she had exceptional rhythm, grace, and poise. The school told her that with minimal training she would be assured of a spot as a principal dancer in one of the national dance companies. On the basis of this encouragement, appellant entered a series of written contracts in which she agreed to pay $10,000 over the next five years for private dance lessons. In reality, appellant is extremely uncoordinated and has no natural aptitude for dance. The trial court held that she was bound by the terms of the contract and dismissed her suit. We disagree.

Courts in this state will not enforce an agreement where there has been a misrepresentation in the inducement to contract. The party seeking to be relieved of the bargain must establish six things: (1) false representations, (2) of material facts, (3) that the defendant knew were false, (4) that the defendant intended the plaintiff to rely on them, (5) that the plaintiff was justified in relying on them, and (6) that the plaintiff suffered damages as a result of this reliance. There is no doubt that there were false representations, that plaintiff relied on them, and that plaintiff was damaged as a result. The only questions here are whether there was a material fact and whether plaintiff was justified in relying on the representation. We hold that while these representations were not material facts in the strict legal sense, they were sufficient to satisfy the requirement. Where there has been some artifice or trick by the representor, or where the parties do not in general deal at arm's length or where the representee does not have equal opportunity to become appraised of the truth or falsity of the fact represented, a material fact in the strict sense is not required. The same reasoning applies to the justifiable reliance element. The dance school held itself out to be an expert. Given plaintiff's lack of knowledge and education, not to mention her dreams, she can properly be said to have relied. This is especially true in cases such as this that smack of undue influence, falsehood, the suppression of the truth, and the lack of free exercise of rational judgment. Reversed.

1. Identify the issues in the Hughes case.

2. What are the most legally significant facts, both favorable and unfavorable to Hughes, for each issue?

3. Draft the Questions Presented for an office memorandum based on your answers to questions 1 and 2. Are they objective and readable?

Exercise 11-B

This exercise is based on the facts and cases from Exercise 8-B on pp. 88–90.

1. What are the legal rules associated with the issues in this case?

2. What are the most legally significant facts for each rule?

3. Draft the Questions Presented for this memorandum based on your answers to questions 1 and 2. Are they objective and readable?

PART D

THE BRIEF

12

Elements of a Brief

THE lawyer as advocate is the counterpart to the lawyer as counselor. Counselor is the role a lawyer presents to his client; advocate is the role he presents to the outside world. As an advocate, the lawyer exercises persuasion to achieve results favorable to his client in a variety of ways. Many times, a lawyer will avoid a lawsuit by convincing a potential adversary that his client's position is solid. At other times, a lawyer may convince a government agency to adopt a more favorable attitude toward his client's position. While effective advocacy can help keep a dispute out of court, it can also increase the likelihood of success if litigation is necessary.

The brief is the formal document a lawyer uses both to convince a court that his client's position is sound and to persuade a court to adopt that position. Briefs are similar to office memos in many respects; consequently, many of the rules for good memos apply with equal force to briefs. Both must honestly state the law, the facts of the case, and the reasons for their conclusions in a clear and concise manner.

Briefs differ from memos, however, in two important respects. The first difference is the attitude of the documents: briefs argue; memos discuss. Rather than developing a legal strategy with other attorneys, the brief writer is submitting a legal argument to opposing counsel and a judge or panel of judges, all of whom will subject it to close scrutiny. Open and honest assessment of the client's position, although required for memos, is absolutely wrong for briefs. The brief writer must attempt to make the client's position seem as strong as possible, emphasizing favorable arguments and minimizing the force of opposing arguments. It is not enough that the client's position appear logical or even desirable; it must seem compelling.

The second difference is the thinking process employed in drafting the documents. The brief writer knows his basic conclusions in advance. His work involves a search for arguments and materials that support those conclusions and that show his client's position is stronger and should prevail. Since the memorandum writer, by contrast, is concerned with objectively determining whose position is most sound, he usually will not come to a conclusion until relatively late in his research and analysis.

Briefs are of two kinds. A trial brief (sometimes called a memorandum of law or memorandum of points and authorities) is the document presented to a trial court in support of, or in opposition to, various motions, or to convince the court to decide the merits in a particular way. An appellate brief is the document presented to a reviewing court challenging or defending a trial court's decision in a case.

Appellate and trial briefs differ in several ways. Appellate briefs focus more on broad policy because appellate courts are more concerned with establishing and applying rules that will work in many situations. Trial briefs tend to focus more on the facts of the individual case since trial courts are closer to the parties and are more concerned with deciding cases in accordance with established precedent than with establishing new law. In addition, appellate briefs, unlike trial briefs, are usually accompanied by an edited transcript of the record from the court below. Appellate briefs also tend to be more formal and contain more elements than trial briefs.

Following is the generally accepted format for appellate and trial briefs:

Appellate Brief	**Trial Brief**
Title Page	Caption
Index	
Authorities Cited	
Opinion(s) Below	
Jurisdiction	
Constitutional Provisions, Statutes, Regulations, and Rules Involved	
Questions Presented	Questions Presented (optional)
Statement of Facts	Statement of Facts
Summary of Argument	
Argument	Argument
Conclusion	Conclusion
Appendix(es)	

The name of each section (except the Title Page and Caption) should be underlined or capitalized and placed immediately above that section.

There are three general considerations you should be aware of when drafting a brief. First, appellate courts usually have specific rules concerning the format and content of briefs. These rules ensure some degree of uniformity and consistency, and make it easier to compare the arguments made in opposing briefs. Specific court rules control when they vary from the general rules provided here. Second, the importance of many of the elements of an appellate brief may seem obscure at first, and many of the court rules will concern such seemingly minor items as length, page size, and citation form. Although some of these elements and rules may seem tedious and overly technical, you should take them seriously. Many courts reject incorrectly presented briefs. Third, briefs are rarely drafted in the order these elements appear. You will usually write the Argument first, then the Summary of Argument, Statement of Facts, and Questions Presented, and then the other elements.

The following is a description of each element of a brief. The discussion is focused primarily on appellate briefs since those briefs contain more elements than trial briefs. Where the element is also found in a trial brief, both styles are discussed and examples of each are provided. Appendix II contains sample appellate briefs using this format, which you should examine in conjunction with this chapter.

1. Title Page (or Caption)

The Title Page of an appellate brief identifies the court, the docket number, the name of the case, the side represented, and the name(s) and address(es) of counsel. The Title Page of briefs filed in a state supreme court or the Supreme Court of the United States also contain the term of the court and the court from which the appeal is taken. The Title Page distinguishes the brief from many others received by the court, and insures that the brief will be placed in the proper file. There are a number of minor stylistic variations in title pages. A standard style for appellate briefs is contained in Appendix II.

The first page of the trial brief contains a Caption, which looks like this:

IN THE UNITED STATES DISTRICT COURT
FOR THE DISTRICT OF SUPERIOR

WESTBROOK NEIGHBORHOOD ASSOCIATION,
                              Plaintiff,
                    v.   Civ. Docket No. CZ-8071-80
ELLISON RECYCLING, INC.,   Hon. F.A. Hollender
                              Defendant.

BRIEF IN SUPPORT OF DEFENDANT'S MOTION TO DISMISS

The Caption substitutes for the Title Page; it identifies the court, the name of the case, the docket number, the motion (or other matter) under consideration, the judge, and the side represented.

2. Index

The Index is a table of contents for the appellate brief, and it is sometimes labeled as such. It lists each element of the brief and the page on which that element begins. In addition, the point headings used in the Argument should be stated in full in the order they appear, with page numbers corresponding to their locations. The point headings, which are described in detail in Chapter 14, are specialized thesis sentences that introduce parts of your argument. This outline of your point headings provides the reader with a concise and easily understandable summary of your argument. The briefs in Appendix II show the basic format for an Index.

3. Authorities Cited

This section (also called Table of Authorities or Citations) lists all of the legal and other materials used to support the Argument in an appellate brief and shows every page on which those materials are cited. This list of authorities is useful because it permits a judge or opposing counsel to determine quickly where you examined specific cases, statutes, or other materials. It also provides a quick reference for complete citations to any materials used in the brief.

The Authorities Cited section is usually divided into several categories, including cases, constitutional provisions, statutes, and miscellaneous materials. Although the material in these four basic categories should usually be kept separate, each category can be further divided. Subdividing is a matter of judgment, and the decision to subdivide should depend on the usefulness of further divisions to the reader. It will often be helpful to have a separate section for cases decided by the court to which the brief is addressed. Cases might, therefore, be listed under the headings, "Michigan Cases," and "Other Cases," or you might list them under "United States Supreme Court Decisions," "Sixth Circuit Court of Appeals Decisions," and "Other Federal Decisions." You might also create categories to emphasize specific statutes, the legislative history of a particular act, administrative rules, or secondary authorities. Avoid numerous subcategories with only a few citations since these will only clutter your organization.

List cases, secondary authorities, and other materials in alphabetical order in each category. Statutory sections, constitutional provisions, and other materials that cannot be listed alphabetically should be listed in numerical order. This section is illustrated in Appendix II.

4. Opinion(s) Below

This section of an appellate brief indicates where the decisions of the lower courts that have decided this case can be located. The reviewing court will then know where to find the previous opinions if it wants to read them. Provide a citation for these previous decisions if they have been reported; if they have not yet been reported, say so and show their location in the record. For example:

> The opinion of the United States District Court for the District of Minnesota is unreported, and contained in the Transcript of Record (R. 18-27). The opinion of the United States Court of Appeals for the Eighth Circuit is reported at 549 F.2d 1564.

5. Jurisdiction

This section of an appellate brief (also called a Jurisdictional Statement or Statement of Jurisdiction) provides a short statement of the jurisdictional basis for the appeal. Since jurisdiction itself is often an issue in trial courts and is also asserted in the complaint, this section is unnecessary for trial briefs. The Jurisdiction section should briefly inform the court of the factual circumstances, court rules, or statutory provisions on which appellate jurisdiction is based. Thus:

> The judgment of the United States Court of Appeals for the Third Circuit was entered on April 30, 1979. The petition for a writ of certiorari was filed on August 30, 1979, and granted on January 7, 1980. 444 U.S. 1075. The jurisdiction of this Court is invoked under 28 U.S.C. § 1254(1).

In moot court competitions and legal writing assignments, the jurisdictional statement is frequently waived:

> Pursuant to Rule 4(c) of the 1977 Rules of the National Moot Court Competition, a formal jurisdictional statement is omitted.

6. Constitutional Provisions, Statutes, Regulations, and Rules Involved

This section indicates to the court what codified provisions are most relevant to the determination of the case and informs the court where in your brief the judge can scrutinize the exact language of these provisions. The name of this section varies with the materials included. When you have one or two provisions and they are relatively short, the exact language should be set out in full. When you have many such provisions, or the provisions are lengthy, provide the name and citation in this section and indicate that they are set forth in one or more appendixes at the end of your brief. Thus:

> Section 29 of the Mobile Home Commission Act, Mich. Comp. Laws Ann. § 125.112a (West Supp. 1980), provides as follows:
> A utility company shall notify the department 10 days before shutoff of service for nonpayment, including sewer, water, gas, or electric service, when the service is being supplied to the licensed owner or operator of a mobile home park for the use and benefit of the park's tenants.

Or:

> The texts of the following statutes relevant to the determination of the present case are set forth in the Appendix: Sections 3(c)(2)(6) and 10(b) of the Federal Insecticide, Fungicide, and Rodenticide Act, 7 U.S.C. §§ 136a(c)(2)(6), 136h(b)(Supp. III 1979); Tucker Act, 28 U.S.C. § 1491 (1976 & Supp. III 1979).

7. Questions Presented

This section states the legal issues involved in a brief and alerts the court to those matters you intend to address. The Questions Presented in a brief are similar to those in a memorandum. Both must include the legal rule and a summary of significant facts, and must also be precise and understandable.

Unlike the Questions Presented in the office memorandum, though, these questions should be slanted toward your client's position and should reflect your interpretation of the law. If you are using that interpretation to emphasize certain facts in your Argument, your questions should contain these facts. In addition, the questions should be stated so that they prompt an affirmative answer. As Chapter 13 (Advocacy) will show in some detail, your brief should project a positive tone; it should argue for a particular conclusion rather than simply against the contrary conclusion. If you are appealing an unfavorable trial court decision, for example, your questions might begin: "Whether the trial court erred . . . ." But if your opponent is appealing the same decision, he might begin: "Whether the trial court properly held . . . ." Both questions suggest an affirmative answer.

There are two styles of presenting the questions in a brief, and these styles differ principally in their argumentative tone and completeness. The better style requires you to state the question so completely and so argumentatively that it answers itself:

> Whether the trial court deprived defendant of his right to due process of law under the Fourteenth Amendment by admitting a

confession that was extracted from defendant after twenty-two consecutive hours of interrogation by rotating teams of detectives?

This question combines the relevant legal rule and the significant facts so that the only reasonable answer seems to be "yes." This style is very effective, although you should not risk your credibility by overstating or distorting your position. The other style states questions in their barest form:

Whether admission of defendant's "confession" violated his right to due process under the Fourteenth Amendment?

This question is affirmative only in the sense that it suggests an affirmative answer. It does not provide any significant facts, nor does it make the answer seem obvious, although it does frame the issue in a way that would be more acceptable to both sides.

Many trial briefs are so short or straightforward that the Questions Presented section is unnecessary. The section is necessary, however, in long or complex trial briefs, which often contain multiple issues. If you use Questions Presented in a trial brief, you should adopt the argumentative style. The trial court's concern with the facts of the case requires the questions to be framed with as much specificity as possible.

8. Statement of Facts

The Statement of Facts in a brief (also known as Statement of the Case or Statement) is a descriptive account of the facts from your client's point of view. Although this statement cannot omit any damaging facts, it should be written to gain the court's sympathy for and understanding of your client's situation. Many lawyers and judges believe that the Statement of Facts, which is discussed in detail in Chapter 15, is the most important section of any brief.

9. Summary of Argument

This section contains a concise statement of your major conclusions and the most important reasons supporting them. The section helps introduce a judge to the core of your argument and is particularly useful to a judge who has not had time to read the entire brief before oral argument. The Summary of Argument should be self-contained; the reader should not have to look elsewhere to understand the essence of your case. Like the Conclusion in an office memorandum, the Summary of Argument should contain no citations to cases, statutes, or regulations unless the authority is well known or absolutely necessary for the reader's understanding.

Each major conclusion should be stated in a single paragraph. The Summaries of Argument provided in the sample briefs in Appendix II illustrate these ideas.

10. Argument

The Argument is the foundation on which the rest of the brief is constructed and, like the Discussion in the office memorandum, is the heart of the brief. Although the Statement of Facts and Summary of Argument are important, and sometimes decisive, your client generally wins or loses on the quality and substance of what you say in the Argument. An effective Argument will incorporate, in large measure, the same lessons required for the Discussion in the office memorandum. The Argument should be well organized and clearly written. It should reflect a sound understanding and thoughtful analysis of the relevant law. Although the Argument is similar to the Discussion in these ways, it differs from the Discussion in two important respects.

First, this section of the brief should be prepared as an argument rather than as an objective discussion of the law. In forceful and affirmative language, state your strongest arguments and issues first, and present your client's position on each issue or sub-issue before you refute that of your opponent. These and other lessons of Chapter 13 (Advocacy) will help you present your case in a more convincing manner.

Second, the Argument should contain point headings. Point headings are specifically stated thesis sentences that preface each logical segment of your argument. The point headings, which are also listed in the Index, make it easier for the reader to understand the structure and content of your Argument. While point headings are always included in appellate briefs, their use in trial briefs is optional. As with Questions Presented, point headings should be included in trial briefs that are lengthy or complex. Point headings are discussed in detail in Chapter 14. The lessons of previous chapters, combined with those concerning advocacy and point headings, should enable you to prepare an effective Argument. Sample Arguments are contained in Appendix II.

11. Conclusion

This section describes what you want the court to do. Precisely state what relief you are requesting from the court, particularly if the relief you seek is more complicated than an affirmance or reversal of the lower court's judgment. The Conclusion is usually one sentence in length. In trial briefs containing complex arguments, you may include a brief summary of the arguments supporting your conclusion. The address, phone number, and signature of at least one of the attorneys who prepared the brief should immediately follow. You should also include the date. A Conclusion in an appellate brief should look like this:

> For all the foregoing reasons, the judgment of the Ingham County Circuit Court should be reversed and the case remanded for a new trial.
>
> Respectfully submitted,
>
> _____
> Charles McGrady
> Attorney for Appellants
>
> Smith, Dunmore & Coffin
> 420 Brookshire
> Greensboro, N.C. 27402
> (919) 423-0706

March 1, 1978

The Conclusion in a trial brief has the same form, but requests different relief from the court. For example:

> For the foregoing reasons, plaintiffs respectfully request that defendant's motion for summary judgment be denied.
>
> Respectfully submitted,
>
> _____
> Charles McGrady
> Attorney for Plaintiffs
>
> Smith, Dunmore & Coffin
> 420 Brookshire
> Greensboro, N.C. 27402
> (919) 423-0706

March 1, 1978

12. Appendix(es)

This section contains the quoted statutes from the section of your brief called Constitutional Provisions, Statutes, Regulations, and Rules Involved. There can be a separate Appendix for each major category of statutes in the brief. You should also have an Appendix for any diagrams or charts you want to include. If you use more than one Appendix, give each a short title describing its content. The sample briefs in

Appendix II each contain an Appendix showing the relevant statutes involved.

This chapter has identified and described each of the components of a brief. Although assembling a brief may seem overly complicated, everything in a brief is there for the court's convenience or to make your client's position as persuasive as possible.

13

Advocacy

ADVOCACY is the craft of persuasion. It is the means by which an attorney persuades a court to adopt his client's position as its own. The effective advocate will show a court that deciding in his favor would be logical and desirable, and that deciding for the other side would not. Courts in an adversary system depend on advocates to illuminate the strengths and weaknesses of competing positions. The advocate thus assists courts in deciding cases. Many times, the arguments, cases, and even the language of the winning brief will appear in the court's opinion. For better or worse, the skill and resources of counsel are often as important to a decision as the relevant law.

Coherence and credibility are essential to effective advocacy. In this sense, the analytical, writing, and organizational principles from Parts B and C apply here. The advocate's research must be complete, his analysis sound, and his conclusions sensible. Clear organization, thoughtful writing, and a logical progression of argument are essential. A writer who cannot be understood will not be an effective advocate.

Brief writers must also be honest about the law. A brief should rely on shading, emphasis, and overall strength of argument for its persuasive value, rather than on omission or distortion of the relevant law. The subtlety of this distinction in certain cases makes it no less important. The American Bar Association's Code of Professional Responsibility requires attorneys to bring opposing cases and statutes in the jurisdiction to the court's attention if the other side does not do so.*

---

*ABA Code of Professional Responsibility, Ethical Consideration 7-23 states:

Advocacy is more a matter of presentation than of content. Two discussions can be identical in substance but far different in persuasive value. The following rules will help you present your client's position in a forceful and persuasive manner.

1. Present Your Strongest Issues, Sub-Issues, and Arguments First

Where your client's position involves several independent issues, present your client's strongest issue first, followed by the next strongest issue, and the next, and conclude with the weakest. Similarly, where several arguments support your client's position on an issue or sub-issue, present them in descending order of strength. The "strongest" issues, sub-issues, or arguments are those most likely to persuade a judge to rule in favor of your client.

There are several reasons why your brief will be more persuasive if the strongest issues and arguments are presented first. First, to capture the court's full attention, you must demonstrate the impressiveness of your client's legal position. The beginning of a brief or an argument sets the tone for what follows. Since the strongest issues or arguments are necessarily the most compelling ones, beginning with them also enhances your credibility. In addition, the less persuasive issues and arguments are more compelling when they buttress stronger issues and arguments than when they are presented strictly on their own merits. Conversely, stronger issues and arguments seem less compelling in the context of weaker issues and arguments. Finally, crowded dockets (even at the appellate level) often mean that a brief will not necessarily be read in its entirety by all the judges or clerks. If the strongest issues and arguments are presented first, they are much more likely to be read.

A corollary to this rule is: Omit very weak arguments and issues. In prewriting and drafting briefs, think of as many arguments and issues as possible. Some of these arguments will be weak, either because there is scant authority to support them or because the rule in question has never been applied to the facts before the court. Sometimes, of course, you will

---

The complexity of law often makes it difficult for a tribunal to be fully informed unless the pertinent law is presented by the lawyers in the case. A tribunal that is fully informed on the applicable law is better able to make a fair and accurate determination of the matter before it. The adversary system contemplates that each lawyer will present and argue in the light most favorable to his client. Where a lawyer knows of legal authority in the controlling jurisdiction directly adverse to the position of his client, he should inform the tribunal of its existence unless his adversary has done so; but, having made such disclosure, he may challenge its soundness in whole or in part.
See also Disciplinary Rule 7-102(A)(5): "In his representation of a client, a lawyer shall not . . . [k]nowingly make a false statement of law or fact."

have to include such arguments in your brief because you will have nothing stronger. When you do have stronger arguments, however, you should omit the weak ones because frivolous arguments undermine your credibility with the court and divert attention from arguments and issues that matter.

The importance of putting the strongest issues or arguments first diminishes greatly when several are nearly equal in strength. As questions about placement become more difficult, they may be resolved by trying to ascertain which arguments will be most appealing to the particular courts or individuals who will be reading the brief. An intermediate state court of appeals with a heavy caseload may be best reached with a brief that is short and pointed. A federal court of appeals or state supreme court may prefer briefs that are longer and more scholarly. Good advocates also recognize that judges, particularly at the trial level, have differing value systems and will prepare briefs that are addressed to their preferences.

*   *   *   *   *

On November 5, Paula Jennings was elected to her first term as Justice of the Peace for Monroe County, a position that enabled her to perform civil weddings and hear small claims cases. Immediately after her election, she reversed her previous support for a highly controversial court reform proposal—one which was an issue in many of the election races, including hers. After she took office on January 2, a group of citizens circulated petitions for her recall. The petitions, filed with the appropriate county official on March 15, contained a statement that the basis for the recall was her "opposition to the court reorganization plan." Section 5 of the State Elections Act provides:

> The petition or petitions, which shall clearly state the reason or reasons for the recall, shall not be filed against an officer until the officer has actually performed the duties of that office to which he or she has been elected for a period of six months during the current term of that officer.

After filing a suit to prevent her recall, her attorney filed a motion for summary judgment. Relying on section 5, he prepared two outlines of a brief in support of that motion:

ANSWER A: The petitions are invalid under the Elections Act because they do not meet the section 5 requirement for a clear statement of the reasons for recall. The statement on the petitions that Jennings opposes the court reorganization plan does not clearly inform voters whether it is her position, her change of position, or both, that motivates the recall.

The petitions are also invalid because, contrary to section 5, they were submitted before Jennings had been in office for six months. Since the petitions were submitted on March 15, less than two-and-one-half months after Jennings took office on January 2, the six-month requirement was not fulfilled.

ANSWER B: The petitions are invalid under the Elections Act because, contrary to section 5, they were submitted before Jennings had been in office for six months. Since the petitions were submitted on March 15, less than two-and-one-half months after Jennings took office on January 2, the six-month requirement was not fulfilled.

The petitions are also invalid because they do not meet the section 5 requirement for a clear statement of the reasons for recall. The statement on the petitions that Jennings opposes the court reorganization plan does not clearly inform voters whether it is her position, her change of position, or both, that motivates the recall.

Answer B is preferable because the six-months argument is stronger than the clear-statement argument. The six-months argument deals with an unmistakable error; section 5 is explicit and leaves little doubt about what is required. The clear-statement issue is less well defined. In the absence of any relevant case law, "opposition to the court reorganization plan" may or may not be reasonably understood as a clear statement. Beginning with an argument so debatable, as Answer A does, is a less forceful way of presenting the case.

2. Where Issues Are of Equal Strength, Present Your Most Significant Issues First

The most significant issues are not necessarily the strongest issues. The most significant issues are those whose favorable resolution would help your client most. In a criminal case involving two equally strong issues, for example, you should first discuss the issue that would completely exonerate the defendant, and then the issue that would merely win him a new trial.

This rule is subordinate to Rule 1 because a strong but less significant argument is more persuasive than a weak argument of greater significance. Likelihood of success should be the dominant consideration. Assume, for example, that a convicted pickpocket could raise two issues on appeal. He could argue with much precedent that the judge erred in permitting him to be convicted solely on the basis of hearsay, and he could argue with tenuous support that the statute under which he was convicted was unconstitutionally vague. The hearsay issue should be presented first, even though it is less significant than the constitutional question, simply because it is more likely to succeed. If, however, the vagueness issue were at least as strong as the hearsay issue, it should be presented first.

Presenting the most significant issues first is important for the same basic reasons as presenting the strongest issues first. If a serious issue is presented first, the court is more likely to take the entire brief more seriously than if the brief begins with an issue concerning a technical violation of an obscure law. In addition, less significant issues seem more compelling when they buttress important issues than when they introduce an argument. Finally, presenting the most significant issues first insures that your brief will be read, and read seriously.

* * * * *

Consider again the Jennings example:

The petition drive against Paula Jennings raised 7,850 signatures. In the last election, 32,000 people in Monroe County voted for a candidate for governor. The State Elections Act further provides:

> Sec. 2. Every elective officer in the state except a judicial officer is subject to recall by the voters of the electoral district in which the officer is elected.
>
> Sec. 6. The petitions shall be signed by a number of qualified and registered voters equal to not less than 25% of the number of votes cast for candidates for the office of governor at the last preceding general election in the electoral district of the officer sought to be recalled. The person or organization sponsoring such recall shall have 10 days to file additional signatures after any determination that the petitions submitted contain an insufficient number of qualified and registered voters.

Jennings's attorney has prepared two outlines of a trial brief concerning these sections:

ANSWER A: The petitions are invalid because they challenge an officer specifically exempted from recall by the Elections Act. Section 2 expressly excepts "a judicial officer" from the Act, a term that necessarily includes a justice of the peace performing such judicial activities as deciding small claims cases.

Even if there were no such exemption, the petitions would still be invalid because, contrary to section 6, they do not contain the signatures of twenty-five per cent of the number of the qualified and registered voters for governor in the last election. Since the petitions contain only 7,850 signatures and 32,000 people voted for a candidate for governor in the last election, they are 150 signatures short of the section 6 requirement.

ANSWER B: The petitions are invalid because, contrary to section 6, they do not contain the signatures of twenty-five per cent of the number of the qualified and registered voters for governor in the last election. Since the petitions contain only 7,850 signatures and 32,000 people voted for a candidate for governor in the last election, they are 150 signatures short of the section 6 requirement.

Even if there were enough signatures, the petitions would still be invalid because they challenge an office specifically exempted from recall by the Elections Act. Section 2 expressly excepts "a judicial officer" from the Act, a term that necessarily includes a justice of the peace performing such judicial activities as deciding small claims cases.

———

Answer A is better because it places the issue of the substantive validity of the petitions before the issue of sufficient signatures, even though both issues are very strong. A favorable decision of the exempt-officer issue would foreclose the recall effort altogether, but the sufficient-signature issue may only delay the recall because of the corrective provision in the statute for insufficient signatures. Answer A emphasizes the more significant issue, and gives additional strength to the sufficient-signature issue because it is discussed after, and therefore in light of, the exempt-officer question. Answer B, by contrast, emphasizes the less compelling procedural issue and obscures the most significant question.

Answer A also shows a more logical progression of thought than does Answer B. Answer A states, in effect, that the Elections Act does not apply, and even if it does apply, its requirements were not met. Each issue is independent of the other. Answer B, on the other hand, is illogical. Answer B states that the requirements of the Elections Act were not met, and even if they were, the Act does not apply. Answer B assumes that the Elections Act applies in the first issue, but then denies its application in the second issue. Answer A is better, then, because it arranges the issues both logically and in order of significance. How should the arguments and issues for sections 2, 5, and 6 of the Elections Act be combined? Why?

3. Present Your Client's Position on Each Issue or Sub-Issue before Refuting the Opposition

This rule is a slight modification of the rule in Chapter 8 requiring you to state the reasons supporting a conclusion before responding to those reasons opposing it. You must show a court why it should decide for your client, as well as convince the court to decide against the opposition. Your client's position should define the order and tone of argument on any given issue or sub-issue. That position will be much clearer if it is stated and justified before opposing arguments are answered. Lawyers who attack their opponents' arguments before advancing their own invite two unfavorable consequences. First, they risk not stating their position intelligibly, or worse yet, not having their main argument read at all. Second, they sound defensive and imply that the oppositions' point of view is more important or of greater interest to the court.

If there are several arguments opposing your client's position on an issue or sub-issue, answer the strongest such argument first after presenting your client's position. The opposition's strongest arguments are likely to be those of most interest to the court, and you gain credibility by readily confronting them. Do not ignore your opponent's arguments.

* * * * *

Ian LeVasseur was convicted of second degree murder on the strength of a voiceprint identification made possible because the victim had been operating a tape recorder just before the crime occurred. He has appealed on the ground that voiceprint identification is inherently unreliable. Although courts in his state have not decided this issue, courts in two neighboring states with identical evidence rules have decided the following cases:

People v. Decker (1963)

Appellant was convicted of arson on the basis of a voiceprint identification from the recording of a wiretapped telephone conversation. The sole issue on appeal is the propriety of the trial judge's ruling that permitted the voiceprint to be admitted into evidence. Our law does not permit evidence of a scientific test to be admitted unless its scientific basis and reliability are generally recognized by competent authorities. Voiceprint analysis, however, is not so recognized; there is little literature on the subject and great disagreement among experts as to its efficacy. For that reason, we reverse and remand for a new trial.

State v. Manning (1973)

Margerita Manning was convicted of second degree murder in connection with the bombing of an office building that led to the death of a secretary employed there. Some twelve minutes before the explosion, local police received a phone call warning that the building should be evacuated. That call was taped and was used in a subsequent voiceprint identification that formed the evidentiary basis for Manning's conviction. Her appeal challenges the reliability of voiceprint identification. We affirm.

The record before this court indicates that voiceprint analysis is a widely accepted and scientifically accurate method of identification which has received the support of many experts. Since its scientific basis and reliability are generally recognized, the trial judge committed no error in admitting the voiceprint identification into evidence.

The prosecutor's brief on appeal might be organized in either of the following ways:

ANSWER A: The voiceprint analysis was properly admitted in evidence. Scientific tests are admissible when their reliability and scientific basis are generally recognized by competent authorities. In *People v. Decker,* the court held that a voiceprint test was improperly admitted because of the lack of scientific literature and disagreement among experts as to its accuracy. *Decker* is distinguishable because it was decided in 1963 when voiceprint analysis was at an early stage of development. In the 1973 case of *State v. Manning,* however, the court held that a voiceprint was proper evidence since by that time the reliability and scientific basis for voiceprint analysis were widely recognized by experts. *Manning* reflects significant developments over ten years in the field and underscores the correctness of the trial judge's ruling in this case.

ANSWER B: The voiceprint analysis was properly admitted in evidence. Scientific tests are admissible when their reliability and scientific basis are generally recognized by competent authorities. In the 1973 case of *State v. Manning,* the court held that the reliability and scientific basis for voiceprint analysis are widely recognized by experts and, hence, that voiceprints could be admitted in evidence. *Manning* reflects significant developments in this field and underscores the correctness of the trial judge's ruling in this case. Although a 1963 case, *People v. Decker,* held to the contrary, it is not controlling because it was decided before voiceprint analysis had become a widely accepted and scientifically reliable identification technique.

———

Answer B is preferable because it describes the favorable case before it responds to the unfavorable case, rather than the other way around. Answer B states that voiceprint analysis is widely accepted and was thus proper in this case, and then distinguishes *Decker* as out of date. This response to *Decker* is consistent with the prior analysis of *Manning,* and is persuasive in that context. Answer A is less clear because the older case is distinguished before the affirmative argument is even stated. Even when *Manning* is discussed, the analysis is not as sharply focused as it is in Answer B. In addition, Answer A is defensive, and gives greater weight to the opposition's point of view. Always present your client's position first.

4. Use Forceful and Affirmative Language

Word choice is as important as structure of argument. Words can make an argument seem confident or defensive, bold or halting, credible or dubious. They can also make a position seem conservative or radical. Words cannot substitute for quality argumentation, but they can greatly enhance it. A court is more likely to be convinced by a lawyer who sounds convinced, one whose arguments are stated with authority and confidence. The following guidelines are illustrative of this rule.

   a. Present Arguments from Your Client's Point of View   The tone of your brief should be one affirming your client's position, rather than simply denying that of your opponent. Both the affirmative arguments and those of opposing counsel must be stated from your client's point of view. Since the most persuasive briefs are those in which the writer seems to have complete control over the arguments, your client's position should thus be clear and positive rather than defensive.

*   *   *   *   *

Plaintiffs brought an action under the Federal Noise Control Act of 1972, alleging section 1337 of the Judicial Code as the sole basis of jurisdiction. The defendant has filed a motion to dismiss on the ground that plaintiffs did not allege an amount in controversy of $10,000 or more. Plaintiff's argument to the federal district court might be stated in either of the following ways:

ANSWER A: Defendant incorrectly contends that plaintiffs' failure to allege $10,000 as an amount in controversy deprives the court of jurisdiction. Section 1337 of the Judicial Code provides original jurisdiction to the federal courts of "any civil action or proceeding arising under any Act of Congress regulating commerce," but does not require an allegation of amount in controversy. Since the federal Noise Control Act, under which plaintiffs brought this action, is a Congressional regulation of commerce, defendant's contention is not true. Section 1331(a) requires an allegation of amount in controversy for federal jurisdiction, but plaintiffs do not rely on section 1331(a).

ANSWER B: This court has jurisdiction to hear this case. Section 1337 of the Judicial Code provides original jurisdiction to the federal courts of "any civil action or proceeding arising under any Act of Congress regulating commerce," but does not require an allegation of amount in controversy. Plaintiff has alleged jurisdiction under the federal Noise Control Act, a Congressional regulation of commerce. Since defendant's claim that an amount in controversy was not alleged is thus irrelevant, this court has jurisdiction. Plaintiffs do not rely on section 1331(a), which requires an allegation of amount in controversy for federal jurisdiction.

Both answers cover the same ground, but they convey different messages. Answer B says the plaintiffs have jurisdiction; Answer A says defendant's claim that the plaintiff is without jurisdiction is not true, but never clearly says the plaintiff has jurisdiction. Answer B is preferable because it is more positive and lucid. Answer B turns defendant's denial of jurisdiction into an affirmative argument that the court has jurisdiction, and shows control over the direction and tone of the argument. Answer A shows a lack of control because it is dominated by the defendant's viewpoint.

b. Present the Law from the Client's Point of View Office memoranda require objective or balanced descriptions of the state of the law, but such descriptions have no place in legal briefs. The law should be characterized to favor, and be consistent with, the client's position. The legal rules and principles, of course, determine what arguments can be made. But they should also be an integral part of the Argument, stated with the same forcefulness and tone as the application of the law to the facts. The description of the law would otherwise disrupt the flow and direction of the Argument.

* * * * *

Mary Elston brought an action against Juan Guerrero, the driver of a car which struck her van from the rear, causing Elston a serious back injury. At trial, Guerrero's attorney attempted to introduce evidence to show that Elston's van had seat belts, and that much, if not all, of Elston's injury could have been avoided had she been wearing one. The case was tried under the state's comparative negligence rule, and Guerrero's attorney was attempting to mitigate damages. The trial judge refused to admit that evidence. The jury returned a verdict for Elston and awarded $225,000 in damages. On appeal, Guerrero's attorney might characterize the relevant law in two ways:

ANSWER A: Where seat belts are available to the plaintiff in an auto negligence action, and plaintiff's failure to use them caused or contributed to his injuries, defendant is entitled to have the damage award reduced accordingly. *Bentzler v. Braun* (1967). This rule is based on the reasonable view that the use of seat belts reduces serious injuries and fatalities from automobile accidents, and that those riding in cars should know of this additional safety factor. *Braun.* Cases to the contrary are based on the questionable premises that the duty to fasten seat belts arises only if plaintiff anticipates the accident, that not all vehicles have seat belts, and that not all people use them. *See, e.g., Kopischke v. First Continental Corp.* (1980). Where seat belts are available, though, it is manifestly unfair to penalize a defendant for plaintiff's failure to exercise a simple precaution that is surely in plaintiff's best interest.

ANSWER B: The courts are divided on whether a defendant in an auto negligence action is entitled to have the damage award reduced where seat belts are available to the plaintiff, and plaintiff's failure to use them caused or contributed to his injury. Most courts, however, deny mitigation. A minority hold the view that the use of seat belts reduces serious injuries and fatalities from auto accidents, and that those riding in cars should know of this additional safety factor. *Bentzler v. Braun* (1967). The majority of cases are premised on the view that the duty to fasten seat belts arises only if plaintiff anticipates the accident, that not all vehicles have seat belts, and that not all people use them. *See, e.g., Kopischke v. First Continental Corp.* (1980). The issue is which party should bear the cost of plaintiff's failure to use seat belts, and *Braun* probably represents the better reasoned view because the use of seat belts reduces injuries.

Answer A is preferable because it is confident, forceful, and presents the law in the light most favorable to Guerrero. Answer B, by contrast, is passive and balanced in tone. The writer does not sound convinced and thus is not convincing. Answer A shows the court how to decide in Guerrero's favor; it states the position favoring mitigation, presents the merits of that approach as if it were clearly better, and encourages the court to select *Braun* as preferable policy. Unlike Answer B, it de-emphasizes the division of the courts and the minority position of the *Braun* case by merely implying these facts. Answer A, in short, describes the law so as to further the Argument.

   c. Make Your Client's Position Sound Objective Since courts generally do not like to innovate, your client's position should appear reflective of the existing law. Even when a decision in your client's favor would break new legal ground, you must make it seem that a favorable decision is required by law, justice, and common sense. Avoid self-conscious references to your client's position, suggestions that the position is merely an interpretation of the law, or any explicit indication that there is divergence between that position and the law. Conversely, you should characterize the opposition's case as distant from the existing law or as mere interpretation. You should, however, avoid a sarcastic or insulting tone.

*   *   *   *   *

A complaint filed with the State Bar charged Leon Gibbon, an attorney, with depositing in his personal checking account the funds of several estates for which he was doing probate work, and converting $147,000 of these funds to his personal use. A hearing panel of the State Bar agreed with the complaint after an evidentiary hearing and voted to suspend Gibbon from the practice of law for five years. Gibbon appealed to the State Bar Grievance Board, which affirmed the panel's findings and increased the suspension to a lifetime disbarment. Gibbon appealed the Board's disbarment decision to the state's highest appellate court. The State Bar's attorney might characterize its position on appeal in either of these ways.

ANSWER A: Appellee interprets the State Bar Grievance Rules to provide the Grievance Board the discretionary authority to increase a five-year suspension to a disbarment. Appellee agrees with the Grievance Board's conclusion, after reviewing the detailed records, that "the uncontradicted evidence of serious violations of the Code of Professional Responsibility warrants disbarment." The Board's failure to make a detailed statement of the reasons for disbarment is therefore irrelevant, notwithstanding the obvious importance of this matter to Gibbon.

ANSWER B: The State Bar Grievance Board has discretionary authority to increase a five-year suspension to disbarment. After reviewing the detailed record, the Board concluded that "the uncontradicted evidence of serious violations of the Code of Professional Responsibility warrants disbarment." In light of that conclusion, a more detailed statement of reasons would serve no useful purpose.

Answer A emphasizes appellee's position, but Answer B emphasizes the correctness of the Grievance Board's decision. Answer B is preferable because it focuses on the issue in a more objective sounding way than the self-conscious position stated in Answer A. Answer A is also verbose because the reader knows appellee takes that position. Finally, Answer A contains some language ("Board's failure," "obvious importance of this matter to Gibbon," and "interprets the . . . Rules") that suggests more weakness in appellee's position than necessary. The difference between the two answers is one of emphasis, but the skillful use of emphasis makes a more persuasive argument.

5. Fully Argue the Client's Position

Since the brief is a statement of reasons for adopting a certain position, these reasons should be stated as completely as possible. The rule in

Chapter 9 requiring an explicit statement of all the analytical steps needed to reach a conclusion takes on a new dimension in advocacy. There are two guidelines:

    a. Make Effective Use of the Facts   As Chapter 15 will show in some detail, the facts have both logical and emotional value. The application of law to facts is the essence of legal reasoning, but the facts may also be used to gain empathy for the client. By marshaling and emphasizing the appropriate facts, you will often be able to overcome a fairly weak legal position to make a court see the desired outcome as compelling. Similarly, damaging facts should be de-emphasized by explaining them, summarizing them, or describing them blandly. Always use facts to the client's advantage.

*   *   *   *   *

    Edgar Brown was convicted of first degree murder. Defense counsel has two drafts of the brief on appeal.

ANSWER A: The trial judge erred by not charging the jury with the lesser included offense of voluntary manslaughter. A defendant is entitled to a jury charge for manslaughter whenever there are enough facts to convince a reasonable person that the homicide was committed under the influence of an irresistible passion caused by an insult or provocation sufficient to excite a reasonable person. *People v. Valentine.* The defendant in that case was convicted of first degree murder for killing a man who repeatedly insulted the defendant in a brief quarrel by calling him a window peeper and a liar, among other things. The court held that these facts would justify a verdict of voluntary manslaughter and that the trial court erred by giving jury instructions that precluded conviction for that crime.

    Brown's case is similar to *Valentine* because the record shows that Brown committed the homicide after being taunted on an extremely sensitive personal matter. Brown described the decedent as "my best friend from army days," even though the decedent had broken Brown's nose in a fight the previous year. Brown was depressed and unemployed, and the killing occurred during a weekly poker game after the decedent called him a "welfare bum" and a "loser." Any reasonable person in Brown's position would have been similarly provoked.

ANSWER B: The trial judge erred by not charging the jury with the lesser included offense of voluntary manslaughter. A defendant is entitled to a jury charge for manslaughter whenever there are enough facts to convince a reasonable person that the homicide was committed under the influence of an irresistible passion caused by an insult or provocation sufficient to excite a reasonable person. *People v. Valentine.* The defendant in that case was convicted of first degree murder for killing a man who repeatedly insulted the defendant in a brief quarrel by calling him a window peeper and a liar, among other things. The court held that these facts would justify a verdict of voluntary manslaughter and that the trial court erred by giving jury instructions that precluded conviction for that crime.

Brown's case is similar to *Valentine* because the record shows that Brown committed the homicide after being taunted on an extremely sensitive personal matter. Brown was extremely depressed after his layoff at the auto plant, where he had worked for seventeen years. He had been unable to find other work because of high local unemployment. Both he and his wife testified that he had trouble concentrating after he was laid off, that he frequently forgot things, and that their marriage was under great strain. The homicide was committed during a weekly poker game with friends. The record shows the decedent, Brown's "best friend from army days," began to taunt Brown about "being a loser," "a welfare bum," and a social parasite." Although Brown and the decedent engaged in a brief fist fight a year earlier, several persons, including the decedent's wife, testified they had long since made up. After decedent ignored repeated warnings to quit, Brown suddenly lunged at him with a paring knife they used to make sandwiches. Brown could remember nothing of the homicide later except a blind rage. A reasonable person in Brown's position would have been similarly provoked.

Answer B is preferable because its greater vividness and detail force the court to see the issue from Brown's viewpoint. The additional facts not only place the incident within the elements of the manslaughter rule, but they also paint a sympathetic portrait of a harassed man pushed to the breaking point. The facts are set out in chronological order, showing Brown's growing frustration and unhappiness. Answer A's summary of the facts, by contrast, is unsatisfactory because it is badly assembled, omits important facts, and does not describe precisely what happened. Answer A also mentions the fist fight in a damaging way. Answer B carefully excused and blended this point into the argument. Answer A is unpersuasive because it does not provide any insight or empathy for Brown's situation. The facts have enormous advocacy value, and they should be strategically woven into your legal argument.

     b. Make Effective Use of Legal Policies   The relationship between rules and policies is important in writing briefs. Policies define the reasons for the legal rules in question. The result you advocate must be significant from a policy standpoint; technical infractions of the law, therefore, are not enough. Policy arguments are also important when the legal rules or the facts do not provide you with a strong position, particularly at the appellate level. The most complete and compelling arguments are those based on both the letter and spirit of the law.

* * * * *

Section 8 of the Township Rural Zoning Act requires a public referendum on the "adoption of a zoning ordinance" when eight per cent of the registered voters in the township sign petitions requesting a referendum. Seymour Township adopted its zoning ordinance in 1962. Several weeks ago, the Township Board rezoned an eighty-acre tract from agricultural to residential. Township residents gathered sufficient signatures to request a referendum, but a trial court ruled that section 8 applied to the initial decision to zone, not to subsequent zoning amendments. The citizens' brief to the court of appeals could be summarized in the following ways:

ANSWER A: Section 8 of the Township Rural Zoning Act requires the requested referendum. Section 8 applies to the "adoption of a zoning ordinance," a term that includes not only the initial decision to zone but also subsequent amendments. Since such amendments obviously become part of the ordinance, they should be treated in the same manner.

ANSWER B: Section 8 of the Township Rural Zoning Act requires the requested referendum. Section 8 applies to the "adoption of a zoning ordinance," a term that includes not only the initial decision to zone but also subsequent amendments. Since such amendments obviously become part of the ordinance, they should be treated in the same manner. This conclusion is important to the underlying purpose of section 8—insuring that the ordinance is acceptable to a majority of those living in the township. Since zoning amendments might make the ordinance unacceptable to those citizens, the referendum requirement should be equally applicable to zoning amendments and the original ordinance. Zoning amendments, moreover, significantly affect the quality of life of township residents by prescribing the existence, location, and density of new developments. The public ought to have the ability to vote on these important decisions. Finally, since the right to vote is a fundamental one, any perceived ambiguities about the scope of a legislative grant ought to be resolved in favor of that fundamental right.

Answer B's completeness makes it far more compelling than Answer A. Answer A is merely an argument about the meaning of the language in section 8, an argument that sounds uninspired and lame because it does not make effective use of the underlying policies. Answer B draws the same conclusion, but it relies far more on the underlying principles of majority approval for zoning decisions than on the meaning of the words.

It states that the legislative intent in enacting section 8 requires that section's application to zoning amendments, regardless of the statute's ambiguous language.

The exercises that follow provide an opportunity to apply these rules:

Exercise 13-A

Yvonne Hardy, an employee of Tri-State Fuel Co., was driving a fuel tanker truck loaded with an expensive and highly flammable grade of oil. She had been following a pickup truck filled with pumpkins for several miles on a two-lane highway when the latch on the back of that truck suddenly came loose, spilling pumpkins on the right side of the highway. The driver of the pickup immediately pulled over. Hardy swerved into the left lane to avoid the pumpkins, forcing a car driven by Rolf Hansen off the road. Hansen, who was coming from the opposite direction in the correct lane, suffered severe injuries.

Hansen sued Tri-State for negligence and claimed that Hardy (and thus Tri-State) was negligent *per se* under State Code § 98.01. Hardy testified at trial that she had driven fuel trucks for eight years. She stated that she did not think she could maintain control of the truck if she struck the pumpkins and that she did not have time to stop. She also testified that there was no shoulder on the right side of the highway and that it dropped off sharply into a small river valley. She said she had reason to believe the truck would explode if she went off the road or lost control, and that she did not see Hansen's car until just before he drove off the road. The driver of the pickup truck testified that he recovered eleven pumpkins, ranging from fifteen to twenty pounds in size, from the road. About half of these pumpkins shattered when they struck the road, he said, and several cars ran over unbroken pumpkins after the incident. The trial court found Tri-State negligent *per se* and awarded Hansen $75,000 for his injuries. Tri-State has appealed.

State Code § 98.01(c) provides:

> Upon all roadways of sufficient width, a vehicle shall be driven upon the right half of the roadway except as follows:
>
> . . . .
>
> (c) When an obstruction exists making it necessary to drive on the left half of the roadway.

The highest appellate court in the state has decided the following cases:

Meekhof v. Golden (1939)

Meekhof brought an action against Golden for injuries Meekhof sustained when the automobile Golden was driving forced Meekhof off the road. Golden, who was intoxicated, was in the left lane of a two-lane highway at the time. The trial court awarded Meekhof $6,100 in damages, and we affirm. State Code § 98.01 requires all vehicles to be driven on the right side of the roadway except in specifically defined situations. The obvious purpose of this statute is to protect persons and property on the left side of the roadway. Golden's violation of the statute constitutes negligence *per se,* and the trial judge so instructed the jury. None of the exceptions stated in the statute are applicable here.

Yerrick v. Boughton (1956)

Appellee Cecelia Boughton was seriously injured when appellant's automobile, which was fast approaching hers in the same lane, forced her off the road to avoid an accident. Appellee brought an action for negligence to recover for her injuries and argued that appellant's violation of State Code § 98.01 constituted negligence *per se.* The trial court agreed and awarded judgment to appellee. Although appellant admitted that he was driving in the left lane of the highway, he argued pursuant to subsection (c) that an obstruction made it necessary for him to drive in the left lane. The obstruction was a bumpy and somewhat uneven forty-yard stretch of the right lane, which appellant told the trial court "might have severely bent a tie rod or wrecked the alignment of my car." We agree with the trial court.

The purpose of § 98.01, as we said in *Meekhof v. Golden* (1939), is protection of persons and property on the left side of the roadway. There is no obstruction within the meaning of § 98.01(c) unless there is an obstacle that prevents, or is likely to prevent, the driver's safe passage on the right side of the roadway. In any case, it is not intended simply for the convenience or financial self-interest of the driver. A bumpy and uneven road, without more, does not meet that test. Affirmed.

James v. Strange (1964)

Appellee was driving about twenty miles per hour on a two-lane street in a residential neighborhood when a child suddenly ran in front of him, chasing a ball. Knowing he did not have time to stop, appellee swerved suddenly and sharply into the left lane. In so doing, he crashed into appellant's vehicle, which was traveling in the opposite direction. The child was not hurt. Appellant, who also was not injured, sued appellee for damages to his vehicle, arguing that appellee was negligent *per se* under State Code § 98.01. Appellee admitted he did not see the other car until he struck it. The trial court dismissed the suit.

This court has often stated that § 98.01 is designed to protect persons and property on the left side of the roadway. *E.g., Yerrick v. Boughton* (1956). Drivers have a right to believe the statute will be observed. At the same time, it would shock the conscience to force a driver to choose between killing a child and subjecting himself to a negligence lawsuit. Section 98.01(c), which permits travel on the left side of the road when an obstruction makes such travel necessary, encompasses small children who run into the roadway. There is no negligence *per se* here. Affirmed.

1. Assume you are representing Tri-State:

(a) Will your argument emphasize the general rule in the statute or the exception? Why?

(b) Affirmatively state your client's position in one sentence.

(c) What argument(s) will you use to support that position?

(d) How will you arrange your discussion of the cases under each argument? Why?

(e) What facts will you emphasize? Why?

(f) What policies will you emphasize? Why?

(g) Identify and refute the strongest argument against your client's position.

(h) Draft the argument for Tri-State based on your answers to these questions.

2. Assume you are representing Hansen:

(a) Will your argument emphasize the general rule in the statute or the exception? Why?

(b) Affirmatively state your client's position in one sentence.

(c) What argument(s) will you use to support that position?

(d) How will you arrange your discussion of the cases under each argument? Why?

(e) What facts will you emphasize? Why?

(f) What policies will you emphasize? Why?

(g) Identify and refute the strongest argument against your client's position.

(h) Draft the argument for Hansen based on your answers to these questions.

Exercise 13-B

Read the following selections from the transcript of the record in *Wong v. PlayChem Corporation:*

Excerpt from Complaint of Susan Wong
Page 4 of the record

1. Plaintiff, Susan Wong, is a resident of the City of Clear Lake, County of Clear Lake, State of East Carolina. Plaintiff is a minor of the age of five (5) years.

2. On October 16, 1980, on application duly made on her behalf, Kim Wong, plaintiff's natural father, was, by an order of court duly given and made, appointed guardian *ad litem* of plaintiff for purposes of this action.

3. Defendant, PlayChem Corporation ("PlayChem"), is a corporation organized and existing under the laws of Delaware, engaged in the business of manufacturing and distributing chemistry sets for educational and other purposes, with its principal place of business in the City of Muskegon, Michigan.

Excerpt from Complaint of Susan Wong (cont.)
Page 5 of the record

6. On May 30, 1980, Kim Wong purchased a Chem VIII chemistry set from defendant PlayChem. This particular set contained no instructions for its use, contrary to the custom and practice of PlayChem.

7. On September 21, 1980, plaintiff mixed three chemicals in the set (crushed charcoal, powdered sulfur, and potassium nitrate), forming gunpowder. Not knowing the danger of this mixture, she heated it, causing an explosion which

severely injured plaintiff, blinding her in her left eye and severely disabling her right hand.

8. Plaintiff's injuries were proximately caused by defendant PlayChem's failure to observe reasonable care in the manufacture and distribution of the particular chemistry set in question in the following respects:

(a) In not including instructions for the use of the set,

(b) In not inspecting each set to determine whether instructions were included, and

(c) In failing to respond to Kim Wong's request for instructions for the set.

9. As a proximate result of the negligence of defendant PlayChem, plaintiff will be permanently restricted to one-eyed vision, and will never again be able to engage in activities that require binocular vision. Furthermore, plaintiff will never be able to engage in activities that require two hands, which will severely restrict a highly promising career in almost any field she could have chosen. Finally, plaintiff has endured great pain and suffering, and will in the future endure great pain and suffering, all to her damage of $2,500,000.

Answer of Defendant PlayChem Corporation
Page 11 of the record

The facts alleged in Paragraphs One through Seven of plaintiff's complaint are admitted, excepting those allegations concerning plaintiff's alleged injuries. Defendant specifically denies each and every allegation in Paragraphs Eight and Nine of plaintiff's complaint.

Affirmative Defense

At the time in question, plaintiff's parents, Kim and Li Wong, were guilty of negligence by reason of their failure to use the degree of care that would have been used by an ordinarily reasonable and prudent person under the same or similar circumstances, in that they:

1. Gave a highly complicated and dangerous chemistry set to their five-year-old child,

2. Failed to provide any supervision over the child's use of the set, and

3. Failed to prevent the child from using the set after discovering that it did not contain the necessary instructions for its use.

Such negligence on their part caused, or contributed to, the matters complained of in plaintiff's complaint.

Affidavit of Ronald York
Page 33 of the record

My name is Ronald York and I am the manager of the sales division of the PlayChem Corporation, Muskegon, Michigan. PlayChem manufactures and sells chemistry sets, primarily for educational purposes, and has done so since 1936. Our advertising literature states truthfully that dozens of college professors, Nobel Prize nominees, and corporate chemists got their start with a PlayChem chemistry set.

The Chem VIII chemistry set contains 78 different kinds of chemical elements and compounds, a Bunsen burner, and a variety of laboratory equipment. Detailed instructions are included with each set. It is a very complicated chemistry set, and we sell relatively few of them.

On June 2, 1980, I received a telephone call from a Mr. Kim Wong of Clear Lake, East Carolina. He said he had just purchased a Chem VIII set for his daughter, but that the set did not contain instructions. We sent the instructions immediately after he called, but the envelope came back. We apparently had not gotten his proper address, and I did not know how to reach him.

Deposition of Kim Wong by Defendant's Attorney
Page 51 of the record
Q: When was your daughter Susan born?
A: Susan was born on June 1, 1975.
Q: Could you tell me about Susan's special abilities?
A: Well, Susan began to speak English when she was six months old. She could read and write by her second birthday, which was right after we arrived in Clear Lake. A neighbor in our apartment building told us there were some child development experts at State University who could help us, so we made an appointment to see them. They tested Susan. They said she has a genius-level IQ. We then enrolled her in a special learning program for gifted children at the University.

Deposition of Kim Wong by Defendant's Attorney (cont.)
Page 55 of the record
Q: Could you tell me about why you bought Susan a chemistry set?
A: She was very good at science. She had also been taught some chemistry in her special program.
Q: Is that why you bought her an advanced chemistry set?
A: Well, yes. She was able to learn very quickly, if you know what I mean.
Q: Why did you buy her a Chem VIII set? That was about the most advanced set, was it not?
A: As I just said, she was very able. The Chem VIII set is designed for sixteen-to-eighteen-year-old children. I asked her teacher if he thought Susan could handle such a difficult set. He said he thought so, so I bought it for her fifth birthday and gave it to her.
Q: Had Susan done any experimentation with chemicals in school?
A: No.
Q: Had Susan ever used another chemistry set?
A: No, but the teacher was confident she could follow the instructions.

Deposition of Kim Wong by Defendant's Attorney (cont.)
Page 61 of the record
Q: What happened just before the accident?
A: I was finishing with the dishes after dinner when Susan said she was going downstairs to play with the chemistry set. I said OK. Everything was quiet for about two hours, and then there was an explosion. It was very horrible, really, I would rather not go into the details . . . .
Q: I appreciate that, Mr. Wong. Could you tell me how often she had used the set before this incident?
A: It is hard to say, but perhaps a dozen times.
Q: Did you ever assist her or watch her when she played with the set?
A: Not really. I asked her questions about what she was doing, but I did not oversee her in any sense.

Q: Was anyone else with her at the time?
A: No.

Deposition of Kim Wong by Defendant's Attorney (cont.)
Page 62 of the record
Q: This chemistry set was not part of her formal study or homework at the University, was it?
A: No, it was not. It helped her a lot, though, and the teachers said she made some very good contributions in class because of her use of the set.
Q: Let me come back to that program for just a minute. This program was optional, right?
A: Yes, in that Susan began when she was four, and that she wasn't required to attend school until she was six. But everyone we spoke to recommended it highly, and said it would help her a great deal.

Deposition of Kim Wong by Defendant's Attorney (cont.)
Page 69 of the record
Q: When did you first notice that there were no instructions in the chemistry set?
A: After Susan played with it the first time, she said there weren't any instructions for it.
Q: Did you seek to procure a set of instructions for the set?
A: I did. I called the company and asked for them.
Q: Did you get an answer?
A: No.
Q: Did you try to stop Susan from playing with the set until you got an answer?
A: No.

Excerpt from Opinion of Judge Gleit
Page 78 of the record
    The principal legal issue here is whether the plaintiff's parents were contributorily negligent in permitting plaintiff to use the chemistry set alone and without instructions. The law in this state does not permit a minor child to be charged with contributory negligence, so defendant has attempted to pin that charge on her parents. Counsel for the Wongs argues that the doctrine of parental immunity for negligent torts applies here, and I must reluctantly agree. The doctrine is a useless and counterproductive bit of legal baggage, but it is the law in this state. *Lanir v. Lanir* (1929). The doctrine bars the contributory negligence claim. Plaintiff's motion for partial summary judgment on the issues of parental immunity and contributory negligence is hereby granted. A trial for determination of defendant's negligence will be scheduled shortly.

Excerpt from Order of Judge Gleit
Page 180 of the record
    In summary, I find that the allegations concerning plaintiff's injuries as specified in Paragraph 9 of the complaint are true, and that defendant's negligence caused those injuries. I hereby find and adjudge defendant to be liable for the sum of $400,000 for the damages it caused to plaintiff. So ordered.
    The following case is the only relevant decision by the Supreme Court of the State of East Carolina:

Lanir v. Lanir (1929)

Jacob Lanir was injured when the 20-gauge shotgun he was using to hunt deer accidentally discharged into his foot. He brought an action against his father for negligently instructing him in the use of the gun. The trial court sustained the father's demurrer, and we affirm. A proper respect for the role of the family in our society counsels us to conclude that the courts are no place to air such grievances between father and son.

Each of the following three cases is from a different state:

Kates v. DeSantis (1968)

Six-year-old Emily Kates completed her first day of school by getting off the school bus, waiting for the bus to drive away, and then being struck and injured by a car driven by Emil DeSantis as Emily attempted to cross the highway to get home. The child's parents sued DeSantis for negligence. DeSantis in turn claimed that they were contributorily negligent in failing to properly instruct her on how to leave a school bus and cross a highway. The trial court disregarded this defense because of the rule we established in *Geller v. Geller* (1963) and awarded damages for the child's injuries. We affirm.

This case involves the interplay between parental immunity and contributory negligence. Where parental immunity is applicable, it bars contributory negligence claims for injuries caused by third parties to their children.

In *Geller v. Geller*, we set aside the traditional rule making parents immune from personal injury actions for negligence brought by their children except in two areas: (1) the exercise of parental authority or discipline over the child, and (2) the provision of food, clothing, housing, medical care, and other care. The phrase, "other care," must be narrowly understood or it will swallow these exceptions and re-establish complete parental immunity. "Other care" does, however, extend to actions dealing with a child's education. These and other actions relating to the provision of food, clothing, housing, and medical care deal with basic necessities of health, morals, and well-being for which society imposes a legal obligation upon the parents. The state requires parents to provide for a child's education, and for this reason the *Geller* exception applies.

Peterson v. Peterson (1971)

We are asked to reconsider our long-established doctrine that parents are immune from negligence actions for personal injuries brought by their children. We replace that doctrine with one that makes parents liable only if they do or fail to do what an ordinary and reasonably prudent parent would have done in similar circumstances.

Ernest Peterson and his twelve-year-old son, Fritz, were riding home from a fishing trip when the elder Peterson stopped on the highway. The father believed that a tire on the boat trailer he was towing had gone flat and asked Fritz to go out on the road to inspect it. While doing so, Fritz was struck and injured by another vehicle. Fritz sued his father for negligence. His father filed a motion to dismiss, and the trial court dismissed the suit. We reverse.

Parental immunity is a useless doctrine based on reasons that are no longer persuasive. The argument that tort immunity prevents the disruption of family harmony is unsound because there is no such immunity for property disputes within a family. In addition, there should be less disruption for tort actions because adverse judgments will normally be paid by the defendant's insurance company rather than, as in property actions, out of the defendant's pocket. The rationale that immunity prevents collusive lawsuits actually goes to that possibility in any lawsuit, and should not be a basis for denying one kind of lawsuit. The threat to parental authority and discipline is the only plausible rationale for preserving any part of the doctrine. Surely a parent should be able to spank a child or order a child to stay in his room without being sued for battery or false imprisonment.

The court in *Geller v. Geller* (1963) abolished parental immunity except in two areas: "(1) the exercise of parental authority or discipline over the child, and (2) the provision of food, clothing, housing, medical care, and other care." We reject that approach because it draws arbitrary distinctions about different kinds of parental behavior for purposes of immunity. We also believe it to be wrong that a parent can shield negligent behavior by bringing it under the umbrella of the exceptions described.

For these reasons, we adopt a "reasonable parent" rule similar to that existing in other areas of negligence. We reverse and remand for further proceedings on the merits.

Wilkes v. Torkko (1980)

Nine-year-old Sarah Wilkes was floating on an old automobile inner tube in Lake Winnebago when she was struck and seriously injured by a speed boat operated by Amos Torkko. She had come to the lake with her mother, Martha Wilkes, who was sitting on the shore at the time. Sarah Wilkes brought an action against Torkko for negligence. Torkko sought to join her mother for contribution since, he alleged, she was negligent in failing to properly supervise her daughter. Martha moved for summary judgment on the basis of parental immunity, and the trial court granted the motion. We affirm.

This case involves both contributory negligence and parental immunity. The record provides good reason to believe that Martha Wilkes was contributorily negligent in the injury of her daughter. There was testimony that many speedboats were cruising the lake that day, that many of them were cruising near the shore, and that Sarah Wilkes had never been on a lake in an inner tube before. The record also shows that Martha Wilkes was reading a novel the entire time rather than watching her daughter. Although Martha was contributorily negligent, parental immunity bars that defense in this case.

This state has long shielded parents from negligence actions by their children, and for good reason. The integrity of the family is essential to the growth and development of our society. We are unwilling to permit judges and juries to intrude on the difficult and sensitive problems of raising children. In that regard, we disagree with the approach taken by another state in *Peterson v. Peterson* (1971), which would permit recovery by children when parents "do or fail to do what an ordinary and reasonably prudent parent would have done in similar circumstances." The people of our state are too diverse to be judged by a common standard. We do not believe, for example, that the same standard could apply to suburban parents in a major city and rural parents in the smallest hamlet.

Finally, we reject the notion that third parties can recover from immune parents since recovery would put a strain on the family relationship. In addition, allowing recovery by a nonparent defendant from a negligent parent would affect the child's recovery, since both parent and child are a single economic unit.

1. What issues are involved in this problem?

2. Assume you are representing the Wongs:
   (a) What is your client's strongest issue?
   (b) What is your client's most significant issue? Is it the same as your client's strongest issue? Why?
   (c) State your client's position on each issue in the order you would present these issues. Outline the arguments you would use to support that position on each issue. State the arguments PlayChem would use in response, and your answers to them.
   (d) Draft the argument for the Wongs on appeal. Make effective use of the facts of this case and the policies of the decided cases to support your position.

3. Assume you are representing PlayChem:
   (a) What is your client's strongest issue?
   (b) What is your client's most significant issue? Is it the same as your client's strongest issue? Why?
   (c) State your client's position on each issue in the order you would present these issues. Outline the arguments you would use to support that position on each issue. State the arguments the Wongs would use in response, and your answers to them.
   (d) Draft the argument for PlayChem on appeal. Make effective use of the facts of your case and the policies of the decided cases to support your position.

14

Point Headings

POINT headings are statements of the legal conclusions the advocate is asking the court to adopt. They correspond to the issues, sub-issues, and other salient points in the brief, and are usually capitalized or underlined to stand out from the rest of the text. Point headings serve two important functions; one is organizational, and the other is related to advocacy.

Point headings serve a useful organizational function because they provide a court with additional guidance in understanding the direction and content of the brief. They are located within the body of the Argument and are also listed in the Index. When located in the Argument, point headings serve as conspicuous thesis sentences for the different sections of the brief. In the Index, they provide the court with a complete and concise summary of the Argument. A judge interested in reading only about a particular point can scan the Index and then turn to the appropriate page. In addition to assisting the court, point headings assist the advocate in drafting the brief, since they magnify organizational errors and provide a useful check on the content of the argument under each heading.

Point headings are also related to advocacy because they are basic statements of the advocate's contentions and, as such, make the Argument more accessible to the court. Since judges are required to decide a variety of complicated matters, they are more likely to be persuaded by briefs that are easily understood. In addition, the special placement of point headings in the Index, coupled with their special treatment in the Argument, impresses the structure of your argument more sharply in the reader's mind.

The logic of argument in the brief unfolds in the point headings. Point headings are arranged in outline form from the most general to the most specific. State your primary arguments in capitalized point headings known as major headings. Each major heading is prefaced with a Roman numeral corresponding to its place in the argument. State the basic components of your argument supporting each primary contention in minor headings. Each minor heading is prefaced by a capital letter corresponding to its place under the major heading. Some advocates underline minor headings to distinguish them from subheadings. Finally, state the significant components of the argument supporting a minor heading in subheadings. Each subheading is prefaced with a numeral indicating its location under the minor heading. You will only rarely need to provide headings for the arguments supporting a subheading.

As with basic outlining, never use minor headings or subheadings under a heading unless you use two or more of them. If you can only formulate one heading under a larger heading, then consolidate that lesser heading into the larger heading.

Thus:

   I. FIRST MAJOR HEADING.
      A. First minor heading.
      B. Second minor heading.
        1. First subheading.
        2. Second subheading.
        3. Third subheading.
  II. SECOND MAJOR HEADING.

The basic rules for formulating and placing point headings are as follows:

1. State Your Legal Conclusions and the Basic Reasons for These Conclusions

Point headings should be an integral part of your Argument. They should be confident, forceful statements cast in terms most favorable to your client. Since they are thesis sentences for parts of your Argument, each point heading should indicate the issue being discussed (including the relevant legal rule), your position on this issue, and the basic reasons for that position. When lesser headings are used under a larger heading, however, the general heading need contain only your position concerning the application of a particular legal rule, since the lesser headings will provide the reasons for that position. A major heading, for example, may draw a general legal conclusion whose underlying rationale is provided by several minor headings. Each minor heading, then, will contain a legal rule, a conclusion concerning its application to your case, and your basic reasons for that conclusion. Case or statutory citations should not be used as a shorthand reference to the applicable legal principle because the reader is usually not afforded any direction by a bare citation.

* * * * *

The Williams Act is a federal statute that imposes disclosure requirements and restrictions concerning tender offers. A tender offer is the term used to describe an offer by an individual or group of individuals to purchase a certain percentage of the outstanding stock of a corporation. The state of Huron has enacted a similar statute regulating tender offers, but imposes more stringent requirements than the Williams Act. You represent a client seeking to make a tender offer who would like to avoid the requirements of the Huron statute. Your research indicates that state statutes sometimes can be declared unconstitutional under the supremacy clause of the United States Constitution when there is a federal law governing the same subject. The supremacy clause makes the federal constitution or statutes "the supreme law of the land." This "preemption doctrine" may be invoked when the Congressional purpose in enacting the federal law is frustrated by the operation of the state statute. You might frame a major point heading on this issue in any of these ways:

ANSWER A: THE PREEMPTION DOCTRINE REQUIRES THAT A STATE LAW NOT FRUSTRATE THE PURPOSE OF CONGRESS.

ANSWER B: THIS CASE IS GOVERNED BY *HINES V. DAVIDOWITZ, PEREZ V. CAMPBELL, KEWANEE OIL CO. V. BICRON CORP.,* AND THEIR PROGENY.

ANSWER C: THE HURON STATUTE IS PREEMPTED UNDER THE SUPREMACY CLAUSE BECAUSE IT CONFLICTS WITH THE OBJECTIVES OF THE WILLIAMS ACT, THEREBY FRUSTRATING THE PURPOSES OF CONGRESS.

Answer C is best because it is an assertive and positive statement of your client's position. It states a legal conclusion and provides a reason for that conclusion, thus introducing the court to the argument that follows. It also incorporates the basic legal rule. Answers A and B provide far less information or direction. Answer A is merely a statement of a legal principle without any application to the present case. The heading draws no conclusions and provides no reasons supporting the client's position.

Although a legal conclusion might be implied from the argument that follows, the writer of Answer A has forfeited an opportunity to advance the client's position. Answer B is worse because it does not even describe the basic legal principle involved. Unless the reader is familiar with the cases cited, he has been given no direction by the point heading. Even if the reader is familiar with the cases, all he will learn is the applicable legal rule. To this extent, Answer B is simply another way of stating Answer A. Point headings must further your argument.

2. Be Both Specific and Readable

Point headings must relate legal rules to specific factual situations. The more specifically these rules and facts are stated, the more persuasive the point headings will be. There is a limit, however, to the amount of information that can be compressed into a single sentence without making a heading incomprehensible. Framing a point heading is essentially a balancing process. When considering how general or specific you should be, remember that point headings must adequately summarize the argument and still remain readable.

*   *   *   *   *

The state Environmental Protection Act provides in part that any person may bring a lawsuit for injunctive relief against any other person whose actions are "likely to pollute, impair, or destroy the air, water, or other natural resources, or the public trust therein." A sportsmen's club brought a lawsuit under that Act to prevent oil drilling in a state forest. After a bench trial, the court granted judgment for the defendants. Counsel for the plaintiff might use one of these point headings on appeal:

ANSWER A: Plaintiff presented uncontradicted evidence of likely pollution, impairment, or destruction of the air, water, or other natural resources, or the public trust therein because plaintiff showed that oil development activities at the proposed sites, including seismic survey work, exploratory drilling, new roads, and other activities would substantially diminish elk populations in the forest by diminishing their habitat, and would also adversely impact bear and bobcat populations, and that it would take these species at least forty to fifty years to recover from these effects.

ANSWER B: Plaintiff presented uncontradicted evidence of likely pollution, impairment, or destruction by showing that oil drilling activities would have a substantial and prolonged impact on elk, bear, and bobcat populations in the forest.

ANSWER C: Plaintiff presented uncontradicted evidence that oil drilling activities would adversely affect the forest.

———

Answer B is the best of the three answers because it states and applies the statutory rule, summarizes the relevant facts, draws a conclusion, and is still very readable. It is a persuasive introduction to the argument that will support and expand on the conclusion reached in the point heading. Answer A contains a more complete statement of the applicable law and the relevant facts, but it is very difficult to read and understand. Its additional detail contributes nothing of significance to the statement, and the heading is almost useless as a persuasive or organizational tool. Answer C errs in the other extreme; the message is easy to read but too vague to be of much use. There is no clear statement or reference to the statutory rule concerning the likelihood of pollution, impairment, or destruction of the environment, nor is there any clear reference to how the forest is likely to be adversely affected. Answer B reconciles the two extremes.

3. Place Headings at Logical Points in Your Brief

Point headings must directly reflect your organizational scheme. You should outline your brief before drafting it, and the headings you eventually formulate for the Argument should correspond with the specific points in your outline. A separate point heading should generally be included for each issue and sub-issue. The major contentions under each issue or sub-issue may also require separate point headings. In addition to using point headings to make the Argument more specific, you may need point headings that are more general than your issues and sub-issues. For example, when you have two or more large categories of issues (such as several objections to the constitutionality of a statute and several jurisdictional issues), each category should receive a separate point heading.

Placement of headings is a matter of balance and good judgment. As a general rule, point headings should simplify your organization by providing logical breaks in your Argument. A well-written brief carries the reader smoothly from one point to another. An insufficient number of point headings makes your brief more difficult to understand and invites long-winded and poorly organized Arguments. If you divide the brief into too many segments, however, it will lose its momentum and persuasive force. An overabundance of headings can interrupt an Argument inappropriately, make the organizational scheme confusingly complex, and draw excessive attention to relatively insignificant points. As a further consideration, although it may be logical to divide the contentions or arguments under a heading into subheadings, it may not be prudent to do so. Several weaker arguments often can be strengthened by combining them rather than by presenting them individually. Each will lend support to the others and give the appearance of a stronger overall Argument.

*   *   *   *   *

A state law provides for the licensing of persons and medical establishments using x-rays and other sources of ionizing radiation. The act also provides that a court "may grant temporary and permanent equitable relief" against persons who have violated the act. Your client, Health Scan Associates, specializes in giving x-rays. A trial court has enjoined your client from giving any x-rays until its equipment and technicians are licensed under the act, even though they meet nearly all of the safety and training requirements of the act. The licensing process could take six months or more. The trial court held that "an injunction is automatically required when the act is being violated." Traditionally, injunctions are issued only when the harm they will prevent outweighs the harm they will cause to the defendant. In addition, injunctions may be issued automatically, with no balancing of interests, when there are repeated or continuing violations of the statute. You are drafting a brief supporting your motion for a stay of the injunction pending appeal and plan to argue that the injunction was wrong under both theories. Your point headings might be drafted in the following ways:

ANSWER A:
II. THE TRIAL COURT ERRED IN GRANTING THE INJUNCTION.
    A. The injunction should not have been issued automatically because appellant did not commit significant and continuing violations of the act.
    B. The injunction should not have been issued because the harm to appellant from its loss of income for six or more months, possible bankruptcy, and unemployment of thirty-four workers outweighs the state's interest in technical compliance with the act.

ANSWER B:
II. THE TRIAL COURT ERRED IN GRANTING THE INJUNCTION.
    A. The injunction should not have been issued automatically because appellant did not commit significant and continuing violations of the act.
    B. Even if the act purported to make injunctive relief mandatory, it could not do so because such relief is always within the trial court's discretion.
    C. The injunction should not have been issued because the act makes such relief discretionary rather than mandatory.

D. The injunction should not have been issued because the harm to appellant far outweighs the state's interest.
  1. The injunction will greatly injure appellant by causing a total loss of income for six or more months, possible bankruptcy, and unemployment of thirty-four workers.
  2. The injunction will only slightly accelerate the time by which appellant technically complies with the act.

ANSWER C:
II. THE TRIAL COURT ERRED IN GRANTING THE INJUNCTION BECAUSE THE INJUNCTION WAS NOT MANDATORY UNDER THE ACT AND BECAUSE THE BALANCE OF EQUITIES FAVORS APPELLANT.

Answer A provides a straightforward and yet complete outline of the client's position, and is the best of the three answers. The organizational scheme is smooth and understandable because each of the client's basic contentions is dealt with in a single minor heading. Answer B is too choppy to be effective. It contains too many headings and thus obscures the basic thrust of the Argument. The second minor heading should be incorporated under the first because the two are so closely related, and because these points are more forceful when made together. Similarly, the third and fourth minor headings should be combined. The subheadings following "D," moreover, add little to the single heading on that issue in Answer A. Answer C represents the other extreme by omitting the use of minor headings. The organizational scheme of the Argument is hard to understand because it is stated only in the vaguest terms, and its persuasive value is diminished accordingly. Point headings should provide a logical outline of the Argument.

Working through the following exercises should improve your understanding of these concepts.

Exercise 14-A

Edward Hinkle is appealing an order of the State Industrial Commission denying his claim for worker's compensation benefits. Hinkle was employed by the Goff Medical Supply Co. to deliver medical supplies to clinics, doctors, and hospitals. The boxes containing the supplies were secured by rubber bands about twelve inches long and one-half inch wide. There was testimony before an administrative law judge that Hinkle and several other Goff employees engaged in rubber band "fights" at least two or three times each week. Hinkle's supervisor said he observed such fights several times per month and discouraged them on at least one occasion.

One day, when Hinkle was loading supplies in his truck as part of his regular work, two other employees flipped rubber bands at him. Hinkle immediately flipped a rubber band back at them. One of these employees then found an eighteen-inch sliver of wood and stepped toward Hinkle, brandishing it like a sword. Hinkle took the wood from her and attempted to use a rubber band to shoot the wood through the air at the employee. The other employee batted the sliver with a trash can lid she had been using as a shield, and the deflected sliver struck Hinkle in the face, blinding him in the right eye. Section 45 of the State Worker's Compensation Act provides for compensation of injuries that are not self-inflicted to "every employee who is injured by accident arising out of or in the course of his employment."

There is one pertinent appellate decision:

Sperry v. Industrial Commission (1979)

Petitioner asks this Court to review an order of the State Industrial Commission denying him worker's compensation benefits for serious injuries he sustained when he fell from a truck that a co-worker was driving around the parking lot at the warehouse where they worked. Petitioner testified that the incident occurred during regular working hours, that they were using the truck to make "figure eights" in the light snow that had just fallen, and that they had never done this before. Petitioner and his co-worker worked in the shipping department at the warehouse, and neither drove nor loaded trucks as part of their regular work. We affirm the Commission's order and we hereby adopt the following four-part test for determining whether a particular act of horseplay arises "out of or in the course of" employment and thus is compensable under section 45 of the Worker's Compensation Act.

1. Extent and seriousness of the deviation. We fully recognize the value of a little nonsense in any employment situation, and we understand that workers cannot be expected to attend strictly to their jobs every minute. The injury here, however, resulted from a lengthy and serious departure from petitioner's job.

2. Completeness of the deviation. It is one thing for an employee to engage in a bit of horseplay as part of the performance of his duty. It is another to completely abandon the employment and concentrate one's energies on something unrelated to one's job, as occurred here.

3. Extent to which horseplay has become a part of the employment. The act of horseplay here occurred only once. It was not a custom in the warehouse.

4. Extent to which the nature of employment may be expected to include some horseplay. Relevant considerations here include the existence of things in the work environment that are readily usable for horseplay and the presence of lulls in the work. We do not believe that, given petitioner's work environment, a truck especially lends itself to horseplay.

For all of these reasons, the Commission's order is affirmed.

1. Assume you are representing Hinkle:
   (a) What is the basic outline of your Argument?
   (b) Draft point headings to correspond to each point in your outline. Are these headings thesis sentences for the text you would draft under them?

Do they incorporate the rule of law and the relevant facts? Are they specific and readable?

2. Assume you are representing the Industrial Commission:
    (a) What is the basic outline of your Argument?
    (b) Draft point headings to correspond to each point in your outline. Are these headings thesis sentences for the text you would draft under them? Do they incorporate the rule of law and the relevant facts? Are they specific and readable?

Exercise 14-B

This exercise is based on the Arguments drafted in response to the advocacy questions from Exercise 13-B on pp. 151–157.

1. Assume you are representing the Wongs:
    (a) What is the basic outline of your Argument?
    (b) Draft point headings to correspond to each major point in your outline. Are these headings thesis sentences for the text under them? Do they incorporate the rule of law and the relevant facts? Are they specific and readable?

2. Assume you are representing PlayChem:
    (a) What is the basic outline of your Argument?
    (b) Draft point headings to correspond to each major point in your outline. Are these headings thesis sentences for the text under them? Do they incorporate the rule of law and the relevant facts? Are they specific and readable?

15

Statement of Facts: Brief

THE Statement of Facts in an office memorandum relates the facts necessary to understand and resolve the legal issues presented. The Statement of Facts in a brief does that and more; it subtly persuades the court that fairness requires a decision in your client's favor. Many advocates believe the Statement of Facts is the most significant part of a brief because it defines the setting in which the case will be decided. Although the Statement of Facts may or may not be the most significant part of a brief, it does have substantial persuasive value.

Factual statements in office memos and briefs are similar in many respects and, therefore, many of the basic rules are the same. The Statement of Facts must be an honest and accurate description of the events which gave rise to the litigation. All legally significant facts must be included and precisely stated, whether or not they are helpful to the client's position. Key background facts should be included, but distracting detail should not. The facts must be stated in an understandable and logical fashion.

Although similar to the Statement of Facts in an office memo, the Statement of Facts in a brief contains two additional kinds of information. First, the factual statement contains emotionally significant facts. These facts are omitted from office memos unless they are also legally significant, but should be included in a brief because they can have a substantial effect on a court's decision-making process by playing on its sympathies and sense of justice. The strongest cases are both emotionally appealing and

167

soundly based on the relevant law, but weak legal cases can often be overcome by a sympathetic factual situation. Second, the factual statement in a brief describes the procedural background of the case, including the major events that led to this point in the litigation, the decisions of any lower courts that heard the case, and brief explanations of their decisions. These procedural facts give both trial and appellate courts a more complete understanding of the case and what relief the advocate requests.

Appellate briefs, unlike trial briefs, are accompanied by a transcript of the record. The transcript includes the pleadings, affidavits, exhibits, and other documents submitted to the courts below, and the decisions of these courts. The record also includes the transcribed oral proceedings before the courts, such as arguments on motions or the testimony at trial. The transcript of the record thus provides the complete factual and procedural background of the proceedings in the lower courts. The Statement of Facts in a brief should show the pages in the record where the stated facts can be found. For example: "The police found the pistol under Anderson's pillow (R. 33)." This citation, of course, shows the source of this fact to be page 33 of the record. Generally, a single fact or group of related facts should be followed immediately by a citation. Where you are paraphrasing or summarizing facts spread through several pages in the record, such as pages 13, 14, 15, and 16, you can group them together and cite them as follows: (R. 13-16). At other times, you will need to mention specific pages: (R. 11, 28, 30). Once you have provided a citation to the record in your Statement of Facts, you no longer need to refer to the record when using those facts.

The basic rules for persuasively stating the facts are best set forth in the context of a hypothetical problem.

* * * * *

You represent Iris Monge in a sex discrimination case. The trial court dismissed her complaint, and she is appealing that decision. The following excerpts are taken from the transcript of the record in *Monge v. Shannon Development Co.:*

Excerpt from Complaint of Iris Monge
Page 6 of the record

III

That plaintiff was employed by defendant from August 1977 to January 30, 1979, when she resigned her position.

IV

That during her employment plaintiff advanced from a Class IV secretary to a Class II secretary and consistently received excellent job evaluations.

V

That from September 1978 to the time of her resignation, plaintiff was subjected to severe, excessive, and inexcusable sexual harassment by her supervisor, Clarence Dudley. Specific instances of this sexual harassment include: making obscene jokes to other male employees in plaintiff's presence, making loud remarks about personal parts of plaintiff's anatomy, suggesting to other employees that he had engaged in sexual relations with plaintiff, asking plaintiff to have sexual relations with him during lunch hour, placing his hands on plaintiff, and referring to plaintiff as "my little girl."

Excerpt from Complaint of Iris Monge (cont.)
Page 8 of the record

VIII

That plaintiff is thirty years of age, divorced, and the sole provider for her two young children, that plaintiff has exhausted her savings, and that defendant has refused to reinstate her to her former position.

IX

That on January 15, 1979, plaintiff filed a sexual discrimination charge with the Equal Employment Opportunity Commission (EEOC), and that as of the date of this complaint, the EEOC has taken no action except to inform plaintiff that it would be unable to process her charge until November 1979.

WHEREFORE, plaintiff prays that this court grant a preliminary injunction requiring defendant to reinstate plaintiff to her former position pending the EEOC investigation of her charge.

Excerpt from Affidavit of Earl Shannon
Page 20 of the record

I am Earl Shannon, and I am the sole owner and manager of Shannon Development Company. My company has branch offices in four states and employs more than 150 persons. Clarence Dudley was a supervisor in my design department for six years, and he had always performed satisfactorily. I was unaware of the situation between Monge and Dudley until February 20, 1979, when Monge informed me of the true reasons for her resignation. At that point I questioned Dudley and promptly fired him when he confirmed Monge's story. My purpose in firing Dudley was to make an example of him. I refuse to tolerate such immoral activity in my company.

Excerpt from Affidavit of Earl Shannon (cont.)
Page 21 of the record

Since her discharge I have written a letter to Monge informing her of my deep regret over the incident and her treatment by Dudley. Also, when Monge approached me and informed me of her hardships, at two consecutive times, I offered to rehire her, but she would have had to start at a lower position than her previous one. I cannot reinstate her to her previous position because that position has been filled by a new employee, and it would be unfair to discharge that employee.

Excerpt from Deposition of Clarence Dudley
Page 42 of the record
Q: Do you admit that you committed the acts of harassment that plaintiff enumerated in Count 5 of plaintiff's complaint?
A: I don't think it was harassment but I did them, yes.
Q: If it was not harassment, how would you classify such actions?
A: Mostly, I was just joking around and sometimes I was honestly showing my appreciation. For example, when I touched her and called her my little girl, it happened like this: She would do a good job for me on something. I would pat her on the shoulder to show my appreciation for her good work. And I did call her "my little girl," but there again, it was just a way of showing my appreciation.
Q: Did you always treat her like this?
A: No.
Q: Why did you treat her like this after September of 1978?
A: I guess I was just hurt and angry.
Q: Why? Could you explain this further?
A: Well, when Monge came to work we really hit it off, if you know what I mean. We started dating and things got serious between us. We became very intimate and we even talked of marriage. I was going to divorce my wife, of course, when all this was going on. Then all of a sudden, in September, she told me she wanted to break the relationship off. I felt hurt and used.

Trial Court Order
Page 50 of the record
This action was heard on the Defendant's motion to dismiss for want of subject matter jurisdiction. The parties filed documents in support of and in opposition to the motion.
The court being fully advised, it is
ORDERED that the motion be granted, and Plaintiff's Complaint be and hereby is dismissed.

Excerpt from Trial Court Memorandum Opinion
Page 52 of the record
A litigant filing suit based on Title VII must first follow certain procedures. Specifically, the litigant must present a "right to sue" letter to the court or satisfy the court that 180 days have expired since the filing of the charge with the Equal Employment Opportunity Commission. A federal district court lacks subject matter jurisdiction unless one of these prerequisites is satisfied. Plaintiff has shown neither in this case. The waiting period was imposed by Congress and serves the beneficial function of resolving many claims of discrimination outside of court. This

conciliation process must be protected. Therefore, this court refuses to allow a litigant to circumvent the statutory requirements.

The following federal court of appeals opinion is from this circuit:

Knowles v. Armond Tool & Die Co. (1978)

Appellant Sheila Knowles worked as a press operator in appellee's plant for more than five years. Since she began her employment in January 1972, she was continuously paid one dollar less per hour than the male employees with the same seniority who were doing the same work. She complained several times to the management that she should be paid the same wage, and these complaints eventually led to her discharge on April 18, 1977. She filed a sex discrimination complaint pursuant to Title VII of the Civil Rights Act of 1964 with the Equal Employment Opportunity Commisssion (EEOC) on April 30, 1977. On May 30, she wrote the EEOC inquiring about the status of her case. The Commission informed her that because it was backlogged it could not process her claim for at least six months. The company refused to reinstate her to her former position or give her any job at all, saying that she was a "liberal and a troublemaker" and that "we don't want this kind of person working for us." She is married and is the only source of support for her husband, who has been unemployed for two years. Appellant filed suit on June 9, 1977, seeking an injunction reinstating her to her former position. The district court dismissed the case for lack of subject matter jurisdiction. We reverse.

Title VII of the Civil Rights Act of 1964 forbids employers to discriminate against employees on the basis of sex. A Title VII plaintiff must normally satisfy the procedural provisions of the Act to be heard in federal court. First, the person must file a charge with the EEOC. Second, the complainant must receive a "right to sue" letter from the EEOC or permit 180 days to elapse from the filing of the charge. Although the Congressional purpose of encouraging conciliation must be respected, it makes little sense to force a complainant to wait 180 days when the EEOC has indicated it will not attempt conciliation prior to the expiration of that period. This is especially true where, as here, it appears unlikely that the parties will voluntarily resolve their differences. In such situations, no Congressional policy will be undermined by allowing the suit to proceed. In fact, a valuable Congressional purpose—elimination of invidious discrimination based on sex—will be preserved. In this case, the company refused to attempt negotiation or other resolution of the problem. A district court has implied jurisdiction in such situations to issue a preliminary injunction ordering reinstatement of plaintiff and preserving the status quo pending the EEOC investigation of the matter. Reversed.

The following rules should help you draft the Statement of Facts for a brief:

1. Describe the Facts from Your Client's Point of View

The old adage that there are two sides to every story assumes a new meaning in advocacy. Show the court how your client saw the events unfolding and describe them in a way that generates sympathy for your client's position. This does not mean that you omit all facts except those that favor your client's side. Rather, your factual statement should place the court in your client's shoes and influence the court to see and respond to the situation as your client did.

In the Monge case, your factual statement should emphasize the injustice of her situation and her innocence of any responsibility in the matter. By so characterizing the situation, you will make it easier for the court to decide the case in her favor. You might start by highlighting her early promotions with the company. Then you would describe how intolerable her working conditions had become, placing the supervisor and the company in as poor a light as possible. After showing that Monge was forced to resign because of her supervisor's behavior, you should show that she is suffering extreme hardship as a result of the company's actions. You should state that she has unsuccessfully tried to find other work, has exhausted her savings, and has two small children to support. Your statement should also convey the idea that it would be insulting for her to accept a lesser position with the same company. This is the way Monge sees it, and this is how the court should see it.

2. Vividly Describe Favorable Emotional Facts and Neutralize Your Opponent's Emotional Facts

Emotional facts that favor your client's position are valuable persuasive tools when used effectively. The more vividly you describe these facts, the more likely it is that a court will be sympathetic to your client's position. At the same time, however, you cannot ignore hostile emotional facts without undermining your credibility, since the other side is sure to raise them. In addition, by raising unfavorable facts in your statement, you can blunt their force. You can bleach hostile facts of their color by summarizing, explaining, paraphrasing, or otherwise minimizing them.

In Monge's case, you should describe all the facts relating to Monge's suffering and the conditions that prompted her resignation exactly as they occurred. Be as detailed and graphic as space will allow. Summarizing favorable facts will diminish the persuasive value of your statement. On the other hand, the facts regarding Shannon's reasons for firing Dudley and Monge's relationship with Dudley should be stated blandly. You should be honest and indicate that Monge and Dudley had a social relationship, for example, but you need not and should not provide the details. While you should raise hostile emotional facts, you have no obligation to make your opponent's emotional appeals.

3. Organize Your Statement to Emphasize Favorable Facts and De-Emphasize Unfavorable Facts

You should, of course, never omit or distort legally significant facts, whether they help or hurt your position. You should also never totally ignore hostile emotional facts. You can, however, emphasize, de-emphasize, and shade facts by properly arranging them in the Statement of Facts. This rule differs from the previous one in that it concerns location rather than description of specific facts, and is particularly important when your case involves few emotionally favorable facts.

You should begin and end the Statement of Facts with favorable facts, and locate unfavorable facts in the middle. The most helpful facts are often those that tend to show just how wrong the other party's actions were, how correct your client's actions were, and the significant consequences of these actions for your client. Placing these facts at the beginning will immediately invoke the court's sympathy for your client. Facts that explain, mitigate, or justify actions by your client are often, but not always, appropriate at the end of the statement. This location minimizes the force of previously stated unfavorable facts and ends the statement on a more favorable note. Placing unfavorable facts in the middle of the statement insures that they will get less of the reader's attention. Another way to minimize unfavorable facts is to place them next to facts that favor or explain your client's position, or to hide them in a group of favorable facts. Background facts should be located to enhance the persuasive quality of your factual statement when possible, but they should never be located where they detract from its persuasive value.

Be careful that in your zeal to give facts appropriate emphasis you do not make your statement nonsensical or hard to follow. Your first priority is to tell a story the reader can understand.

In Monge's case, you should begin with facts that show the degree of sexual harassment to which she was subjected. By showing how severe and inexcusable the harassment was, you place her supervisor and her employer in as poor a light as possible. Only then should you indicate that Monge had been involved with her supervisor in a nonprofessional capacity. By placing the facts of the discrimination first, you have minimized any importance the court might place on the fact that she had had an affair with her supervisor. In the same vein, you should emphasize that Monge had sought and been denied a reinstatement to her former position. After you have revealed this fact, you should state the facts showing that Shannon had investigated the discriminatory treatment, fired Dudley, written Monge an apology, and twice offered her another position. All of these facts are legally relevant under the *Knowles* case because they tend to show that Monge and Shannon might have reconciled their differences. These facts also tend to place Shannon in a favorable light, and you should make sure that the court sees these facts only in the shadow of the company's refusal to reinstate Monge.

You can further minimize Shannon's honest-appearing intentions by stating that Monge is the sole supporter of two children, that she has been unable to find other work, and that she has exhausted her savings. This will end your statement on a note of sympathy for Monge and minimize Shannon's conciliatory actions by hiding these facts between two blocks of favorable facts. Place the necessary background facts about the Shannon Company after describing Shannon's refusal to reinstate her.

By arranging the facts in this manner you will highlight the unfair treatment and helplessness of Monge, and place the company and Dudley in an unfavorable light. A persuasive factual statement is especially important in Monge's case because of the questionable strength of her legal position on the conciliation issue. In *Knowles,* the lack of effort to resolve the matter was much greater than it was here.

* * * * *

Now that you have seen the techniques for drafting a persuasive statement, examine the following:

ANSWER A: The appellant, Iris Monge, accepted a position with appellee Shannon Development Company in August 1977. On January 30, 1979, she was forced to resign because of sexual harassment by her supervisor, Clarence Dudley (R. 6). Dudley made obscene jokes and crude comments about personal parts of appellant's anatomy to other male employees in appellant's presence. In addition, he often implied or suggested to others that he had engaged in sexual relations with appellant, frequently touched appellant, and called appellant "my little girl." He also repeatedly asked her to have sexual relations with him during the lunch hour. This situation, which was prompted by appellant's refusal to continue seeing her supervisor socially, led to her resignation (R. 6, 42). Appellant's work had always been satisfactory; in one year she had advanced from a Class IV to a Class II Secretary (R. 6).

On January 15, 1979, appellant filed a charge with the Equal Employment Opportunity Commission (EEOC) alleging a violation of Title VII of the Civil Rights Act of 1964 due to her supervisor's sexual harassment of her at her job. On March 1, 1979, appellant contacted the EEOC and was informed that her charge would not be processed until November 1979 (R. 8). Appellant twice asked appellee to reinstate her to her former position. Shannon refused to reinstate her, although he apologized for Dudley's actions. Appellee claimed that appellant's former position was filled and offered appellant a lower position at a lower rate of pay, which she refused (R. 8, 20-21). Earl Shannon is the sole owner of the Shannon Development Company, which has offices in four states and employs more than 150 people. Dudley was fired after Shannon learned of his activities (R.20).

Appellant, who is divorced and the sole provider for two children, is in dire financial straits. She has been unable to locate work. She has tried unsuccessfully to obtain credit, and she has exhausted her meager savings (R. 8). She filed suit in federal district court on March 15, 1979, alleging a violation of Title VII and seeking a preliminary injunction ordering Shannon to reinstate her to her former position pending the EEOC determination of her charge (R. 8). The court held that it lacked jurisdiction and dismissed the case (R. 50). The court stated that a litigant must receive a "right to sue" letter or wait 180 days before filing suit for the court to have jurisdiction. Since Monge had satisfied neither requirement, the court concluded that the case must be dismissed. The court reasoned that the conciliation process should be protected and refused to make any exception (R. 52). Plaintiff appealed to this Court.

ANSWER B: The appellant, Iris Monge, accepted a position with the Shannon Development Company in August 1977. Her supervisor was consistently satisfied with her work and she advanced from a Class IV to a Class II secretary in a very short period of time. Shannon Development Company has offices in four states and employs more than 150 people. Earl Shannon is the sole owner of the company. Monge filed a complaint on January 15, 1979, with the Equal Opportunity Employment Commission (EEOC), alleging sexual harassment on the part of her employer. She resigned from her job on January 30, 1979, because she could no longer tolerate the situation as it existed. Her supervisor was subjecting her to verbal and physical abuse. Monge is currently in a precarious financial position. She twice requested reinstatement to her former position and both times Shannon refused her request. He offered her a lesser position, but she refused. After learning of Dudley's harassment of Monge, Shannon fired him to make an example of him because Shannon stated he would not tolerate such immoral activity in his company. He also wrote a letter of apology to appellant expressing his sympathies for Dudley's abuse of appellant.

Monge contacted the EEOC in February to ask what was happening on her charge and was informed that it would not be processed until November. Monge filed suit in federal district court on March 15, 1979, alleging a violation of Title VII, and seeking a preliminary injunction ordering Shannon to reinstate her to her former position pending the

EEOC determination of her charge. The court held that it lacked jurisdiction and dismissed the case.

Answer A is the better of the two answers. It relates Monge's story from her perspective in a concise and understandable manner, and it shows where these facts are located in the record. Answer A highlights the extent of discrimination by vividly relating the facts of Monge's treatment, and closes on a note of sympathy by describing Monge's desperate financial position. In addition, it neutralizes the legally significant and emotional facts that favor Shannon. The legally significant facts are neutralized by their placement in the center of the statement, immediately after the facts concerning the discrimination and Shannon's refusal to reinstate Monge, and immediately before the facts of Monge's financial condition. The force of the emotional facts favoring Shannon's position, such as Monge's relationship with Dudley, is weakened by the bland description. Shannon's desire to eliminate immoral activity in the company and the reasons for his discharge of Dudley are not detailed. Answer A, in short, has utilized the three rules of perspective, description, and organization to make a forceful and persuasive factual statement.

Answer B, on the other hand, is not persuasive at all. Several introductory sentences contain unimportant background facts instead of facts that favor Monge's position. In addition, Answer B concludes by showing the sincerity of Shannon's efforts to correct the problem. Facts that show the severity of sexual discrimination and Monge's destitute financial position are summarized and, therefore, used ineffectively. On the other hand, the facts showing Shannon's willingness to remedy the problem are described in detail, tending to place Shannon in a more favorable light. In addition to other deficiencies, the answer contains no citations to the record and fails to completely relate the procedural facts. Answer B is a poor example of how factual statements should be drafted.

The following exercises should help you write a persuasive Statement of Facts for a brief.

Exercise 15-A

Ellen Brummer is appealing a trial court decision refusing to declare a release and settlement agreement executed between herself and Ivan Pearce to be void. The following information is extracted from the transcript of the record.

Direct Examination of Ellen Brummer
Page 41 of the record
Q: Could you refresh the court's memory about how this got started?
A: Sure. About two years ago, now, April 14, 1978, my daughter, Nancy, was hurt

in a car accident. She was five at the time and already a very good violin player. Her tutor said that with normal development she might be able to play for a major symphony orchestra. Mr. Pearce's car collided with the one I was driving, and Nancy was thrown against the back of the front seat. She was sitting in the back seat. Her face was severely lacerated, and the doctor said there was a chip fracture in her nasal bones. Well, we were able to settle with Mr. Pearce and his insurance company shortly after we filed a lawsuit. The agreement was for about $7,500, which we thought was the extent of her injuries.

Q: Then what happened?

A: We settled on August 18, 1978. Then in October, the 14th, we had another doctor, Dr. Dion, perform an electroencephalogram on her. He said she had severe brain damage. We didn't know that when we signed the settlement.

Cross Examination of Ellen Brummer
Page 45 of the record

Q: Did you read the settlement before you signed it?

A: Yes.

Q: You read it so that you would know what you were signing, is that correct?

A: Yes.

Q: Didn't you think you understood the settlement when you signed it?

A: Well, I thought so at the time, but I didn't think much about it.

Direct Examination of Dr. Francis Dion
Pages 56-57 of the record

Q: Could you describe what you found from your tests?

A: Well, to summarize, Nancy is suffering from a post traumatic seizure disorder. Her brain was physically damaged in the accident. I will probably be able to control the disorder, but there is no question in my mind that she will require the care of physicians for her seizures for her entire life. I might add that she has impaired reading and hand-eye coordination, and will require special help for her education.

Cross Examination of Dr. Francis Dion
Page 63 of the record

Q: An electroencephalogram taken immediately after the accident would have disclosed this abnormality, would it not?

A: I think there is a reasonable medical probability of that, yes.

Release and Settlement Agreement between Ellen Brummer and Ivan Pearce
Page 88 of the record

FOR THE SOLE CONSIDERATION of Seven Thousand Five Hundred and 00/100 Dollars ($7,500.00), the receipt and sufficiency whereof is hereby acknowledged, the undersigned, Ellen Brummer, individually and as a parent and natural guardian of Nancy Brummer, a minor, hereby releases and forever discharges Ivan Pearce and Ajax Insurance Company, their heirs, executors, administrators, agents and assigns, and all other persons, firms or corporations liable or who might be liable, none of whom admit liability but all expressly deny any liability, from any and all claims, demands, damages, actions, causes of action, or suits of whatsoever kind or nature, and particularly on account of loss or damage to the property and on account of bodily injuries, known and unknown, and which have resulted or may in the future develop, sustained by Nancy Brummer, a minor, or arising out of damage or loss direct or indirect sustained by the undersigned in consequence of an automobile accident occurring on April 14, 1978 . . . .

Oral Opinion of Judge Miles Maloney
Page 92 of the record

Well, I think I've heard enought to decide this matter. The briefs of counsel and the testimony of the witnesses fill out the picture pretty well. Since there is no controlling law in this state, I find the case of *Nokovich v. Myles Insurance Exchange* persuasive. That case says, in essence, that the words of a settlement agreement mean what they say. The agreement the parties signed is airtight, as near as I can tell. I sympathize with Mrs. Brummer, but she signed the agreement. Defendant's motion for a directed verdict is granted.

The following cases are from different states:

Nokovich v. Myles Insurance Exchange (1962)

Appellant signed a settlement relieving appellee of "any and all claims" that "have resulted or may in the future develop" from injuries appellant sustained when she was struck by an automobile whose driver was insured with appellee. She now claims that she intended to release only her claim under the liability section of the insurance policy and not her claim under the section concerning medical payments. The trial court disagreed with her, and we affirm.

Settlement agreements are contracts and governed by the law of contracts. Where there is clear and unambiguous language, the test is not what the parties intended the contract to mean, but what a reasonable person would have thought the language meant. The language of the settlement here plainly bars all subsequent claims, and we so hold.

Brooks v. Pingel (1941)

Appellant learned of a severe brain injury suffered by his eight-year-old son several months after he had signed a settlement agreement with appellee holding appellee "forever harmless" of any further claims arising from a fight between his son and appellee's son. This injury is so severe that appellant's son has developed a permanent paralysis on his right side. The trial court refused to void the contract on the grounds of mistake, but we reverse.

Settlements for personal injury claims are much different from normal contract matters. Appellant has shown here that neither party to the release knew about the hidden injury. This is not a case where there is lack of knowledge of unexpected consequences of a known but apparently negligible injury. The parties knew that appellant's son had been struck on the head and back, but they did not know about the brain injury. The release clause is therefore inapplicable.

1. What are the legally significant facts of this problem?

2. What other facts are emotionally favorable to Brummer?

3. What other facts are emotionally favorable to Pearce?

4. What are the important procedural facts of this case?

5. Draft a Statement of Facts for Brummer on appeal. How did you start the statement? How did you end it? How did you emphasize her favorable facts and de-emphasize those of Pearce?

6. Draft a Statement of Facts for Pearce on appeal. How did you start the statement? How did you end it? How did you emphasize his favorable facts and de-emphasize those of Brummer?

Exercise 15-B

This exercise is based on the facts and cases from Exercise 13-B on pp. 151–157.

1. What are the legally significant facts in this problem?

2. What other facts are emotionally favorable to the Wongs?

3. What other facts are emotionally favorable to PlayChem Corporation?

4. What are the important procedural facts of this case?

5. Draft a Statement of Facts for the Wongs on appeal. How did you start the statement? How did you end it? How did you emphasize their favorable facts and de-emphasize those of PlayChem Corporation?

6. Draft a Statement of Facts for PlayChem on appeal. How did you start the statement? How did you end it? How did you emphasize its favorable facts and de-emphasize those of the Wongs?

APPENDIXES

MEMORANDUM

To: Sheldon Light

From: Lynn Wright

Re: Possible objection to federal jurisdiction in Westbrook
Neighborhood Association v. Ellison Recycling, Inc.,
file no. 1417.

Date: July 7, 1980

QUESTIONS PRESENTED

I. Whether Plaintiff can assert citizen suit jurisdiction for
violation of the Federal Clean Air Act, which requires that 60
days' advance notice be given to Defendant before a suit may be
filed, when Plaintiff files suit after providing only 37 days'
notice and when Defendant took some corrective action but indicated that further corrective action was unlikely until after
the notice period expired?

II. Whether Plaintiff can assert federal question jurisdiction
for violation of the Federal Clean Air Act when Plaintiff has met
all the requirements for federal question jurisdiction and the
Act states that it does not restrict any right a person may have
under any statute or common law, even though permitting such jurisdiction allows Plaintiff to avoid the 60-day notice requirement
of the Act?

BRIEF ANSWERS

I. No. Plaintiff's failure to comply with the 60-day notice
requirement is fatal to citizen suit jurisdiction. An exception
to this rule, permitting jurisdiction where defendant says it
will take no corrective action, is inapplicable because defendant indicated it was taking corrective action.

II. Probably yes. Plaintiff has satisfied the statutory requirements for federal question jurisdiction, and the citizen
suit provision expressly permits the assertion of other jurisdictional bases for citizen enforcement suits.

<u>STATEMENT OF FACTS</u>

Ellison Recycling, Inc. (Ellison) began operating its oil
recycling plant on the outskirts of Westbrook on April 14, 1980.
On April 15, a number of local residents began complaining of
intermittent but strong odors from the plant's emissions. Many
of these people are members of the Westbrook Neighborhood Association, an organization of residents and landowners in the Westbrook area. On the same day, the Association wrote Ellison and
the Superior Air Resources Board asking for corrective measures.

The Board responded to the Association's request by stating
that the plant's emissions were not regulated by the Superior
State Implementation Plan (SIP) under the Federal Clean Air Act
except for the opacity limitation in section 33.1301 of the
State Administrative Code. That section prohibits the discharge
of visible atmospheric contaminants with a density of more than
20 percent opacity for more than three minutes in any twenty-
four hour period. Opacity measures the darkness of smoke or
emissions from a polluting source. Ellison did not respond to
the Association's letter.

On May 20, 1980, the Association notified Ellison, the
Board, and the United States Environmental Protection Agency
(EPA), that it intended to file suit against Ellison within 60
days (July 19) unless Ellison complied with the opacity limitation. On June 22, Ellison wrote the Association, stating that it
had recently hired a consultant to conduct a national search of
air pollution control technologies available to oil recycling
plants. Ellison said the consultant was scheduled to report back
to the company on July 15 and it would know better how to proceed

-2-

after that time. Ellison also said that air pollution from the
plant had diminished to some extent because of adjustments made
in the shakedown process for the new plant, and that it hoped
the consultant's information would help it improve on the degree of control required by the opacity regulation.

The Association filed suit in federal district court on
June 26, 1980, seeking declaratory and injunctive relief against
Ellison for violations of the opacity regulation. The Association alleged 28 violations of the regulation in April, 17 in
May, and 12 to the date suit was filed, and claimed that several
of its members were damaged in excess of $10,000 each by emis-
sions from the plant. The Association bases jurisdiction on the
citizen suit provision of the Federal Clean Air Act and on
federal question jurisdiction.

DISCUSSION

I.   Whether Plaintiff can assert citizen suit jurisdiction for
violation of the Federal Clean Air Act, which requires that 60
days' advance notice be given to Defendant before a suit may be
filed, when Plaintiff files suit after providing only 37 days'
notice and when Defendant took some corrective action but indicated that further corrective action was unlikely until after
the notice period expired?

Plaintiff does not have jurisdiction under the citizen suit
provision of the Clean Air Act because it failed to provide Defendant with the required 60 days' notice before filing suit.
An alternative theory used by several courts, which permits less
than 60 days' notice in citizen suits against defendants who refuse to act during the notice period, is inapplicable here because Plaintiff filed suit while Defendant was working to correct
the problem.

The Clean Air Act, 42 U.S.C. §§7401-7626 (Supp. III 1979),
was Congress's first comprehensive attempt to prevent and control
air pollution. Section 304(a) of the Act, 42 U.S.C. §7604(a)(1)
(Supp. III 1979), permits citizens to bring actions against

-3-

industrial sources and others in violation of emission standards or limitations under the Act to obtain court-ordered compliance. Jurisdiction is proper "without regard to the amount in controversy or the citizenship of the parties." 42 U.S.C. §7604(a). Section 304(b)(1), however, limits this right by providing that "no action may be commenced" under section 304(a)(1):

> prior to 60 days after the plaintiff has given notice of the violation (i) to the [EPA] administrator, (ii) to the state in which the violation occurs, and (iii) to any alleged violator of the standard, limitation, or order.

42 U.S.C. §7604(b)(1)(A).

The language of the statute is clear; a federal district court lacks subject matter jurisdiction unless a plaintiff provides the state, the EPA, and the defendant with 60 days' advance notice before commencing suit. Strict compliance with the 60-day notice provision is mandatory since statutes must be understood in terms of their plain meaning. E.g., Tennessee Valley Authority v. Hill, 437 U.S. 153 (1978). The legislative history also supports this interpretation. The conference report for the 1970 Clean Air Act Amendments, in which section 304 was added to the Act, stated that a citizen suit plaintiff "must have provided the violator, the Administrator and the State with sixty days' notice" before filing suit. H.R. Rep. No. 1783, 91st Cong., 2d Sess. 56 (1970)(emphasis added).

A number of courts have required strict compliance with the 60-day notice requirement. The leading case is City of Highland Park v. Train, 519 F.2d 681 (7th Cir. 1975), cert. denied, 424 U.S. 927 (1976). In Highland Park, plaintiffs sought to have the EPA promulgate indirect source and significant deterioration regulations under the Clean Air Act in an attempt to preclude construction of a shopping mall and attendant road expansion. The district court dismissed plaintiff's section 304 jurisdictional claim because plaintiffs had provided defendant with no notice whatsoever. The court of appeals affirmed, reasoning that Con-

-4-

gress's intent in enacting section 304 would be frustrated if it were ignored.

Similarly, the court in <u>Loveladies Property Owners Association v. Raab</u>, 430 F. Supp. 276 (D.N.J. 1975), <u>aff'd</u>, 547 F.2d 1162 (3d Cir. 1976), <u>cert. denied</u>, 432 U.S. 906 (1977), required strict compliance with the 60-day notice provision in the Federal Water Pollution Control Act (FWPCA), 33 U.S.C. §§1251-1376 (1976 & Supp. III 1979). (The FWPCA citizen suit provision is similar in all material respects to the one in the Clean Air Act.) In that case, property owners sued Raab and the United States to prevent landfilling by Raab on the edge of a bay. Plaintiffs later amended their complaint by naming EPA and certain EPA officials, among other persons, as additional defendants. Although plaintiffs notified the EPA regional administrator more than 60 days before filing this amended complaint, the court held that their failure to provide notice before filing suit was fatal to the citizen suit claim. The court reasoned that since courts are not free to ignore statutory language, jurisdiction depends on strict adherence to the notice provision.

Although the courts in these and similar cases requiring strict compliance emphasized the need to abide by statutory language, they based their decisions on several important policy considerations. First, the full notice period provides an opportunity for out-of-court settlements of disputes and thus lessens the likelihood of lawsuits that will add to the burden of the courts. <u>City of Highland Park v. Train</u>, 519 F.2d at 690-91. Second, the notice period allows government lawyers to better integrate the concerns identified in the lawsuit into their overall enforcement efforts. <u>Id</u>. at 690. Third, jurisdictional provisions permitting suits against the government abrogate the traditional doctrine of sovereign immunity and should be strictly construed. <u>West Penn Power Co. v. Train</u>, 378 F. Supp. 941 (W.D. Penn. 1974).

Although the factual pattern and policies relevant to West-

brook's case differ somewhat from the cases cited, there is ample
support for requiring strict compliance with the 60-day notice
provision here. The Association sent its notice of intent to sue
on May 20, 1980, but brought suit only 37 days later on June 26,
1980. The statutory language requiring 60 days' notice and the
policy of encouraging out-of-court settlements are thus compelling
reasons to deny citizen suit jurisdiction. By bringing an early
suit, the Association precluded any possibility of resolving the
problem without litigation. The other policy concerns of inte-
grating citizen enforcement suits into the government enforcement
scheme and of sovereign immunity, however, are inapplicable to
the present case since those concerns are only applicable to governmental defendants and Ellison is a private party.

In response to the perceived rigidity of the strict compliance approach, several courts have permitted citizen suit jurisdiction where the plaintiff has "substantially complied" with the
60-day notice requirement. These courts have reasoned that there
is no point in waiting the full 60 days when the defendant responds prior to the end of the period that he plans to take no
action on the notice. Natural Resources Defense Council v. Callaway, 524 F.2d 79 (2d Cir. 1975); Massachusetts v. United States
Veterans Administration, 541 F.2d 119 (1st Cir. 1976). Although
these cases are inconsistent with the strict compliance approach,
their insistence that section 304 must be interpreted in light of
its remedial purposes may have great force, particularly for a
citizens' organization claiming exposure to pollution. These
cases, however, are inapplicable here due to the particular facts
of Westbrook's situation.

In Callaway, plaintiffs brought a citizen suit to enjoin the
use of an ocean disposal site for dredge materials. The district
court dismissed the suit because plaintiffs had provided only 48
days' notice. The court of appeals reversed, holding that strict
compliance was not required where the EPA and other agencies are
given notice of the alleged violations, and the defendant informs

the plaintiff prior to the commencement of the suit that no action will be taken. The court reasoned that the purpose of the
notice provision had been served since waiting longer would have
been futile. 524 F.2d at 84 n.4. See also Conservation Society
of Southern Vermont v. Secretary of Transportation, 508 F.2d 927,
938 n.62 (2d Cir. 1974), vacated on other grounds, 423 U.S. 809
(1975) (dicta concerning the district court's strict, and therefore "crabbed construction," of the 60-day notice provision).

The court in Veterans Administration reached a different
conclusion because plaintiff had not stated a "prima facie-claim
of futility" sufficient to justify jurisdiction after only 40
days' notice. 541 F.2d at 121-22. Plaintiff in that case alleged that a veterans hospital had violated the FWPCA by failing
to comply with a timetable for tying into a municipal sewage system. Although plaintiff claimed that notice would not cure past
violations of the permit condition, the court of appeals affirmed
the dismissal of the citizen suit. The court reasoned,"even conceding that no administrative action could cure the failure of
the VA to meet past deadlines for planning and construction of
the sewer tie-in, increased administrative attention could still
expedite completion of the project." Id. at 121. The court suggested that the substantial compliance theory is inapplicable if
it is possible that some administrative action "could" correct
the problem. Id.

The Westbrook Association did not substantially comply with
the 60-day notice requirement because Ellison was taking corrective action, and so informed Plaintiff prior to the end of the
notice period. This case is thus similar to Veterans Administration because "increased administrative attention" seems to be resolving the problem. Plaintiff's complaint alleged a significant
but diminishing number of opacity violations following the start-
up of the plant--28 in April, 17 in May, and only 12 in the first
25 days of June. Defendant's consultant was to examine different
control technologies and report back by July 15, four days before

the end of the notice period. Although significant work remained after that period, and it is not clear whether anything would be done, Ellison said it was correcting the problem. Even if that response can be considered ambiguous, the Veterans Administration case precludes substantial compliance where there is a possibility of further corrective measures. Westbrook's situation, therefore, is a far different case from the "no action" reply considered in Callaway because Ellison documented its progress and indicated its plans to abate the problem.

The most compelling argument for applying the substantial compliance approach in Westbrook's case focuses on Defendant's continuing violations and the injunctive relief Plaintiff seeks. This argument, however, does not change the conclusion that there is no legitimate claim of futility here. In Callaway, where the court found substantial compliance, plaintiffs sought to enjoin the use of certain ocean dump sites. In Veterans Administration, where the court found no substantial compliance, plaintiff sought fines for a past failure to comply with the law, rather than injunctive relief against continuing violations. But since section 304 conditions a citizen's ability to obtain court-ordered compliance on adherence to the notice procedure, the absence of futility is controlling.

A third theory for jurisdiction under section 304, constructive compliance, can be discredited but not distinguished from Westbrook's case. Although the cases use the terms constructive compliance and substantial compliance interchangeably, constructive compliance here refers to an approach permitting jurisdiction if 60 days pass between the time notice is given and the time of the court's first hearing on the lawsuit.

The only case that has used constructive compliance is City of Riverside v. Ruckelshaus, 4 E.R.C. 1728 (C.D. Cal. 1972). In that case plaintiffs filed suit to force the EPA to promulgate an air pollution control plan for part of California. Plaintiffs provided no advance notice under section 304. The court refused

to dismiss the case since 60 days had passed between the date
suit was filed and the time the court completed its hearing on
plaintiff's request for an injunction. The court reasoned that
the lapse of these 60 days was sufficient for purposes of section 304 because the EPA had the beneficial effect of the 60-day
notice provision during that period. 4 E.R.C. at 1731.

Constructive compliance would, if applied, permit jurisdiction in Westbrook's case since in all likelihood more than 60
days will have elapsed between the May 20 notice and the court's
first hearing. The court is unlikely to apply this theory, however, due to its weak legal basis. Constructive compliance
abrogates the language in section 304(b) that "no action may be
commenced" before plaintiff has provided 60 days' notice. It
also removes the notice provision from the Act since almost any
imaginative plaintiff would obtain 60 days of notice before the
court's first hearing. Constructive compliance, therefore, is
not a valid basis for citizen suit jurisdiction.

II.   Whether Plaintiff can assert federal question jurisdiction
for violation of the Federal Clean Air Act when Plaintiff has
met all the requirements for federal question jurisdiction and
the Act states that it does not restrict any right a person
may have under any statute or common law, even though permitting
such jurisdiction allows Plaintiff to avoid the 60-day notice
requirement of the Act?

The court probably has federal question jurisdiction over
Westbrook's case. Plaintiff has met the statutory requirements
for federal question jurisdiction, and the Clean Air Act and the
better reasoned cases permit the assertion of such jurisdiction,
although there is significant authority to the contrary.

Section 1331(a) of the Judicial Code, 28 U.S.C. §1331(a)
(1976), provides that the federal district courts have jurisdiction over civil actions against private parties where the matter
in controversy exceeds $10,000 and the action arises under
federal law. Plaintiff has satisfied both requirements. Specific members of Plaintiff Association have alleged damages in

excess of $10,000 each from Defendant's emissions. The matter
also arises under federal law because the Clean Air Act requires
state SIPs to be federally approved and enforceable. <u>Citizens
Association v. Washington</u>, 383 F. Supp. 136 (D.D.C. 1974).

The savings clause of the citizen suit provision, section
304(e) of the Clean Air Act, 42 U.S.C. §7604(e) (Supp. III 1979),
expressly permits citizen suit plaintiffs to allege other bases
of jurisdiction:

> Nothing in this section shall restrict any right
> which any person (or class of persons) may have
> under any statute or common law to seek enforcement
> of any emission standard or limitation or to seek
> any other relief (including relief against the
> Administrator or a state agency).

The court in <u>Natural Resources Defense Council v. Train</u>,
510 F.2d 692 (D.C. Cir. 1975), construed a comparable savings
provision in the Federal Water Pollution Control Act (FWPCA), 33
U.S.C. §§1251-1376 (1976 & Supp. III 1979), to permit jurisdiction under section 1331(a) even when plaintiffs had provided no
advance notice of the suit. In <u>Train</u>, plaintiffs filed suit
against the EPA to force it to publish effluent guidelines for
specific categories and classes of point sources. Jurisdiction
was based on section 1331(a). The EPA argued that the court
lacked jurisdiction because suits to compel the EPA to perform a
nondiscretionary duty can only be brought under the citizen suit
provision of the FWPCA. The court rejected this argument and
permitted jurisdiction, reasoning that the citizen suit provision
does not restrict federal court jurisdiction over actions that
could have been maintained even in the absence of that special
authorization. 510 F.2d at 702. The court viewed the savings
clause as confirming that interpretation.

The court in <u>National Sea Clammers Association v. City of
New York</u>, 616 F.2d 1222 (3d Cir. 1980), similarly concluded that
the citizen suit provision of the FWPCA was intended to expand
rather than restrict the rights of injured parties to bring actions. Plaintiffs in that case, who made their living harvesting

fish and shellfish, sought injunctive and other relief against
the discharge of untreated sewage and toxic wastes. The district court dismissed plaintiff's FWPCA claim because they had
not provided adequate notice under the citizen suit provision of
that Act. The court of appeals reversed, holding that plaintiffs
could proceed under section 1331(a). The court reasoned that
the citizen suit provision was particularly intended for persons
who could not meet the existing jurisdictional requirements but
who still had legitimate grounds for an enforcement action. The
court concluded that persons who could previously bring an action
under section 1331(a) now have the option of suing under section
304, but persons who could not previously obtain jurisdiction
may sue only under section 304.

In Westbrook's case, the court probably has federal question jurisdiction even if it does not have jurisdiction under
section 304. Since section 304 was intended to expand the possible jurisdictional bases for citizen lawsuits to enforce the Act
while leaving existing jurisdictional bases intact, Plaintiff's
failure to provide adequate notice is relevant only to the
section 304 claim. Plaintiff, therefore, should be able to proceed under section 1331(a).

There is, however, significant authority to support the
contrary position that Plaintiff's failure to provide adequate
notice precludes jurisdiction under any other statute. The leading case is City of Highland Park v. Train, 519 F.2d 681 (7th
Cir. 1975), cert. denied, 424 U.S. 927 (1976). In Highland Park,
plaintiffs filed suit to have the EPA promulgate indirect source
and significant deterioration regulations under the Clean Air
Act in an attempt to prevent construction of a shopping mall and
attendant road expansion. Plaintiffs based jurisdiction on section 304 and on federal question jurisdiction. The court held
that since the plaintiffs had provided no notice whatsoever it
could not exercise jurisdiction under either section 304 or
section 1331(a). The court reasoned, "the savings provision,

-11-

expressing the general intention of Congress not to disturb
existing rights to seek relief, does not have the affirmative
effect of removing conditions which existing law imposes upon
the exercise of those rights." Id. at 693. The court further
reasoned that since section 304 was an adequate jurisdictional
basis for plaintiffs' claim, they were required to use that and
nothing else.

Although the Highland Park court's reasoning is not without
force, it fails to read section 304(e) for its plain meaning.
The court's analysis imposes a 60-day notice requirement on section 1331(a) in Clean Air Act cases, even though section 304(e)
expressly preserves "any right" that a person may have under
"any statute." The right to bring suit under section 1331(a) as
it is written must be considered one of those rights. In addition, there does not appear to be a valid basis for making section 304 the exclusive jurisdictional basis for Clean Air Act
suits when it provides to the contrary by its own terms. The
court in Westbrook's case, therefore, will probably reject the
Highland Park reasoning and exercise jurisdiction over Plaintiff's Clean Air Act claim under section 1331(a).

CONCLUSION

The court does not have citizen suit jurisdiction but it
probably does have federal question jurisdiction. The Clean Air
Act requires that a plaintiff in a citizen enforcement suit must
provide the defendant with 60 days' notice before filing suit.
Plaintiff in the present case failed to meet the 60-day requirement because it provided only 37 days' notice. The substantial
compliance exception to this requirement, which applies when a
defendant responds to the notice by stating it will take no further action prior to the end of the notice period, is inapplicable here. Defendant responded to the notice by stating it was
taking corrective action and would continue to do so before the

end of the period. A second exception, constructive compliance, will most likely be rejected by the court. This little-used theory permitting notice after suit is filed is of questionable legal validity because it effectively renders the notice period meaningless in most cases.

The court, however, probably has federal question jurisdiction over Plaintiff's suit. Plaintiff has met the statutory requirements for federal question jurisdiction because the amount in controversy exceeds $10,000, and the claim arises under federal law. In addition, such jurisdiction is a permissible alternative to citizen suit jurisdiction. The better reasoned cases have concluded that the citizen suit provision was intended to expand rather than restrict the existing bases of federal jurisdiction over suits to enforce the Act. This interpretation is confirmed by the savings clause in the Act which preserves any right a person may have under any other statute. Plaintiff's failure to provide the requisite 60-day notice is thus irrelevant to federal question jurisdiction.

IN THE UNITED STATES
COURT OF APPEALS FOR THE
THIRTEENTH CIRCUIT

No. 80-152

WESTBROOK NEIGHBORHOOD ASSOCIATION,

Appellant,

v.

ELLISON RECYCLING, INC.,

Appellee.

ON APPEAL FROM THE
UNITED STATES DISTRICT COURT
FOR THE DISTRICT OF SUPERIOR

BRIEF FOR APPELLANT

Truman LaFoote
Wayne State University
Law School
Detroit, Michigan 48202

INDEX

AUTHORITIES CITED

OPINIONS BELOW

The opinion of the United States District Court for the District of Superior is unreported, and contained in the Transcript of Record (R. 22-25).

JURISDICTION

The judgment of the United States District Court for the District of Superior was entered on August 8, 1980. The appeal was filed on August 20, 1980 and was granted on December 1, 1980. The jurisdiction of this court is invoked under 28 U.S.C. § 1291.

STATUTES INVOLVED

The texts of the following statutes relevant to the determination of the present case are set forth in the Appendix: Federal Clean Air Act, §§ 304(a), 304(a)(1), 304(b)(1), 304(e), 42 U.S.C. §§ 7604(a), 7604(a)(1), 7604(b)(1), 7604(e) (Supp. III 1979); Judicial Code, 28 U.S.C. § 1331(a) (1976).

QUESTIONS PRESENTED

I.   Whether the district court erred in refusing to exercise citizen suit jurisdiction under the Clean Air Act when Appellant substantially complied with the Act's 60-day notice provision by giving notice and bringing suit only when Appellee's response indicated that waiting further would be futile?

II.   Whether the district court erred in refusing to exercise citizen suit jurisdiction under the Clean Air Act when Appellant constructively complied with the Act's 60-day notice provision because more than 60 days elapsed between the notice and the district court's first hearing on the case?

III.   Whether the district court erred in declining to exercise general federal question jurisdiction over a citizen enforcement action under the Clean Air Act when Appellant has met the requirements for federal question jurisdiction and the Act expressly states that it does not restrict any right a person may have under any statute or common law?

STATEMENT OF FACTS

The Appellant, Westbrook Neighborhood Association, is an
organization of approximately 250 members, most of whom are
residents and landowners in and around the town of Westbrook,
Superior. The Appellee, Ellison Recycling, Inc., is a corporation which has its sole plant located on the outskirts of
Westbrook (R. 1-2).

On April 15, 1980, one day after the plant commenced operation, local residents, many of them members of Appellant Association, began complaining of intermittent, noxious odors from
plant emissions. These emissions in all likelihood contain a
large number of substances with carcinogenic, mutagenic, and
toxic properties. On the same day, Appellant wrote the company
and the Superior Air Resources Board, asking them to take
measures to correct the problem. Neither the company nor the
Board responded (R. 2, 22-23).

The odors continued. On May 20, 1980, Appellant again wrote
the company, and requested that it take some action to reduce the
pollution. Appellant informed the company that unless action was
taken within 60 days a suit would be instituted against it for
violation of section 33.1301 of the Superior Administrative Code
(R. 10-12). That section prohibits any person from discharging
into the atmosphere visible contaminants with a density of more
than 20 percent opacity for more than three minutes in any 24-
hour period. Opacity measures darkness of the smoke or emissions
from a polluting source (R. 8-9). Appellant sent copies of that
letter to the Board and the United States Environmental Protection Agency (EPA) (R. 10).

The excess emissions were not abated, and Appellee's response did not come until more than one month later. On June 22,
1980, the company informed Appellant that it had recently hired
a consultant to make a survey of pollution control technology and
that it "hoped" to install control equipment that would at least
reduce emissions to comply with the regulation. The consultant,

however, was not scheduled to report back to the company until
July 15, 1980, three months after the plant had begun polluting
the air and only five days before the end of the notice period.
Although the number of violations diminished somewhat after
April because of "minor adjustments . . . in the shakedown process," the company violated the regulation on 57 separate times
between April 15 and June 25. There were 28 violations in
April, 17 in May, and 12 in the first 25 days of June. The pollution was causing extensive corrosion to buildings and automobiles in the neighborhood (R. 3). Neither the Board nor the EPA
responded to the notice (R. 10).

     Finally, on June 26, 1980, Appellant filed suit for declara-
tory and injunctive relief in federal district court, alleging
violations of the opacity regulation. Appellant predicated
jurisdiction on the citizen suit provision of the Federal Clean
Air Act, 42 U.S.C. § 7604, and on federal question jurisdiction.
28 U.S.C. § 1331(a) (R. 1-4). Several members of Appellant
Association were by that time damaged in excess of $10,000 each
by emissions from Appellee's plant (R. 3).

     The court heard argument on Appellant's motion for a pre-
liminary injunction and Appellee's motion to dismiss on July 28,
1980. The district court dismissed the complaint on August 8,
1980, holding that it did not have jurisdiction to consider the
case. The court found that Appellant complied with the requirements for content and form of notice contained in 40 C.F.R.
§ 54.1-.3 (1979). The court also found that neither the Board
nor the EPA was prosecuting the Appellee for these violations.
The court, nonetheless, refused to exercise jurisdiction under
the Clean Air Act because it concluded that Appellant had not
complied with the 60-day notice requirement of that Act. The
court also declined to exercise federal question jurisdiction
because it concluded that Congress had precluded alternative
jurisdictional bases when it enacted the citizen suit provision
of the Clean Air Act (R. 22-25). This Court granted the appeal.

SUMMARY OF ARGUMENT

The district court erred in dismissing this case for want of jurisdiction. The court had jurisdiction under section 304 of the Federal Clean Air Act, which provides jurisdiction for citizen enforcement actions against violators of the Act where the plaintiff has given 60 days' advance notice of the suit. Appellant substantially complied with the 60-day notice provision by giving notice and bringing suit only after Appellee implied that waiting longer would be futile. Appellee's response stated that a consultant would not report until several days before the end of the notice period, indicating that no action would occur before the end of the period, if at all. The purpose of the notice period, promoting out-of-court settlements where possible, was served, since waiting the entire period would have been pointless and counterproductive.

Appellant also constructively complied with the 60-day notice provision since more than 60 days elapsed between the formal notice and the date of the court's first hearing in the case. In fact, Appellant's prior complaints and requests for action, coupled with this period after formal notice, provided Appellee with more than 100 days of notice during which to correct the air pollution problem it was causing.

Finally, even if Appellant failed to comply with the 60-day notice provision, the district court erred because Appellant met the requirements of federal question jurisdiction as an independent basis for the lawsuit. Several members of Appellant Association were damaged by Appellee's emissions in excess of $10,000 each, and Appellant brought this suit under the federal Clean Air Act. Section 304 expands the opportunities of citizens to bring actions to enforce the Act because it is expressly available to plaintiffs regardless of the amount in controversy. At the same time, section 304 expressly preserves "any right" that any person may have to proceed under "any statute," thus permitting the assertion of independent jurisdictional bases.

4

Since Appellant met the requirements for federal question jurisdiction, the district court should have permitted Appellant to
seek relief on the merits.

ARGUMENT

I.   THE DISTRICT COURT ERRED IN REFUSING TO EXERCISE CITIZEN
     SUIT JURISDICTION UNDER SECTION 304 OF THE CLEAN AIR ACT.

The nation's serious efforts to prevent and control air pollution and its adverse effects on human health and the environment began with the passage of the 1970 Clean Air Act Amendments,
42 U.S.C. §§ 7401-7626 (Supp. III 1979). The basic purpose of
the Amendments, Congress stated, is "to protect and enhance the
quality of the Nation's air resources so as to promote the public
health and welfare and the productive capacity of its popula-
tion." 42 U.S.C. § 7401(b)(1) (Supp. III 1979). Congressional
concern about controlling air pollution was so great that Congress took the unprecedented step of permitting citizens to aid
in the enforcement process. This provision was necessary,
observed the late Senator Philip A. Hart, because "the Government
simply is not equipped to take court action against the numerous
violations of legislation of this type which are likely to
occur." 116 Cong. Rec. 33104 (1970).

Section 304(a) of the Act, 42 U.S.C. § 7604(a), permits "any
person" to bring a civil action against any other person alleged
to be in violation of "an emission standard or limitation under
this act." Although section 304(b) of the Act, 42 U.S.C.
§ 7604(b), provides for 60 days' advance notice to the potential
defendant, section 304 was intended to widen citizen participation in the enforcement of the Act by removing technical hind-
rances to jurisdiction. Natural Resources Defense Council v.
Train, 510 F.2d 692 (D.C. Cir. 1975). The district court's ele-
vation of form over substance is thus wholly at odds with both
the intent and language of the Act.

A. Appellant substantially complied with the 60-day notice
   provision by bringing suit only after Appellee's response indicated that corrective action was highly
   unlikely before the period expired.

Congress intended the 60-day notice provision to give
industrial polluters and governmental agencies an opportunity to
administratively resolve problems and avoid lawsuits. S. Rep.
No. 1196, 91st Cong., 2d Sess. at 37 (1970). Where the potential
defendant indicates prior to the expiration of the notice period
that it will take no action on the matter before the end of that
period, the purpose of the 60-day notice provision has been
served and plaintiff may immediately bring suit. Massachusetts
v. United States Veterans Administration, 541 F.2d 119 (1st Cir.
1976); Natural Resources Defense Council v. Callaway, 524 F.2d
79 (2d Cir. 1975).

In Callaway, plaintiffs brought suit under the Federal Water
Pollution Control Act (FWPCA), 33 U.S.C. §§ 1251-1376 (1976 &
Supp. III 1979), and the Marine Research, Protection, and Sanc-
tuaries Act, 33 U.S.C. §§ 1401-1444 (1976), seeking to enjoin the
use of an ocean disposal site for dredge materials. Both statutes have a citizen suit provision identical to section 304 in
all material respects. The district court dismissed the action
because the plaintiffs filed suit only forty-eight days after
giving notice. The court of appeals reversed, holding that the
plaintiffs had substantially complied with the notice provision.
The court reasoned that the purpose of the notice provision had
been served since the EPA and other agencies were given notice of
the alleged violations, and the defendants indicated that no
action would be taken before the suit was commenced. 524 F.2d
at 84 n.4.

Similarly, in Conservation Society of Southern Vermont, Inc.
v. Secretary of Transportation, 508 F.2d 927 (2d Cir. 1974),
vacated on other grounds, 423 U.S. 809 (1975), the court of appeals held that Congress did not intend the 60-day notice provision to erect an absolute barrier to earlier suits by private

6

citizens. The court described the district court's dismissal of a citizen suit claim for failure to comply with the notice provision as a "crabbed construction" of the provision. Id. at 938 n.72.

Appellant substantially complied with the 60-day notice provision by not bringing suit until Appellee stated, in effect, that waiting longer would be futile. Appellee responded to Appellant's May 20, 1980 notice by stating that it had hired a consultant to study technological options and that the consultant's report was due July 15. Appellee said only that it "would know better what to do" after it saw the report, indicating that Appellee would not begin to formulate options until immediately before the 60-day period expired. Although Appellee said it "hoped" to install better controls, it did not make a firm commitment to resolve its severe air pollution problem, nor did Appellee commit itself to a timetable for resolving it.

During this period, moreover, the number of opacity violations stabilized. Appellee made some progress in controlling its emissions after it violated the opacity regulation 28 times in the last half of April, but there were 17 violations in May and 12 in the first 25 days of June. Appellee's inability to further improve air quality after April 30 indicated that "the minor adjustments . . . during this shakedown process" were insufficient to meet the opacity limitation. Appellant had every reason to believe that the controls described in the consultant's report would be necessary. During this entire period, moreover, emissions from Appellee's plant were causing economic and potentially severe health injury to the members of the Association; several members alleged damage of more than $10,000 each. These emissions in all likelihood contain a large number of toxic, mutagenic, and carcinogenic substances. Appellant was amply justified in bringing suit before the 60-day period formally expired.

This is thus a very different case from Massachusetts v. Veterans Administration, 541 F.2d 119 (1st Cir. 1976), which involved a citizen suit for civil penalties to correct a past failure rather than injunctive relief to correct a continuing one. In <u>Massachusetts</u>, plaintiff brought suit after only 40 days' notice, claiming that a veterans hospital had violated a permit requirement under the FWPCA. The court affirmed the dismissal of plaintiff's claim because plaintiff had not shown that waiting the full period would be futile. Increased administrative action, the court reasoned, might resolve the problem just as quickly. In the present case, however, an injunction against the operation of Appellee's plant or even a court order expediting compliance would have resolved this problem far more quickly than administrative action. In light of Appellee's unwillingness to take significant corrective action during the notice period, Appellant had ample evidence of futility.

Cases requiring strict compliance with the 60-day notice provision are distinguishable because they usually involve plaintiffs who made no attempt whatsoever to give notice before filing suit, or special considerations applicable only to governmental defendants. In <u>City of Highland Park v. Train</u>, 519 F.2d 681 (7th Cir. 1975), <u>cert. denied</u>, 424 U.S. 927 (1976), the court of appeals affirmed the dismissal of a section 304 claim because plaintiffs gave no notice at all to the defendants. Courts have repeatedly dismissed citizen suit claims by plaintiffs who provided no notice whatsoever. <u>E.g.</u>, <u>City of Evansville v. Kentucky Liquid Recycling, Inc.</u>, 406 F.2d 1008 (7th Cir. 1979), <u>cert. denied</u>, 444 U.S. 1025 (1980); <u>Pinkney v. Ohio Environmental Protection Agency</u>, 375 F. Supp. 305 (N.D. Ohio 1974). These cases, therefore, do not require strict (as opposed to substantial) compliance at all; they merely rejected claims by plaintiffs who made no effort to obey the law. Since the Westbrook Association made an effort to comply with the law, these decisions are inapplicable to the present case.

The concerns in these cases are also inapplicable to private defendants. The court in <u>West Penn Power Co. v. Train</u>, 378

F. Supp. 941 (W.D. Penn. 1974), dismissed a citizen suit claim
by plaintiffs who failed to give any notice, relying on the
sovereign immunity principle that the terms of Congressional
consent to sue the government must be strictly construed. See
also, Smoke Rise, Inc. v. Washington Suburban Sanitary Commission, 400 F. Supp. 1364 (D. Md. 1974) (strict compliance required
by sovereign immunity). Similarly, the court in Highland Park
reasoned that the notice requirement was designed to give EPA
time to respond to complex lawsuits and minimize the interruption such lawsuits have on the ongoing regulatory process. 519
F.2d at 690. Both of these concerns are inapplicable to the
present case.

The few remaining cases requiring strict compliance, e.g.,
Loveladies Property Owners Association v. Raab, 430 F. Supp. 276
(D.N.J. 1975), aff'd, 547 F.2d 1162 (3d Cir. 1976), are inappropriate because they place technical considerations before substance in interpreting a statutory provision designed to involve
citizens in the enforcement process. The danger of elevating
form over substance in statutory interpretation was recognized at
an early date by the Supreme Court when it stated, "A thing may
be within the letter of the statute and yet not . . . within the
intention of its makers." Church of the Holy Trinity v. United
States, 143 U.S. 457, 459 (1892), cited in United Housing
Foundation, Inc. v. Forman, 421 U.S. 847, 849 (1975).

Air pollution control is more important than procedural
nicety. The undeniable effect of the district court decision is
to force members of the Appellant Association to breath and live
with obnoxious and health damaging emissions from Appellee's
plant for a longer period than they would have otherwise. Appellant could file another notice, wait 60 days, and bring suit
again, but its members would continue to suffer through an additional two months of pollution, a penalty manifestly inconsistent
with the spirit of the Clean Air Act. Appellant substantially
complied with the 60-day notice requirement, and the district

9

court should thus have heard its claim.

    B.   <u>Appellant constructively complied with the 60-day</u>
        <u>notice requirement of section 304 since 60 days elapsed</u>
        <u>between the notice and the district court's first hear-</u>
        <u>ing on the case.</u>

Even if section 304(b) rigidly requires 60 days' notice,
Appellant complied with that requirement because 60 days elapsed
between the notice and the court's first hearing. In <u>City of</u>
<u>Riverside v. Ruckleshaus</u>, 4 E.R.C. 1728 (C.D. Cal. 1972), plain-
tiffs sued the Administrator of the EPA for his failure to publish an air quality implementation plan. The court held it had
jurisdiction because 60 days passed between the filing of the
complaint and the date that the hearing on plaintiffs' request
for a preliminary injunction was complete. The court reasoned
that the EPA had the beneficial effect of the 60-day notice provision during this time. 4 E.R.C. at 1731. In <u>National Sea</u>
<u>Clammers Association v. City of New York</u>, 616 F.2d 1222, 1226
(3d Cir. 1980), the court noted that it would be permissible to
"adopt the pragmatic approach" requiring merely that 60 days
elapse prior to district court action on the complaint.

The underlying reasons for this "pragmatic approach" are
sound. First, impermissible pollution occurs throughout the inherent delay between the time when the complaint is filed and
the time when the district court takes action on it. Second,
potential defendants often receive notice of the violation long
before formal notice is sent, and thus have an early opportunity
to correct the problem. <u>Save Our Sound Fisheries Association v.</u>
<u>Callaway</u>, 429 F. Supp. 1136, 1143-44 n.11 (D.R.I. 1977). Third,
negotiation or resolution of a violation can occur as easily
after suit is filed as before.

Appellee knew on April 15 that its emissions were causing
problems and learned a short time later that it was violating
the state's opacity limitation. The district court held its
hearing on Appellant's motion for a preliminary injunction and
Appellee's motion to dismiss on July 28, 1980, 69 days after

Appellant gave notice on May 20, and about 104 days after it
first learned of the violations. Appellee thus had far more
than the 60 days provided by section 304(b) to correct its violations. To require even more time would prolong a serious
problem, discourage settlement of litigation, and encourage
industrial dischargers to ignore citizen complaints until re-
ceiving formal notices under section 304(a). Congress intended
the contrary in creating section 304.

II. THE DISTRICT COURT ERRED IN REFUSING TO EXERCISE FEDERAL
     QUESTION JURISDICTION.

   A. The amount in controversy exceeds $10,000 and arises
       under the Federal Clean Air Act.

Section 1331(a) of the Judicial Code, 28 U.S.C. § 1331(a)
(1976), provides that the federal district courts shall have
jurisdiction in civil suits against private parties where the
amount in controversy exceeds $10,000 and arises under federal
law. The district court erred in denying jurisdiction under
section 1331(a) because Appellant unmistakably met its requirements. First, Appellant Association alleged that each of the
several members were damaged in excess of $10,000 by unlawful
emissions from Appellee's plant. Second, the matter arises under
federal law because the Clean Air Act requires State Implementation Plans to be federally approved and federally enforceable.
Citizens Association v. Washington, 383 F. Supp. 136 (D.D.C.
1974). The opacity limitation is part of the Superior State
Implementation Plan under the Clean Air Act.

   B. The language and purpose of section 304 permit indepen-
       dent assertion of federal question jurisdiction for
       citizen enforcement suits under the Clean Air Act.

Whether or not Appellant complied with the 60-day notice
provision of section 304(b), the district court should have
heard its claim under section 1331(a). Section 304(e) of the
Clean Air Act expressly preserved such independent jurisdictional
bases for citizen enforcement lawsuits:

> Nothing in this section shall restrict <u>any right</u> which
> any person (or class of persons) may have under <u>any</u>
> <u>statute</u> or common law to seek enforcement of any emis-
> sion standard or limitation or to seek any other relief
> (including relief against the Administrator of a State
> agency).

42 U.S.C. § 7604(e) (Supp. III 1979) (emphasis added). Congress's intent to preserve existing bases of jurisdiction while
providing another is central to the meaning of section 304.

Section 304(a), which expressly provides for jurisdiction
without regard to the amount in controversy, was particularly
intended for those persons who could not meet the $10,000 re-
quirement of section 1331(a) but who nonetheless had a legitimate
need to bring an enforcement action. <u>National Sea Clammers</u>
<u>Association v. City of New York</u>, 616 F.2d 1222 (3d Cir. 1980).
In <u>National Sea Clammers</u>, the plaintiffs brought suit under the
FWPCA (which has a citizen suit provision similar to that in the
Clean Air Act), claiming that the defendants had adversely affected shellfish populations by improperly permitting sewage to
be dumped into the Atlantic ocean. In rejecting defendant's
claim that the citizen suit provision of the FWPCA precludes the
assertion of section 1331(a) jurisdiction, the court observed
that the "more persuasively reasoned cases" recognize that section 304(a) gives the district court jurisdiction over a new
class of plaintiffs, while section 304(e) "preserves jurisdiction over the preexisting right of injured parties to sue to
enforce the Act." 616 F.2d at 1228. Section 304(a), therefore,
expands the opportunities citizens have to participate in the
enforcement of the Federal Clean Air Act. Where there are
existing jurisdictional bases such as section 1331(a), plaintiffs
have the option of proceeding under either section 1331(a) or
section 304(a).

Similarly, the Court of Appeals for the District of Columbia
Circuit in <u>Natural Resources Defense Council v. Train</u>, 510 F.2d
692 (D.C. Cir. 1975), held that the plaintiff could bring an
action under section 1331(a) notwithstanding its failure to give

60 days' notice. The legislative history, the court said, re-
flected a deliberate choice by Congress to widen citizen access
to the courts, as a supplemental and effective assurance that
the Act would be implemented and enforced. Id. at 700. The
court further reasoned that the provisions of section 304(b)
were not intended to restrict or to curtail federal court jurisdiction over suits that would have been maintainable even in the
absence of section 304. Id. at 701. Since section 1331(a) was
such an existing jurisdictional basis, it was preserved for
Clean Air Act enforcement actions by section 304(e).

Cases to the contrary ignore this distinction and render
section 304(e) meaningless. These cases are premised largely on
a view that Congressional delineation of a judical review scheme
within a statute means the scheme should be exclusive. E.g.,
Loveladies Property Owners Association v. Raab, 430 F. Supp. 276,
281 (D.N.J. 1975), aff'd, 547 F.2d 1162 (3d Cir. 1976) (citing
Weinberger v. Salfi, 422 U.S. 749 (1975)). In Weinberger, the
Court's decision that section 1331(a) could not be asserted as a
jurisdictional base for benefit claims arising under the Social
Security Act was based on language in that Act expressly prohibiting the use of section 1331(a) for that purpose. There is
no indication, however, that Congress intended section 304 to be
the exclusive grant of jurisdiction for claims under the Clean
Air Act. Indeed, section 304(e) says the opposite.

There is also no merit to the reasoning in City of Highland
Park v. Train, 519 F.2d 681 (7th Cir. 1975), cert. denied, 424
U.S. 927 (1976), for the exclusiveness of section 304. The court
there held, in effect, that the Clean Air Act imposes the 60-day
notice provision of section 304(b) on section 1331(a). The court
stated, "the saving provision, expressing the general intention
of Congress not to disturb existing rights to seek relief, does
not have the affirmative effect of removing conditions which
existing law imposes upon the exercise of these rights." 519
F.2d at 693. The court's description of section 304 as "existing

13

law" fails to recognize that section 1331(a) existed long before
the Clean Air Act, and converts the savings clause into a power-
ful weapon to preclude other rights of relief--an interpretation
that is totally at odds with Congressional intent. It is not
necessary to remove any additional conditions from section 1331(a)
because section 304(e) prevents their imposition in the first
place.

Section 304(e) expands rather than narrows the range of
jurisdictional options available to citizen plaintiffs. Since
Appellant met the requirements of section 1331(a), the district
court should have exercised jurisdiction over its claim.

CONCLUSION

For all of the foregoing reasons, the judgment of the United
States District Court for the District of Superior should be
reversed and remanded for proceedings on the merits.

Respectfully submitted,

_____

Truman LaFoote
Attorney for Appellant

Wayne State University Law School
Detroit, Michigan 48202
(313) 577-4822

November 3, 1980.

APPENDIX

Clean Air Act

Section 304(a), 42 U.S.C. § 7604(a):

The district courts shall have jurisdiction, without regard to the amount in controversy or the citizenship of the parties, to enforce such an emission standard or limitation, or such an order, or to order the Administrator to perform such act or duty, as the case may be.

Section 304(a)(1), 42 U.S.C. § 7604(a)(1):

Except as provided in subsection (b) of this section, any person may commence a civil action on his own behalf--

(1)   against any person (including (i) the United States, and (ii) any other governmental instrumentality or agency to the extent permitted by the Eleventh Amendment to the Constitution) who is alleged to be in violation of (A) an emission standard or limitation under this chapter or (B) an order issued by the Administrator or a State with respect to such a standard or limitation. . . .

Section 304(b)(1), 42 U.S.C. § 7604(b)(1):

No action may be commenced--

(1)   under subsection (a)(1) of this section--

(A)   prior to 60 days after the plaintiff has given notice of the violation (i) to the Administrator, (ii) to the State in which the violation occurs, and (iii) to any alleged violator of the standard, limitation, or order, or

(B)   if the Administrator or State has commenced and is diligently prosecuting a civil action in a court of the United States or a State to require compliance with the standard, limitation, or order. . . .

Section 304(e), 42 U.S.C. § 7604(e):

Nothing in this section shall restrict any right which any person (or class of persons) may have under any statute or common law to seek enforcement of any emission standard or limitation or to seek any other relief (including relief against the Administrator or a State agency).

Judicial Code

28 U.S.C. § 1331(a):

> The district courts shall have original jurisdiction of all
> civil actions wherein the matter in controversy exceeds the
> sum or value of $10,000, exclusive of interest and costs,
> and arises under the Constitution, laws, or treaties of the
> United States, except that no such sum or value shall be re-
> quired in any such action brought against the United States,
> any agency thereof, or any officer or employee thereof in
> his official capacity.

IN THE UNITED STATES
COURT OF APPEALS FOR THE
THIRTEENTH CIRCUIT

No. 80-152

WESTBROOK NEIGHBORHOOD ASSOCIATION,
Appellant,

v.

ELLISON RECYCLING, INC.,
Appellee.

ON APPEAL FROM THE
UNITED STATES DISTRICT COURT
FOR THE DISTRICT OF SUPERIOR

BRIEF FOR APPELLEE

Amy Scroggins
Wayne State University
Law School
Detroit, Michigan 48202

INDEX

AUTHORITIES CITED

OPINIONS BELOW

The opinion of the United States District Court for the District of Superior is unreported, and contained in the Transcript of Record (R. 22-25).

JURISDICTION

The judgment of the United States District Court for the District of Superior was entered on August 8, 1980. The appeal was filed on August 20, 1980 and was granted on December 1, 1980. The jurisdiction of this court is invoked under 28 U.S.C. § 1291.

STATUTES INVOLVED

The texts of the following statutes relevant to the determination of the present case are set forth in the Appendix: Federal Clean Air Act, §§ 304(a), 304(a)(1), 304(b)(1)(A), 304(e), 42 U.S.C. §§ 7604(a), 7604(a)(1), 7604(b)(1)(A), 7604(e) (Supp. III 1979); Judicial Code, 28 U.S.C. § 1331(a) (1976).

QUESTIONS PRESENTED

I.   Whether the district court properly declined citizen suit jurisdction since a provision of the Clean Air Act expressly conditions jurisdiction on 60 days' advance notice by Appellant and Appellant provided only 37 days' notice?

II.   Whether the district court properly declined citizen suit jurisdiction since Appellant failed to substantially comply with the 60-day notice requirement by bringing suit prior to the expiration of the notice period when Appellee was taking corrective measures and had so informed Appellant?

III.   Whether the district court properly declined federal question jurisdiction in a suit brought under the Clean Air Act because Congress intended the citizen suit provision of that Act, which provides an adequate procedure for judicial review, to be the exclusive basis for jurisdiction?

STATEMENT OF FACTS

The Appellee, Ellison Recycling, Inc., is a small company engaged in the business of recycling oil. The firm converts waste oil from steel treatment plants, car repair facilities, and small shops into usable oil by removing the contaminants. The company operates its only plant on the outskirts of Westbrook (R. 2, 18-19).

The Appellee began operation on April 14, 1980. On April 14, 1980. On April 15, 1980, Appellee received complaints from the Appellant, a citizens' organization, and the Superior Air Resources Board about intermittent odors from the plant. The Board informed Appellant that the plant's emissions were not regulated by the State Implementation Plan of the Federal Clean Air Act except for the opacity requirement of section 33.1301 of the State Administrative Code (R. 2). Opacity is a measure of the darkness of the emissions, and that section prohibits any person from discharging into the atmosphere a visible air contaminant with a density of more than 20 percent opacity for more than three minutes in any 24-hour period (R. 8-9). Appellee made many changes in its plant during the first few weeks of operation to reduce such emissions. Although there were 28 violations of the opacity requirement prior to April 30, Appellant alleged only 17 in May (R. 2).

Notwithstanding this improvement, Appellant sent Appellee a letter on May 20, 1980, stating its intent to file suit against Appellee unless Appellee complied with the opacity requirement within 60 days (R. 10-12). Appellant sent copies of the letter to the Board and the United States Environmental Protection Agency (EPA). Appellee wrote Appellant on June 22, 1980, in response to this notice that it had hired a consultant to conduct a national search of air pollution control technologies available to oil recycling plants. Appellee stated that it hoped to install equipment that would reduce emissions far more than the opacity regulation required, and that it would know better what

to do after the consultant reported back on July 15, 1980. Appellee stated that it had already made progress in reducing
emissions and that it had been meeting with the Board's staff
(R. 15-16).

On June 26, 1980, only four days after Appellee's response,
and only 37 days after Appellee received notice, Appellant filed
suit in federal district court seeking declaratory and injunctive
relief against Appellee for violations of the opacity requirement
(R. 1-4). Appellant charged only 12 violations of the requirement to that date in June (R. 3). Appellant alleged jurisdiction
under two separate theories, both of which were considered and
rejected by the district court.

The court concluded that jurisdiction under the citizen suit
provision of the Clean Air Act was improper because Appellant had
filed suit before expiration of the requisite 60 day waiting
period required by the Act. The court also refused to exercise
federal question jurisdiction. The court reasoned that Congress
intended the citizen suit provision of the Clean Air Act to be
the exclusive basis of jurisdiction for citizen enforcement suits
under that Act. The court, therefore, dismissed the case for
lack of jurisdiction (R. 22-25).

SUMMARY OF ARGUMENT

The district court properly dismissed this case for want of
jurisdiction because Appellant ignored the thoughtful and orderly
procedure Congress established for citizen enforcement claims
under the Clean Air Act. Although the Clean Air Act provides for
citizen suits against alleged violators of the Act, it conditions
that jurisdictional grant on strict compliance with a 60-day
advance notice requirement. Appellant failed to comply with that
requirement because it gave only 37 days' advance notice. Congress intended the provision to avoid unnecessary litigation and
minimize interference with the enforcement process. That intent
would have been frustrated by a premature lawsuit.

Even if it were possible to abrogate the language and intent of Congress by permitting jurisdiction where a plaintiff substantially complied with the 60-day notice requirement, jurisdiction would still have been improper. Substantial compliance can occur only when the potential defendant responds to the notice prior to the end of the 60-day period that it plans to take no action on the notice. In this case, however, Appellee made significant progress in reducing emissions simply by making changes in its operation. In addition, Appellee hired a consultant to investigate control technologies and hoped to reduce its emissions beyond the requirements of state law. Since Appellee's response to Appellant's notice states these facts, Appellant cannot reasonably claim that waiting until the end of the notice period would have been futile.

Appellant's failure to meet the 60-day notice requirement closed the only jurisdictional door open to it since the citizen suit provision of the Clean Air Act is the exclusive jurisdictional basis for such lawsuits. Any other conclusion would permit the notice requirement to be easily eluded and frustrate Congressional intent to avoid premature lawsuits. Where Congress has prescribed adequate procedures for judicial review under a statutory scheme, these procedures are exclusive.

ARGUMENT

I. THE DISTRICT COURT PROPERLY DECLINED JURISDICTION UNDER THE CITIZEN SUIT PROVISION OF THE CLEAN AIR ACT.

The most fundamental attribute of the federal courts is their limited jurisdiction. They are empowered to hear only those cases that are within constitutional limits of the judicial power of the United States, and have been entrusted to them by a jurisdictional grant of Congress. C. Wright, The Federal Courts § 7 (3d ed. 1976). Where Congress provides a statutory method for obtaining review of administrative decisions, that method must be strictly adhered to. Loveladies Property Owners Association v. Raab, 430 F. Supp. 276 (D.N.J. 1975), aff'd, 547 F.2d

1162 (3d Cir. 1976). Since Appellant failed to follow the statutory scheme in this case, the district court properly declined to
exercise jurisdiction over the claim.

    A.   Appellant violated the 60-day notice requirement for
        citizen suits by providing Appellee only 37 days'
        notice before filing suit.

Section 304(a)(1) of the Federal Clean Air Act, 42 U.S.C.
§ 7604(a)(1) (Supp. III 1979), provides a jurisdictional basis
for citizens to bring actions against persons alleged to be violating emissions standards or limitations under the Act. Jurisdiction is proper "without regard to the amount in controversy or
the citizenship of the parties." 42 U.S.C. § 7604(a). Section
304(b)(1)(A), however, provides that no action "may be commenced":

> prior to 60 days after the plaintiff has given notice
> of the violation (i) to the Administrator, (ii) to the
> state in which the violation occurs, and (iii) to any
> alleged violator of the standard, limitation, or order.

42 U.S.C. § 7604(b)(1)(A) (Supp. III 1979).

The legislative history of section 304 shows Congress intended the 60-day notice period to be scrupulously observed. The
Conference Committee for the Act doubled the 30-day notice period
contained in the Senate bill to 60 days. H.R. Rep. No. 1783,
91st Cong., 2d Sess. at 55-56 (1970). The Conference Report observed, "Prior to commencing any action in the district courts,
the plaintiff must have provided the violator, the Administrator,
and the State with sixty days' notice." Id. at 55.

The great majority of courts have recognized the importance
of strictly complying with the 60-day notice requirement. In
City of Highland Park v. Train, 519 F.2d 681 (7th Cir. 1975),
cert. denied, 424 U.S. 927 (1976), the court affirmed the dismissal of a section 304 claim for plaintiff's failure to comply with
the 60-day notice requirement, observing that Congress's intention would be frustrated if the statutory mandate of section
304(b)(1)(A) were ignored. 519 F.2d at 691. Courts have

applied this rule in citizen suits against industrial sources,
City of Evansville v. Kentucky Liquid Recycling, Inc., 604 F.2d
1008 (7th Cir. 1979), cert. denied, 444 U.S. 1025 (1980). They
have also applied this rule where plaintiffs gave less than 60
days' notice, Smoke Rise, Inc. v. Washington Suburban Sanitary
Commission, 400 F. Supp. 1369 (D. Md. 1974), where plaintiffs
gave the EPA Regional Administrator 60 days' notice before filing
their amended complaint, Loveladies Property Owners Association
v. Raab, 430 F. Supp 276 (D.N.J. 1975), and where plaintiff gave
no notice at all. Pinkney v. Ohio Environmental Protection
Agency, 375 F. Supp. 305 (N.D. Ohio 1974). In each case, failure
to strictly comply with the 60-day notice requirement was fatal
to citizen suit jurisdiction.

Congress had good reason for requiring strict compliance
with this notice requirement. First, the full notice period provides an opportunity for the parties to settle the problem, making it less likely that unnecessary lawsuits will add to the
burden of the courts. S. Rep. No. 1196, 91st Cong., 2d Sess. 37
(1970). Second, the notice period provides an opportunity for
government lawyers to more smoothly integrate the interruption
caused by a citizen suit into their overall enforcement concerns.
City of Highland Park v. Train, 519 F.2d 681, 690 (7th Cir.
1975). The government is necessarily involved in any citizen
enforcement action, whether it is a formal party or not, because
the suit will affect its enforcement efforts. Third, a precise
60-day period decreases the judicial time required to process a
citizen suit; plaintiffs either give proper notice or they do
not. In a similar vein, Congress required citizen suit plaintiffs to allege specific violations under the Act--an "objective
evidentiary standard"--rather than generalized claims of pollution. S. Rep. No. 1196, 91st Cong., 2d Sess. at 36 (1970).

Finally, strict compliance is fundamentally equitable because of the substantial power granted to citizen suit plaintiffs
against persons alleged to be violating the statute. In

6

Tennessee Valley Authority v. Hill, 437 U.S. 153 (1978), plaintiffs brought suit under a provision of the Endangered Species
Act modeled after section 304 to prevent completion of the
Tellico Dam and the consequent destruction of the snail darter,
a fish species protected by that Act. The Court affirmed an
order permanently enjoining completion of the dam because the
statutory language permitted no exceptions, and in so doing
brushed aside arguments that the result would cost millions of
dollars and preserve a species of minimal value. Congress, the
court said, "has spoken in the plainest of words." 437 U.S. at
195. Where plaintiffs seek compliance with the letter of the law
through such drastic means as prohibiting completion of a nearly
finished dam or enjoining the operation of an oil recycling
plant, then they must comply with the jurisdictional language
conditioning their right to do so.

In the present case, the district court correctly refrained
from exercising jurisdiction under section 304 of the Clean Air
Act. Appellant filed suit on June 26, 1980, after giving notice
on May 20. Appellant thus failed to comply with the statutory
requirements because only 37 of the required 60 days had elapsed.
This court must not permit Appellant to so easily evade the plain
intent of Congress.

Cases sustaining citizen suit jurisdiction on "substantial"
or "constructive" compliance ignore the language and purposes of
section 304. The Second Circuit has permitted jurisdiction where
there was "substantial compliance" with the 60-day notice requirement, but only in cases where that issue was peripheral, if
relevant at all, to the decision. The substantial compliance
theory, which permits jurisdiction after less than 60 days'
notice when the purpose of the notice period has been served,
originated in dicta in Conservation Society of Southern Vermont,
Inc. v. Secretary of Transportation, 508 F.2d 927 (2d Cir. 1974),
vacated on other grounds, 423 U.S. 809 (1975). Although the
court stated that the 60-day notice provision was not intended

7

to be an "absolute barrier" to an earlier suit, that statement was premised largely on the court's view that other jurisdictional bases were available. In addition, the court never held that the district court wrongly denied jurisdiction for failure to strictly comply with the 60-day requirement; it only assumed there was jurisdiction under some statutory provision to reach a substantive question. The same court of appeals in <u>Natural Resources Defense Council v. Callaway</u>, 524 F.2d 79 (2d Cir. 1975), was similarly influenced by the presence of jurisdictional bases other than the citizen suit provision, an erroneous assumption discussed in Argument II of this brief.

Substantial compliance also makes poor policy. The <u>Callaway</u> court's footnote that the purposes of the 60-day notice requirement are served when the potential defendant says "no action will be taken," 524 F.2d at 84 n.4, permits a plaintiff to seize on the slightest negative response, or even an ambiguous one, as an excuse for a premature lawsuit. The "substantial compliance" principle thus hinders pre-lawsuit communications between the parties, makes it difficult for potential defendants to communicate anything short of total agreement with those giving notice, and raises difficult and unnecessary questions about how much notice is enough.

The slipperiness of this concept is also illustrated by a closely related theory extending jurisdiction if the plaintiff gave notice 60 days before the court's first hearing in the citizen suit, rather than 60 days before filing suit. This "constructive compliance" theory was applied in <u>City of Riverside v. Ruckelshaus</u>, 4 E.R.C. 1728 (C.D. Cal. 1972), and has not been applied since that time. <u>Dicta</u> in <u>National Sea Clammers Association v. City of New York</u>, 616 F.2d 1222 (3d Cir. 1980), states that such an interpretation would be "entirely permissible," but the court in that case added that it "need not pass upon this proposition" because it found independent jurisdiction under another statute. 616 F.2d at 1226.

The <u>Riverside</u> case was wrongly decided because it abrogates the language of section 304(a) requiring 60 days' notice before any action "may be commenced." The case would permit a plaintiff to ignore the 60-day notice period before filing suit, assured that 60 days almost certainly would pass by the time the court began to hear the case. As the court in <u>City of Highland Park v. Train</u> observed, rule 12(b) of the Federal Rules of Civil Procedure provides 60 days for the federal government to respond to complaints in lawsuits where it is a defendant. Although the same rule provides only 20 days for other parties to respond, Congress intended the notice provision to supplement, rather than replace, these and other response periods in the litigation process. Section 304(b)(1)(A) provides a workable and efficient notice procedure, and the district court properly dismissed Appellant's complaint for failure to comply with it.

    B.   <u>Appellant failed to substantially comply with the 60-day notice requirement by bringing suit prior to the end of that period when Appellee was taking corrective action and so informed Appellant.</u>

Even if it was proper to abrogate the statutory language by permitting jurisdiction under section 304(a)(1) when plaintiff provides less than 60 days' notice, Appellant did not "substantially comply" with the 60-day requirement here. This case is analogous to the situation in <u>Massachusetts v. United States Veterans Administration</u>, 541 F.2d 119 (1st Cir. 1976), which involved a citizen suit under the Federal Water Pollution Control Act (FWPCA), 33 U.S.C. §§ 1251-1376 (1976 & Supp. III 1979), for the failure of a veterans hospital to comply with the timetable in a permit requirement for connecting to a municipal sewage system. (The FWPCA contains a citizen suit provision that is similar to the one in the Clean Air Act.) The state brought a citizen suit after giving only 40 days' notice, claiming that notice would not cure past violations of the permit condition. The court of appeals affirmed the dismissal of the citizen suit claim, holding that there was not a claim of futility sufficient

to raise the issue of constructive compliance.   541 F.2d at
121-22.   The court reasoned, "even conceding that no administrative action could cure the failure of the VA to meet past
deadlines for planning and construction of the sewer tie-in,
increased administrative attention could still expedite the completion of the project.   Id. at 121.

Appellant did not substantially comply with the 60-day
notice requirement because Appellee was and is taking corrective
actions, and so informed Appellant prior to the end of the
notice period.   Appellant's complaint alleged 28 violations of
the opacity limitation in the Superior regulations in the last
half of April, 17 in May, and only 12 in the first 25 days of
June.   Appellee was thus making significant progress in meeting
the opacity limitation, the only regulation addressed in the
complaint.   In addition, Appellee responded to the notice on
June 22 by stating that it had hired a consultant to examine different control technologies and that it hoped to install equipment that would improve on the degree of control required by the
opacity limitation.   Appellee wrote that it would know better
what to do after the consultant presented its report on July 15,
five days before the end of the notice period.   Appellant brought
suit four days later, without waiting for the consultant's report
and without asking for any clarifications, even though Appellee's
increased administrative attention was resolving a difficult
technical problem.

Even if Appellee's response can be considered ambiguous,
Appellant cannot claim frustration.   In Veterans Administration,
the court suggested that there can be no substantial compliance
if it is possible that some administrative action "could" correct
the problem.   541 F.2d at 121.   Since in Appellee's case there
was a possibility--and a strong one--of further corrective measures, the substantial compliance theory is inapplicable.

This situation is thus far different from that in Natural
Resources Defense Council v. Callaway, 524 F.2d 79 (2d Cir.

1975), because Appellee did not say that "no action" would be taken. Plaintiffs, in <u>Callaway</u>, brought a citizen suit to enjoin the use of an ocean disposal site for dredge materials. The court of appeals reversed the district court's dismissal of the case for plaintiffs' failure to provide more than 48 days' notice, reasoning that the refusal of the defendants to take any action meant that waiting any longer would be futile. Where a potential defendant responds positively, or at worst ambiguously, to formal notice, there can be no reasonable claim of frustration. In the present case, Appellee had not stated that "no action" would be taken. To the contrary, Appellee responded that it was studying what steps it could take to remedy the problem. Appellant, therefore, had no basis for a premature lawsuit.

II.   THE DISTRICT COURT PROPERLY DECLINED FEDERAL QUESTION JURISDICTION SINCE THE CITIZEN SUIT PROVISION OF THE CLEAN AIR ACT IS THE EXCLUSIVE JURISDICTIONAL BASIS FOR CITIZEN ENFORCEMENT ACTIONS UNDER THAT ACT.

Plaintiffs in a citizen suit cannot claim alternative jurisdictional bases to avoid the 60-day notice requirement. "If Congress has provided adequate procedures for judicial review within a given statutory scheme, the prescribed procedures are exclusive." <u>Pinkney v. Ohio Environmental Protection Agency</u>, 375 F. Supp. 305, 309 (N.D. Ohio 1974).

In <u>Weinberger v. Salfi</u>, 422 U.S. 749 (1975), the Court held that section 405(g) of the Social Security Act, 42 U.S.C. § 405(g) (1976), provided the sole jurisdictional basis for benefit claims under that Act. The Court concluded that since the Social Security Act contains a series of procedural steps that an aggrieved claimant must follow before bringing action in federal district court, plaintiffs were barred from bringing those same claims under general federal question jurisdiction. 28 U.S.C. § 1331(a) (1976). The Court reasoned that where there is an orderly administrative mechanism, it is counterproductive to permit plaintiffs to circumvent its requirements by relying on other jurisdictional statutes. Similarly, the claimant in Califano v. Sanders, 430 U.S. 99 (1977), which also dealt with section 405(g), was barred by procedural irregularities from seeking judicial review under that Act. The Court held he could not rely on the Administrative Procedure Act, 5 U.S.C. §§ 701-06 (1976), as an alternative jurisdictional source.

In the present case, the Clean Air Act provides an adequate procedure for judicial review. The Act expressly allows citizens to sue to enforce the provisions of the Act, but it conditions this right on satisfying the prerequisite of waiting 60 days before bringing suit. As in Califano and Weinberger, plaintiffs seeking relief under the Clean Air Act must adhere to the prescribed procedural steps. The district court, therefore, properly refused to permit Appellant to circumvent the notice requirement by simultaneously claiming general federal question jurisdiction under 28 U.S.C. § 1331(a) (1976).

Section 304(e) of the Clean Air Act, 42 U.S.C. § 7604(e) (Supp. III 1979), which provides, "Nothing in this section shall restrict any right which any person (or class of persons) may have under any statute or common law," does not preserve additional jurisdictional sources for declaratory and injunctive relief. Rather, the legislative history of section 304(e) shows that Congress intended it primarily to preserve common law actions for damages. The Senate Committee emphasized that section 304 contains no provision "for the recovery of property or personal damages. It should be noted, however, that the section would specifically preserve any rights or remedies under any other law. Thus, if damages could be shown, other remedies would remain available." S. Rep. No. 1196, 91st Cong., 2d Sess. 38 (1970). Congress thus required 60 days' advance notice for enforcement actions brought under the Clean Air Act pursuant to section 304(b)(1)(A) while preserving common law actions for damages caused by air pollution through section 304(e).

Even if section 304(e) preserves other jurisdictional
statutes for citizen enforcement claims, it conditions their
use on compliance with section 304(b). <u>City of Highland Park</u> v.
<u>Train</u>, 519 F.2d 681 (7th Cir. 1975), <u>cert. denied</u>, 424 U.S. 927
(1976). In <u>Highland Park</u>, the court specifically concluded that
section 304(e) does not permit citizen suit plaintiffs to seek
jurisdictional refuge in section 1331(a). The court reasoned
that although the saving provision expressed the general intention of Congress not to disturb existing rights to seek relief,
it did not remove conditions which existing law imposes on the
exercise of those rights. 519 F.2d at 693. The court then held
that section 304(b) was "existing law" which imposed its jurisdictional prerequisites, including proper notice, on section
1331(a). <u>Accord</u>, <u>Pinkney v. Ohio Environmental Protection
Agency</u>, 375 F. Supp. 305 (N.D. Ohio 1975).

There is thus no merit to the distinction in <u>National Sea
Clammers Association v. City of New York</u>, 616 F.2d 1222 (3d Cir.
1980), between "injured" parties, who can bring actions under
both the citizen suit provision and section 1331(a), and "non-
injured" parties, who are limited to citizen suit jurisdiction.
The legislative history contains no clear indication that Congress intended two classes of plaintiffs to be involved in citizen enforcement action. The policy considerations behind the
60-day notice requirement--administrative resolution of issues,
minimal disruption of the administrative process, minimal court
clogging--are applicable to all plaintiffs regardless of the
degree of their "injury." This artificial distinction may well
encourage potential plaintiffs to ignore section 304 altogether
and proceed under section 1331(a)--a result manifestly at odds
with Congressional intent.

Where Congress provides a means of judicial review, the
means specified are exclusive and must be followed. Congress
permitted Appellant to sue under section 304 and only under section 304. Appellant's failure to provide the required 60 days'

13

notice before suit precluded the district court from exercising jurisdiction under the citizen suit provision of the Federal Clean Air Act. This court should, therefore, find that the district court correctly refused to exercise general federal question jurisdiction over the claim.

CONCLUSION

For all of the foregoing reasons, the judgment of the United States District Court for the District of Superior should be affirmed.

Respectfully submitted,

_____

AMY SCROGGINS
Attorney for Appellee

Wayne State University Law School
Detroit, Michigan 48202
(313) 577-4823

November 3, 1980

14

APPENDIX

Clean Air Act

Section 304(a), 42 U.S.C. § 7604(a):

The district courts shall have jurisdiction, without regard to the amount in controversy or the citizenship of the parties, to enforce such an emission standard or limitation, or such an order, or to order the Administrator to perform such act or duty, as the case may be.

Section 304(a)(1), 42 U.S.C. § 7604(a)(1):

Except as provided in subsection (b) of this section, any person may commence a civil action on his own behalf—

    (1) against any person (including (i) the United States, and (ii) any other governmental instrumentality or agency to the extent permitted by the Eleventh Amendment to the Constitution) who is alleged to be in violation of (A) an emission standard or limitation under this chapter or (B) an order issued by the Administrator or a State with respect to such a standard or limitation. . . .

Section 304(b)(1), 42 U.S.C. § 7604(b)(1):

No action may be commenced—

    (1) under subsection (a)(1) of this section—

        (A) prior to 60 days after the plaintiff has given notice of the violation (i) to the Administrator, (ii) to the State in which the violation occurs, and (iii) to any alleged violator of the standard, limitation, or order, or

        (B) if the Administrator or State has commenced and is diligently prosecuting a civil action in a court of the United States or a State to require compliance with the standard, limitation, or order. . . .

Section 304(e), 42 U.S.C. § 7604(e):

Nothing in this section shall restrict any right which any person (or class of persons) may have under any statute or common law to seek enforcement of any emission standard or limitation or to seek any other relief (including relief against the Administrator or a State agency).

Judicial Code

28 U.S.C. § 1331(a):

The district courts shall have original jurisdiction of all
civil actions wherein the matter in controversy exceeds the
sum or value of $10,000, exclusive of interest and costs,
and arises under the Constitution, laws, or treaties of the
United States, except that no such sum or value shall be required in any such action brought against the United States,
any agency thereof, or any officer or employee thereof in
his official capacity.

Bibliography—Sources of Law

THE cases and statutes used in this book are intended exclusively to briefly and simply illustrate specific principles of legal writing and legal method. Although they are not intended to teach substantive rules of law, they are based on or inspired by real cases and statutes which are too lengthy to be reproduced in full. This section is provided to show from where the ideas for the illustrations and exercises were derived.

Chapter 1
The text and Exercise 1 require no comment. Exercise 2 is inspired by *People v. Utica Daw's Drug Store Co.,* 16 A.D.2d 12, 225 N.Y.S.2d 128 (1962), and *People v.Walker,* 14 N.Y.2d 901, 200 N.E.2d 779, 252 N.Y.S.2d 96 (1964).

Chapter 2
The first case in the text, *State v. Jones,* is based on *United States v. Castillo,* 524 F.2d 286 (10th Cir. 1975) and *State v. Baxter,* 285 N.C. 735, 208 S.E.2d 696 (1974).

The burglary case under Part 2 is based on *State v. Crawford,* 8 N.D. 539, 80 N.W. 193 (1899).

The case under Part 3 is based on *Jackson v. Brown,* 164 N.W.2d 824, (Iowa 1969).

The first case under part 4 is drawn from *Brown v. Union Trust Co.,* 229 Ind. 404, 98 N.E.2d 901 (1951).

The corporation case under Part 4 is based on the reasoning in *Decker v. Juzwick,* 255 Iowa 358, 121 N.W.2d 652 (1963), although the court in that case concluded the promoters were not liable because there was a novation of the contract by the corporation.

The case under Rule 5 is drawn from *Stratton v. Mt. Hermon Boys' School*, 216 Mass. 83, 103 N.E. 87 (1913).

Exercise 2-A is derived from the principles stated in *Missouri Fed'n of the Blind v. National Fed'n of the Blind*, 505 S.W.2d 1 (Ct.App. 1974), and *Powell v. Zuckert*, 366 F.2d 634 (D.C. Cir. 1966).

Exercise 2-B is drawn from W. PROSSER, LAW OF TORTS § 70 (4th ed. 1971).

Exercise 2-C is inspired by *State v. Glover*, 330 Mo. 709, 50 S.W.2d 1049 (1932), and *Commonwealth v. Redline*, 391 Pa. 486, 137 A.2d 472 (1958).

Chapter 3

The cases in the text are based closely on *Johnston v. Harris*, 387 Mich. 569, 198 N.W.2d 409 (1972) and *Samson v. Saginaw Professional Bldg., Inc.*, 393 Mich. 445, 224 N.W.2d 843 (1976).

Part 1 of Exercise 3-A is drawn from *Ellis v. Butterfield*, 98 Idaho 644, 570 P.2d 1334 (1977), *rehearing denied*, 98 Idaho 663, 572 P.2d 509 (1978). Part 2 of Exercise 3-A is based on a line of cases typified by *Wyman v. Newhouse*, 93 F.2d 313 (2d Cir. 1937). *See generally* Annot., 98 A.L.R.2d 551 (1964). Part 3 is modeled on a trilogy of Rhode Island decisions, *State v. Welford*, 29 R.I. 450, 72 A. 396 (1909), *State v. Scofield*, 87 R.I. 78, 138 A.2d 415 (1958), and *State v. Lunt*, 106 R.I. 379, 260 A.2d 149 (1969).

Exercise 3-B is inspired primarily by *Williams v. Walker-Thomas Furniture Co.*, 350 F.2d 445 (D.C. Cir. 1965).

Chapter 4

The cases in the text are inspired by *Bialac v. Harsh Building Co.*, 463 F.2d 1185 (9th Cir. 1972) (diversity jurisdiction), *Executive Jet Aviation Co. v. City of Cleveland*, 409 U.S. 249 (1972) (admiralty jurisdiction), and *Tayler v. Vallelunga*, 171 Cal. App. 2d 107, 339 P.2d 910 (1959) (emotional distress).

The excerpt from the state encyclopedia are based on 6 AM. JUR. *Assault and Battery* §§ 109, 111, 113, 114, 117 (1963). The cases in Exercise 4-A are loosely based on *Timmons v. Bostwick*, 141 Ga. 713, 82 S.E. 29 (1914), *Lucy v. Zehmer*, 196 Va. 493, 84 S.E.2d 516 (1954), *Olson v. Rasmussen*, 304 Mich. 639, 8 N.W.2d 668 (1943), and the principles find some support in J. CALAMARI & J. PERILLO, THE LAW OF CONTRACTS § 13 (2d ed. 1977).

Exercise 4-B is based on MICH. COMP. LAWS. ANN. §§ 15.231-.246 (West Supp. 1980); TEX. CIV. CODE ANN. tit. 6252-17a, § 3(a)(8) (Vernon Supp. 1978-79); *Ayers v. Lee Enterprises, Inc.*, 277 Or. 527, 561 P.2d 998,

(1977); *Houston Chronicle Publishing Co. v. City of Houston,* 531 S.W.2d 177 (Tex. Civ. App. 1975).

Chapter 5

The cases in the text are based on *Ball v. White,* 3 Mich. App. 579, 143 N.W. 2d 188 (1966), and *Barnes v. Clayton House Motel,* 435 S.W.2d 616 (Tex. Civ. App. 1968).

Exercise 5-A is drawn from *Cooper v. Sisters of Charity, Inc.,* 27 Ohio St. 2d 242, 272 N.E.2d 97 (1971), *Hicks v. United States,* 368 F.2d 626 (4th Cir. 1966), and *Walden v. Jones,* 439 S.W.2d 571 (Ky. 1969).

The cases in Exercise 5-B are based on *Fontainebleau Hotel Corp. v. Forty-Five Twenty-Five, Inc.,* 114 So. 2d 357 (Fla. Dist. Ct. App. 1959) and *Miles v. A. Arena & Co.,* 23 Cal. App. 2d 680, 73 P.2d 1260 (1938).

Chapter 6

The statute and case in the text are drawn from MICH. COMP. LAWS ANN. §§ 15.262(a)-(b), 15.263(1) (West Supp. 1980), and *New-Journal Co. v. McLaughlin,* 377 A.2d 358 (Del. Ch. 1977).

Exercise 6-A is based on MICH. CT. R. 209.1(3), 1 MICH. CT. RULES ANN. 616 (Honigman & Hawkins, 2d ed. 1962), and *D'Agnostini v. City of Roseville,* 396 Mich. 185, 240 N.W.2d 252 (1976).

Exercise 6-B is inspired by MICH. COMP. LAWS ANN. §§ 162.252(6), .269(5) (West Supp. 1980); N.J. STAT. ANN. §§ 19:44A-29(b) (West Supp. 1980-81); *Buckley v. Valeo,* 424 U.S. 1 (1976); *Common Cause v. New Jersey Election Law Enforcement Comm'n,* 74 N.J. 231, 377 A.2d 643 (1977).

Chapter 7

The injunction rule alluded to several times in the chapter is drawn from cases such as *People v. Blacks' Food Store,* 16 Cal. 2d 59, 105 P.2d 361 (1940).

Chapter 8

The cases in the text under Rule 1 are based on W. LAFAVE & A. SCOTT, CRIMINAL LAW §§ 82, 94 (1972).

The cases in the text under Rule 2 are drawn from *Bartram v. Zoning Comm'n,* 136 Conn. 89, 68 A.2d 308 (1949), *Rodgers v. Village of Tarrytown,* 302 N.Y. 115, 96 N.E.2d 731, 96 N.Y.S.2d 58 (1951), *D'Angelo v. Knights of Columbus Bldg. Ass'n,* 89 R.I. 176, 151 A.2d 495 (1959), and *Thomas v. Town of Bedford,* 29 Misc. 2d 861, 214 N.Y.S.2d 145 (1961).

The case under Rule 3 is drawn from *Thompson v. Enz,* 379 Mich. 667, 154 N.W.2d 473 (1967), and *In re County Ditch No. 34,* 142 Minn. 37, 170 N.W. 883 (1919).

The illustration in the text under Rule 1(a) is derived from W. LAFAVE & A. SCOTT, CRIMINAL LAW § 95 (1972).

The problem used under Rule 4 is based on section 102(2)(C) of the National Environmental Policy Act of 1969, 42 U.S.C. § 4332(2)(C) (1976).

Exercise 8-A is inspired by *In re Estate of Kamesar,* 81 Wis.2d 151, 259 N.W.2d 733 (1977), and *In re Estate of Malnar,* 73 Wis.2d 192, 243 N.W.2d 435 (1976).

Exercises 8-B, 9-B, 10-B, 11-B are inspired by sections 109 and 304 of the federal Clean Air Act, 42 U.S.C. §§ 7409, 7604, (Supp. II 1978), MICH. ADMIN. CODE § 336.1401(1) (1980), *Jost v. Dairyland Power Coop.,* 45 Wis.2d 164, 172 N.W.2d 647 (1970), *Amphitheaters, Inc. v. Portland Meadows,* 184 Or. 336, 198 P.2d 847 (1948), and W. PROSSER, LAW OF TORTS § 88-89 (4th ed. 1971).

Chapter 9
The illustration under Rule 1b is based on *Frampton v. Central Indiana Gas Co.,* 297 N.E.2d 425 (Ind. 1973), and *Peterman v. International Bhd. of Teamsters, Local 396,* 174 Cal. App. 2d 184, 344 P.2d 25 (1959).

The problem under Rule 1c, obviously, is based on FED. R. CIV. P. 24.

The illustration under Rule 2 is based on 28 U.S.C. § 1331(a) (1976) and *Zahn v. International Paper Co.,* 414 U.S. 291 (1973).

The illustration under Rule 3 is drawn from *Meadows v. F.W. Woolworth Co.,* 254 F. Supp. 907 (N.D. Fla. 1966), and *Coblyn v. Kennedy's, Inc.,* 359 Mass. 319, 268 N.E.2d 860 (1971).

The illustrations under Rule 4 require no comment.

The cases cited under Rule 5 are *Wilmington General Hosp. v. Manlove,* 54 Del. 15, 174 A.2d 135 (1961), *O'Neill v. Montefiore Hosp.,* 11 A.D.2d 132, 202 N.Y.S.2d 436 (1960), and *Birmingham Baptist Hosp. v. Crews,* 229 Ala. 398, 157 So. 224 (1934).

The principles concerning standing to sue under Rule 6 are from *Village of Arlington Heights v. Metropolitan Hous. Dev. Corp.,* 429 U.S. 252 (1977), *United States v. S.C.R.A.P.,* 412 U.S. 669 (1973), and other cases. The exclusionary rule cases are *United States v. Janis,* 428 U.S. 433 (1976) and *United States v. Calandra,* 414 U.S. 338 (1974).

Chapter 10
The illustration in the text is derived from the principles stated in *Canell v. Arcola Hous. Corp.,* 65 So. 2d 849 (Fla. 1953) and *Romanchuk v. Plotkin,* 215 Minn. 156, 9 N.W.2d 421 (1943) (implied easement by necessity).

Exercise 10-A is similar to *Kline v. Burns,* 111 N.H. 87, 276 A.2d 248 (1971).

Chapter 11
The illustration in the text is based on W. PROSSER, LAW OF TORTS § 11 (4th ed. 1971).

Exercise 11-A is based on the English Statute of Frauds entitled "An Act for the Prevention of Frauds and Perjuries," 29 Charles II, c.3 (1677).

The sale of land case is based on the principles contained in J. CALAMARI & J. PERILLO, THE LAW OF CONTRACTS § 282 (2d ed. 1970). The dance case is inspired by *Vokes v. Arthur Murray Inc.*, 212 So. 2d 906 (Fla. Dist. Ct. App. 1968).

Chapter 12
Chapter 12 requires no further comment.

Chapter 13
The statute described under Rules 1 and 2 is drawn from MICH. COMP. LAWS ANN. §§ 168.951, .952, .955 (West. Supp. 1980). *See also Woods v. Clerk of Saginaw County*, 80 Mich. App. 596, 264 N.W.2d 74 (1978). The cases under Rule 3 are based on the discussion in *People v. Kelly*, 17 Cal. 3d 24, 549 P.2d 1240, 130 Cal. Rptr. 144 (1976).

The illustration under Rule 4(a) is based on 28 U.S.C. § 1337 (1976), and the Federal Noise Control Act, 42 U.S.C. §§ 4901-18 (1976 & Supp. II 1978).

The cases cited under Rule 4(b) are *Kopischke v. First Continental Corp.*, ___ Mont. ___, 610 P.2d 668 (1980), and *Bentzler v. Braun*, 34 Wis.2d 362, 149 N.W.2d 626 (1967).

The illustration under Rule 4(c) is inspired by *State Bar v. Geralds*, 402 Mich. 387, 263 N.W.2d 241 (1978), and *State Bar v. Williams*, 394 Mich. 5, 228 N.W.2d 222 (1975), *modified*, 396 Mich. 166, 240 N.W.2d 246 (1976).

The illustration under Rule 5(a) is inspired by *People v. Valentine*, 28 Cal. 2d 121, 169 P.2d 1 (1946).

The example under Rule 5(b) is based on section 8 of the Michigan Township Rural Zoning Act, MICH. COMP. LAWS ANN. § 125.282 (West Supp. 1980) and *Stadle v. Township of Battle Creek*, 346 Mich. 64, 77 N.W.2d 329 (1956).

Exercise 13-A is inspired by 75 PA. CONS. STAT. ANN. § 3301(a) (Purdon 1977), *Hamilton v. Glemming*, 187 Va. 309, 46 S.E.2d 438 (1948); *Stoll v. Curry*, 115 Pa. Super. Ct. 484, 175 A. 724 (1934).

Exercises 13-B, 14-B, and 15-B are based on *Pedigo v. Rowley*, 101 Idaho 201, 610 P.2d 560 (1980), *Gibson v. Gibson*, 3 Cal. 3d 914, 479 P.2d 648 92 Cal. Rptr. 288 (1971); and *Cole v. Sears Roebuck & Co.*, 47 Wis.2d 629, 177 N.W.2d 866 (1970).

Chapter 14
The Williams Act, cited under Rule 1 is located at 15 U.S.C. §§ 78m(d),(e) & 78n(d)-(f) (1976). The cases are *Hines v. Davidowitz*, 312 U.S. 52 (1941); *Perez v. Campbell*, 402 U.S. 637 (1971); *Kewanee Oil Co. v. Bicron Corp.*, 416 U.S. 470 (1974).

The illustration under Rule 2 is based on MICH. COMP. LAWS § 691.1201-07 (1970) and *West Michigan Environmental Action Council v. Natural Resources Comm'n*, 405 Mich. 741, 275 N.W.2d 538 (1979).

The illustration under Rule 3 is inspired by MICH. COMP. LAWS ANN. §§ 333.13501-36 (West Supp. 1980). It is based on *Hecht v. Bowles*, 321 U.S. 321 (1944), and *Tennessee Valley Auth. v. Hill*, 437 U.S. 153, 193-95 (1978).

Exercise 14-A is based on *Prows v. Industrial Comm'n*, ___ Utah ___, 610 P.2d 1362 (1980).

Chapter 15

The statute in the text is the Equal Employment Opportunity Act of 1972, 42 U.S.C. §§ 2000e—2000e-17 (1976).

The case in the text is inspired by and is a combination of *Berg v. Richmond Unified School Dist.*, 528 F.2d 1208 (9th Cir. 1975), *vacated to consider intervening decision*, 434 U.S. 158 (1977), and *Drew v. Liberty Mut. Ins. Co.*, 480 F.2d 69 (5th Cir. 1973), *cert. denied*, 417 U.S. 935 (1974).

Exercise 13-A is based on *Bernstein v. Kapneck*, Md. App. ___, 417 A.2d 456 (1980), *Thomas v. Erie Ins. Exch.*, 229 Md. 332, 182 A.2d 823 (1962), *Hall v. Strom Const. Co.*, 368 Mich. 253, 118 N.W.2d 281 (1962), and *LeFrancois v. Hobart College*, 31 N.Y.S.2d 200, *aff'd*, 287 N.Y. 638, 39 N.E.2d 271 (1941).